Metaphor and the Slave Trade in West African Literature

Metaphor and the Slave Trade in West African Literature

LAURA T. MURPHY

Ohio University Press
Athens

Ohio University Press, Athens, Ohio 45701
ohioswallow.com
© 2012 by Ohio University Press
All rights reserved

To obtain permission to quote, reprint, or otherwise reproduce or distribute material from Ohio University Press publications, please contact our rights and permissions department at (740) 593-1154 or (740) 593-4536 (fax).

Printed in the United States of America
Ohio University Press books are printed on acid-free paper.∞ ™

20 19 18 17 16 15 14 13 12   5 4 3 2 1

Library of Congress Cataloging-in-Publication Data

Murphy, Laura (Laura T.)
 Metaphor and the slave trade in West African literature / Laura Murphy.
   p. cm.
 Includes bibliographical references and index.
 ISBN 978-0-8214-1995-3 (pb : alk. paper)
 1. West African literature (English)—History and criticism. 2. Slave trade in literature. I. Title.
 PR9340.5.M87 2012
 820.93580966—dc22
                                                                    2011051426

CONTENTS

ACKNOWLEDGMENTS
v

INTRODUCTION
vii

ONE
Against Amnesia:
Metaphor and Memory in West Africa
1

TWO
Magical Capture in a Landscape of Terror:
The Trope of the Body in the Bag in
Amos Tutuola's *My Life in the Bush of Ghosts*
47

THREE
Geographies of Memory:
Mapping Slavery's Recurrence in
Ben Okri's *The Famished Road*
75

FOUR
The Curse of Constant Remembrance:
The Belated Trauma of the Slave Trade in
Ayi Kwei Armah's *Fragments*
106

FIVE
Childless Mothers and Dead Husbands:
The Enslavement of Intimacy and
Ama Ata Aidoo's Secret Language of Memory
133

SIX
The Suffering of Survival
169

EPILOGUE
The Future of the Past:
The New Historical Fiction
180

NOTES
195

BIBLIOGRAPHY
219

INDEX
237

ACKNOWLEDGMENTS

This work was first conceived in conversation with the incomparable Joseph Miller, who encouraged me, before the project was even a vague possibility, to pursue the questions about African literature that his history lectures provoked in me. His enthusiasm became a motivating force and eventually helped pave the road for me to travel to West Africa to begin my research.

Which is where I met Kwadwo Opoku-Agyemang, professor of literature at Cape Coast University, who one day greeted this uninvited but curious scholar with unhesitating warmth and generosity. His research on this topic was a launching pad for my own, and our continuing conversations still enrich my work.

My humblest thanks go to Abiola Irele, who supported my project for so many years, patiently bore its constant reincarnations, and always provided useful suggestions and advice. My other advisers (official and unofficial)—Henry Louis Gates Jr., Werner Sollors, Biodun Jeyifo, Emmanuel Obiechina, Glenda Carpio, and John Mugane—encouraged me at critical moments as well. John Thornton, Joe Miller, Suzanne Blier, and Emmanuel Akyeampong were critical in helping me understand the contexts that inform the texts I study here.

I must also thank Jennifer Wenzel, Gert Buelens, Steph Craps, and Victor Manfredi, all of whom provided careful, dedicated readings of my work without my having to ask. At conferences and other gatherings, I spent long afternoons discussing African literature, history, and culture with Ato Quayson, Paul Lovejoy, Adéléké Adéèkó, Abioseh Porter, Dan Magaziner, Joseph Slaughter, Jennifer Wenzel, Esther deBruijn, Matthew Christensen, Dana Rush, Nicolas Argenti, Eileen Julien, Lokangaka Losambe, Alexander Kakraba, Moussa Sow, and Vincent Odamtten, all of whom inform this work in more ways than I can prove in the footnotes. And though he may not have realized it, Stephen Best posed some questions regarding this project that shook its foundations and helped me shape some of the most exciting aspects of this work.

In West Africa, I especially want to thank Philip Atta-Yawson and Amissane Hackman as well as all of the other tour guides and friends who patiently answered my never-ending questions. I am also grateful for the assistance of Alexander Kakraba, who helped me retrace my steps. To all of the other generous people who showed me around, took me into their homes, gave me unofficial tours, plied me with stories on buses, basically taught me where Southern hospitality (and gumbo) came from, I owe you all more than this book can contain. I'm coming back soon, and I hope I'll be able to host you here sometime as well.

And to my colleagues and friends who have been supportive of this work all along—Julia Lee, Amber Musser, Jen Nash, Peter Geller, Cameron Leader-Picone, Ashley Farmer, Linda Chavers, Andrew Reynolds, Tobin Anderson, Elena Marx, Erin Royston, Ally Field, Mia Bagneris, Michael Jeffries, Derrick Ashong, and the members of the Doktor Colloquium—I cannot be grateful enough. This book is a testament to how well you took care of me and nurtured my ideas.

My brilliant new colleagues in the Junior Faculty Working Group at Loyola University New Orleans immediately invited me into their wildly successful club and forced me to present my work just minutes later, ensuring that I got this book out on time. Hillary Eklund, Christopher Schaberg, Janelle Schwartz, Katherine Fidler: here's to many more years of productive exchanges in the best city in the United States. I really must thank each and every one of my colleagues in the English Department at Loyola who so generously welcomed me into their community, but special thanks go to John Sebastian, Mary McCay, and Kate Adams. Though I was able to spend only two years among the unprecedentedly good and humane folks in the English Department at Ithaca College, I am so much the better person and scholar because of it. Thanks especially to Claire Gleitman and Hugh Egan, to whom I now turn in making all life decisions.

In the final moments of producing this manuscript, several wonderful old and new friends helped me work out a couple of dents in the editing, translations, and images departments. Dana Rush and Christine Mullen Kreamer helped me track down this amazing cover image. Samuel Ray ensured that the French translations were not only correct but also beautiful. And Edward Ewing tidied the whole project up. My student assistants at Loyola dedicatedly provided me with the support I needed to put the finishing touches on this project—thanks, Jessiona Bryant and Jessica Thomas. My editor at Ohio, Gillian Berchowitz, has been enormously supportive since the day I met her.

And my dearest gratitude is reserved for Rian Thum, without whom it would not have been so much fun or so challenging.

This project received the generous support of the National Endowment for the Humanities, the Northeast Modern Language Association, the Fellows of Harvard College, the W. E. B. DuBois Institute for African and African American Research at Harvard, the Jennifer Oppenheimer Grant in African Studies, the Committee on African Studies at Harvard University, the Loyola University Faculty Research Grant, the Ithaca College Summer Grant for Faculty Research, and the Center for Faculty Research and Development Release Time Grant.

Thanks to *Research in African Literatures* and *Studies in the Novel*, where some of this project first appeared. An earlier version of the chapter on Tutuola appeared as "Into the Bush of Ghosts: Specters of the Slave Trade in West African Fiction" in *Research in African Literatures* 38, no. 4 (Winter 2007): 141–52. The chapter on Ayi Kwei Armah was published in a special issue on postcolonial trauma fiction in *Studies in the Novel* 40, nos. 1–2 (Spring/Summer 2008): 52–71. Finally, sections of the chapter on Aidoo were published as "'Obstacles in the Way of Love': The Enslavement of Intimacy in Crowther and Aidoo," in a special issue on the transatlantic slave trade in *Research in African Literatures* 40, no. 4 (Winter 2009): 47–64.

INTRODUCTION

Metaphor and the Slave Trade examines the hidden though significant role the transatlantic slave trade has played in the Anglophone West African imagination and the means by which it has been metaphorized in the literary production of the region. It explores how four canonical authors in particular—Amos Tutuola, Ben Okri, Ayi Kwei Armah, and Ama Ata Aidoo—integrated metaphors of the slave trade into their fictional worlds, metaphors that were inherited from or invented as a reflection of the coded discourse surrounding the slave trade in their cultures. In much of West African fiction—even in works that employ a seemingly timeless folk-style narrative as Tutuola's does—we must read into the spaces where the slave trade lies lurking, beyond the layer of the explicit historical setting and into the realm of the metaphor, the rumor, the bodily expression of a long-resident wound. The slave trade hides in the proverbial bush of ghosts, a past always alive in the present, though it is sometimes unnoticed or obscured.

Conservative estimates established by the Trans-Atlantic Slave Trade Database determined that more than 12.5 million African people were held as cargo on ships destined for the Americas and slavery.[1] Scholars have managed to document almost thirty-five thousand ships that crossed the Atlantic during the era of the slave trade—a significant achievement in coming to terms with the nature and outcomes of the global commerce in human lives that spanned the fifteenth to the nineteenth centuries.[2] However, the estimates they are able to make of the African lives affected are limited to those who made it to the coast and embarked on ships headed for the Americas. This quantitative data cannot account for all the people who died in slave-raiding battles or wars, nor the multitude of people who died marching to the shore or in the barracoons, castles, and forts along the coast. These calculations cannot determine how many more people were brought into African domestic slavery as a result of the increased slave raiding engendered by the trade. They do not tell us how many communities were destroyed or how many new ones were formed in the aftermath of wars waged in the pursuit of slaves.[3]

Nor can these calculations measure the significant personal and social costs of the trade. They do not reveal the suffering of those who lost their homes to warfare and were forced to trek across unknown lands to found new communities. They do not expose the violence people suffered in order to satisfy the desires of an expanding and careless European and American bourgeoisie or the material interests of African tyrants. And most of all, they do not reveal the sheer terror and incurable sorrow people must have felt as their neighbors, husbands, wives, and children were lost to them without explanation. As Carolyn A. Brown indicates, in some regions, there "was scarcely a village, kin group, or family that did not lose a relative to the trade."[4] William H. Clarke's narrative of his journeys through Yorubaland in the 1850s confirms that "nearly every kingdom in Africa could relate stories and adventures connected with" the effects of the "accursed slave traffic."[5]

The transatlantic slave trade had profound economic, demographic, political, and social impacts on African societies and cultures. Patrick Manning notes that "the tragic experience of slavery in the modern world left Africans depleted in population, divided irremediably among themselves, retarded economically, and despised as an inferior race in a world which had built a vision of racial hierarchy based on the inspiration of their enslavement."[6] The tragic centuries of the slave trade did more than simply pit Europeans against Africans; the significant demographic shifts and economic transformations inspired by the slave trade encouraged radical alterations in the political organizations within and among local African communities, which resulted in the favoring of strong centralized powers over smaller acephalous societies. As Joseph E. Inikori has documented, "The transatlantic slave trade seriously retarded the development of markets and the market economy in West Africa," despite a robust economic network that crossed West Africa leading up to the rapid expansion of the slave trade in the middle of the seventeenth century. The shift from a trade based in currency in exchange for African-made goods to an exchange of European-made goods for human labor reduced the economic power of the African trading partners.[7]

Furthermore, as demand for captives to feed the transatlantic trade increased, cultural perceptions of slavery within African communities were altered and domestic demand increased as well. This increased demand and desire for slaves from both external and domestic clients had unintended consequences; for instance, many of those who fled raided villages formed new refugee communities, some of which flourished, others of which fell to renewed warfare and political strife.[8] Class dynamics shifted in communities across West Africa as the disparity in wealth between the rulers and the ruled increased and as warrior and bandit classes took on a new dominant status on account of their role in producing slaves for the Atlantic trade.[9]

Thus, the effects of the slave trade cannot be measured simply in terms of the people who embarked on ships, who experienced the Middle Passage, and who were enslaved in the Americas. Instead, this study seeks to engage the violence and terror that the slave trade imposed upon the African continent, not simply for those African people who were its direct victims as enslaved captives, but for all those who remained in West Africa and their descendants. And these effects are not comprehensible in economic or demographic terms alone. In seeking out some of the ways people have expressed the anguish and suffering that accompanied these more quantifiable changes, we can engage the modes of representation through which West African authors have depicted the slave trade in the last few centuries, as this can expose us to the memory of loss and mourning that continues to shape West African life in the long shadow of the slave trade.

The present work, then, explores the unique forms of representation and remembrance of the slave trade that surface in Anglophone West African literature. While scholars of West African literature have diagnosed an amnesia in communal memory regarding the slave trade and mourn an alleged failure to memorialize it in creative forms, I argue that memories of the slave trade are overlooked in African literature because they are not revealed in the forms of overt narrativization so familiar in African American literature. My readings of West African texts reveal that Africans do not merely remember the slave trade differently from African Americans; they *represent* it differently as well. Drawing methodological inspiration from the work of interdisciplinary scholars such as Achille Mbembe, Ato Quayson, Marianne Hirsch, Luise White, and Rosalind Shaw as well as from trauma theory and work on collective memory, this study contends that the distant past endures in West African culture and literature in forms of "alternative memory" and metaphorization such as tragic repetition, fear and gossip, and tropes of suffering, bondage, and impotent sexuality—all of which expose the continued physical as well as psychological legacy of a past that no individual living now personally experienced. Overt narrativization, archiving, or even explicit cultural discourse are not necessary for a collective memory of the transatlantic slave trade to exist in West Africa. In fact, narratives of that kind are nearly nonexistent in the literature of the twentieth century. And yet metaphors of the slave trade nonetheless memorialize that era in West Africa's past in its literature. West African authors express cultural memories of the slave trade in the alternative, metaphorized forms they encounter in their communities and in metaphors of their own creation that resonate with the distinctively African experience of the slave trade. These forms give expression to the way West Africans have archived the traumatic past for themselves.

In the first chapter of this study, I argue that the discourse of the transatlantic slave trade has largely been dominated by the literature, histories, and criticism written about and by African Americans, those whose lives are defined by the diaspora experience of the trade. There is no doubt, however, that the slave trade did not begin on the coastlines of Africa or on the Middle Passage. If we read West African literature for its own particular means of depicting the slave trade, our image and understanding of the encounter with the slave trade is radically altered. The slave ship is almost invisible, as the depictions of the trade move much further into the continent, into the homes of families who lost their children, into the forest where slave raiders and fears abound, to the suffering on the long march to the shore, to the barracoons where captives were held. These depictions turn away from official narrative histories that might ignore the painful era of the trade, toward whispered rumors, terrorizing fears, and bodily knowledges that express metaphorically the localized and splintered memory of the trade.

Thus, through a shift in contextual perspective, an entirely different system of tropes, figures, and images comes to light and represents both the horrors and the cultures produced by the slave trade. In this first chapter, I explore the implications of reading the literature of West Africa in search of the metaphorized expression of slave trade memory. Those metaphors work to express the lingering memory of the slave trade as well as its long-term effects. Writers employ metaphor as a means to critique contemporary political and social realities in West Africa as well. This chapter describes the mechanisms by which these metaphors of the slave trade function, to reveal their prevalence in the canon, and, through this analysis, I hope to provoke a greater awareness and discussion of the way the slave trade is represented in West African literature and culture.

In the chapters on Amos Tutuola and Ben Okri that follow, I contend that these Nigerian authors represent the means by which the memory of the trade continues to haunt the imagination of West Africa through metaphors of captivity and enslavement in the landscape of the bush. In my chapter on

My Life in the Bush of Ghosts, for instance, I trace a genealogy of a centuries-old African trope I call "the body in the bag." Through this trope, Tutuola depicts a haunting cycle of enslavement in which the African protagonist is chased by terrifying ghosts, made captive by them, forced to labor, and then escapes, only to be recaptured by some more horrible slave master. Tutuola employs this trope to depict continuities of memory and fear regarding captivity and the slave trade's endemic presence in the African landscape. In my chapter on *The Famished Road*, I discuss Okri's appropriation of Tutuola's body in the bag, through which he critiques the project of global capitalism and redefines modernity in uniquely West African terms. For Okri, the haunted bush is not only the place where people like Olaudah Equiano can be captured and made a slave, but also a space that can be transformed into the tool of the captive, wherein the protagonist is able to subvert the power of the captor by inventing a personal independence, one that parallels the recently won independence of Nigeria. These chapters explore the production of anxiety regarding the slave trade and the metaphorical reproduction of those anxieties.

In the next two chapters, I discuss the means by which West African authors turn away from a focus on the fears of external predators associated with the slave trade to investigate African complicity and the way the slave trade permeates and violates even the most intimate of spaces, relationships, and even the body. Ayi Kwei Armah and Ama Ata Aidoo make this turn to the exploration of the African body through a critique of the slave trade's contagious commodification of human lives. In Armah's *Fragments*, the protagonist's return to Ghana is marred by his lack of resources and his inability to provide for his family, which he implicitly and explicitly links with African participation in the slave trade. As a result, each time he contemplates the past, he falls into an undiagnosable illness, which forces him to vomit profusely, figuratively purging himself of this disease and releasing himself from bodily memories of the trade. My reading of Armah contends that his exploration of slave trade memory requires a renegotiation of our understanding of "trauma" and its metaphorical, physical, and psychological expression over long durations. In Aidoo's works, memory of the slave trade surfaces as an unbridgeable division between men and women just as the memory of the trade continues to debase the body as a commodity to be exchanged and discarded. In both her play *Anowa* and her novel *Our Sister Killjoy*, human intimacy is thwarted by the insurmountable memory of the denigration of the value of human life, and the impotent body becomes a metaphor for the effects of the trade on the continent. I argue that Ama Ata Aidoo creates, in response, a "grammar of memory" that aims to transcend the uniquely oppressive nature of slavery's legacy on African bodies and to serve as a model for escaping the captivity that haunts many of the other metaphorical representations discussed in the study.

The final chapter, "The Suffering of Survival," explores the long-term trauma that continues to afflict communities that were "left behind" on the African continent during and after the era of the slave trade. For people all along the coast, the slave trade remains an open wound and their experience of it is one marked by suffering that resulted from surviving a trauma and living to tell it. Brief readings of Soyinka's *Death and the King's Horseman*, Achebe's *Arrow of God*, and T. Obinkaram Echewa's *I Saw the Sky Catch Fire* help to synthesize the claims of the preceding chapters, underscoring the way these metaphorical representations are a reflection of the transgenerational expression of the uniquely West Africa experience of the slave trade.

In the epilogue, titled "The Future of the Past," I turn to the more recent writing of Nigerian author Obi Akwani and Ghanaian Kwakuvi Azasu, whose novels mark a historically driven response to the slave trade. In stark contrast to the metaphorical depictions of the trade that constitute late twentieth-century engagement with the trade, this more recent writing suggests the potential for an African historical novel tradition that seems to be emerging in twenty-first-century West African fiction. In this new mode, young authors attempt an overt and literal examination of the slave trade within its original historical frame. I contextualize this literary shift in the context of recent African apologies for the slave trade as well as the testimonial literature of Truth and Reconciliation Commissions that have followed conflicts in South and West Africa. The epilogue, then, sheds light on this emerging twenty-first-century trend, which indicates a departure from the metaphorical representations discussed in this study and toward a more overtly political and historicized literature of the slave trade.

In order to explore how contemporary African people have experienced and depicted the effects of the slave trade in their own lives, each chapter of this study engages a metaphor associated with the trade by putting a twentieth-century work of literature in conversation with an eighteenth- or nineteenth-century African representation of the slave trade. Reading twentieth-century novels and drama alongside letters, diaries, and autobiographies of the eighteenth- and nineteenth-century witnesses to the transatlantic slave trade reveals compelling continuities of expression. The usage of the trope of the body in the bag, for instance, can be traced back to the language used by victims of the slave trade to describe their own captivity. Such connections suggest that the kind of metaphorization outlined in this book can act as an agent for transforming experiences of the slave trade into durable collective memories shared by members of the communities affected by the trade, even when the slave trade's resonance is sometimes unrecognizable to the people who currently use those metaphors. This, of course, does not exclude the possibility that new metaphors are also invented in contemporary circumstances and literature, which are meant to be suggestive of the African experience of the slave trade without having been employed historically. Indeed in the case of some of the metaphors of the slave trade discussed here, authors evoke the suffering recorded by eighteenth- and nineteenth-century witnesses as a way to create original literary metaphors, which provide a new voice for the African experience of the slave trade. In the turbulent seas of language, symbols and meanings chart irregular courses—receding, reemerging, and reinventing themselves in unpredictable ways. Whether inherited or invented, West African authors utilize the power of metaphor to speak for the seeming silence of slave trade memory.

Though the slave trade is not typically made explicit as the primary historical determinant or even mobilized as a central theme in the twentieth-century texts that are analyzed here, the experience of the transatlantic slave trade nonetheless erupts from scenes of contemporary life in the literature of West Africa. The metaphors studied here provide evidence of the way people remember things they would rather forget. They mobilize the silences enforced by institutionalized histories. They allow for representation when the past seems too difficult to confront. And they allow West African authors to engage a subject so significant to their collective past. As we will see, West African authors use metaphors of the slave trade to refute the false dichotomies of witness and silence, memory and forgetting, past and present, and representation and unutterability.

CHAPTER ONE

Against Amnesia

Metaphor and Memory in West Africa

Metaphors of the Slave Trade

Metaphor and the Slave Trade explores the way the transatlantic slave trade has endured in the cultural memory of West Africa because people continue to generate discourse about the trade and, not insignificantly, because they continue to survive a legacy of suffering associated with it. Within the West African literary tradition, creative writers of all stripes, including many of the most canonical fiction authors as well as other dramatists, poets, popular novelists, and children's authors, have similarly attempted to come to terms with the memory and legacy of the slave trade. The central focus of this study is an analysis of the way the memory of the slave trade is represented in West African literature, paying careful attention to the moments when authors record the whispered stories and metaphors that people produce regarding the slave trade. It is my contention that literature provides an opportunity to better understand the complicated process of metaphorization that characterizes much of the memory of the slave trade in West African discourse.

Reading West African literature through the lens of the slave trade reveals that metaphor is not merely a literary tool. The very root of the word *metaphor* is linked to the notion of transfer. Metaphor carries and transports our often nearly unspeakable meanings for us; it transfers our values, concerns, fears, and recollections to others. Elaine Scarry has described pain as an experience that challenges our expressive capabilities in such a way that we turn to metaphors such as "sharp" or "burning" or "piercing" in order to articulate our suffering.[1] This study explores the way metaphor can also communicate a wide range of otherwise hidden, terrifying, traumatic, controversial, socially unacceptable, or politically dangerous notions and memories. Like Rosalind Shaw's analysis of the way Temne images associated with witches and spirit raiders express memories of the slave trade,[2] Nicolas Argenti's examination of the terrors of slave raiding that have been expressed in the masking and dance traditions in the Cameroonian Grasslands,[3] and Luise White's investigation of how vampire and bloodletting images in East Africa convey anxieties about colonial oppression,[4] this study examines the use of metaphor as a political and social tool that West Africans wield with finesse and deliberation to describe the effects of a traumatizing past on their contemporary experiences. The metaphors West African authors employ are often drawn from cultural discourse and popular culture, and as such, they are both reflective and productive of meaning. They are carriers of meaning passed down through the generations, and can also act as translators, animators, and modifiers of meaning. As vehicles for compressing and transmitting meaning and experience, metaphors of the slave trade testify to the way in which slave trade memory is active in West African society even as it appears to be forgotten.

My investment in this study is not so much about excavating or narrating the history of the slave trade itself as it is about analyzing the power of metaphor to communicate our past in ways that resist dominant narratives and produce a countermemory for those who have been dispossessed and silenced as a result of violent pasts. The slave trade is just one example of the many ways the past has been metaphorized to accommodate transmission and mobilization. I am interested in the way a formal device is able to convey such a complex legacy as the global commodification of human lives that we call the slave trade. Metaphor is a form of transgenerational conversation that we can overhear, a conversation that imparts the values and anxieties of generations scarred by the reality of oppression and terror, at the same time as it conveys to us the concerns of those who come to live in the aftermath of such violence. The use of metaphor is often necessitated by particular contemporary political and economic concerns that silence other forms of narration—circumstances that the authors studied here suggest are themselves engendered by the legacy of the slave trade. In identifying formal strategies that activate the memory of the slave trade as a mode of contemporary cultural critique, we have the opportunity to explore the political and social function of metaphor.

This study, then, is grounded in literature, while still very much invested in highlighting the voices and experiences of the West African people being represented in the literature. Utilizing first-person interviews, oral narratives, slave narratives, diaries, folklore, and African philosophy, the discussion of metaphors of the slave trade found in this book puts fiction in the context of and in conversation with the real, lived experiences of people living along the coast of Africa. It reminds us of the political potential of metaphor and of the historical significance of seemingly abstract signifiers.

Castle "Lies" and Community Knowledge

Perhaps the most lasting physical remnants of the transatlantic slave trade as well as the most readily recognized metaphors for its legacy are the more than sixty slave-trading "castles" and "forts" that stand as monuments to that era along the coast of present-day Ghana. They were built along the Atlantic coast between the fifteenth and eighteenth centuries by powerfully mobile European powers—the Dutch, the Portuguese, the French, the Brandenburg-Prussians, the British, the Danes, the Swedes. Conceived first as trading warehouses for luxuries such as gold, they were soon transformed to accommodate the sinister trade in human lives. The remains of some of the posts of the former Gold Coast still face boldly and proudly toward the Atlantic Ocean today, while others are tucked away in small coastal villages. In some of those villages, townspeople have nestled their own homes between and against these formidable centuries-old edifices.

The people who live in the cities and villages surrounding the old posts harbor a wide range of ideas about what the structures symbolize. Perhaps the most significant of the structures is Christiansborg Castle (also known as Osu), which peeks out over the edge of the Atlantic on the coast of Accra. Originally built by the Danish in 1661, it was transferred to the British and later used as the home of their colonial government.[5] When Ghana gained its independence in 1957, Christiansborg became the seat of the new postcolonial government, and in 1960 its newly elected president, Kwame Nkrumah, took up residence there. It remained the seat of government until 2008, when President John Kufuor, responding to controversy over the tainted historical implications of governing from a slave castle, moved into a newly constructed, federally funded $50 million presidential palace called Golden Jubilee House.[6] President John Atta Mills returned to Osu Castle after his election in 2009,

FIGURE 1.1 The remains of Komenda Castle in Ghana are a make-shift home to many families. *Photo courtesy of Laura Murphy (2006).*

ignoring historical arguments and favoring austerity instead, citing the enormous expense of maintaining the residence at Golden Jubilee (now officially renamed Flagstaff House). Today, after that short and highly politicized hiatus, Ghana's presidential residence is located at Osu Castle once again, and access to the castle is strictly monitored.

The castle continues, through successive governments, to signify the inheritance of political power—whether that power is exploitative or benevolent, foreign or indigenous. The legacy of exploitation that mars the site is central to continuing public debates over the propriety of fixing the seat of government at a site haunted by the most devastating reminders of violence in the nation's history, but the signification of power is so convincing that president after president returns to it as their own seat of political authority. Proponents of transforming the castle into a museum seek a corresponding transformation of the concept of political power in the country, which they think could be effected by relegating the slave trade and its monuments to a narrative of Ghana's past, exiling the trade from the landscape of contemporary politics.

Certainly, the abolition of the slave trade in West Africa did not mark the end of its effects. Those locations related to the trade took on the metaphorical pall of slave trade violence to such an extent that the government housed there appears to many as tainted by the specter of torture and the commodification of human life. Ongoing governmental attempts to redefine the function of many of the other slave trade forts reiterate that brutality as well. Ussher Fort in Accra, Fort Patience in Apam, Fort William in Anomabu, Fort St. Jago in Elmina, and Fort Metal Cross in Dixcove have all been used as police stations; Elmina Castle was used for many years as a police training station before becoming an official historical site. James Fort Prison in Accra was closed as recently as 2007.[7] Ussher Fort in Accra, which was also used as a prison for decades, was the site of an abysmal refugee camp for young men fleeing Sudan in 2005, despite its prison-like structure and lack of upkeep. As these formidable sites are transformed into police stations, prisons, and asylums, they continue to reproduce in their dungeons, their sleeping quarters, and their thick impenetrable walls the aura of violence that the slave trade imposed on them. Thus, the castles themselves metaphorize the slave trade and the detrimental toll it took on Africa, even as they are literal spaces in which the slave trade took place.

Cape Coast Castle, perhaps the most famous of the trading forts, is known for both its role as a reminder of slave trade violence and its accessibility to inquisitive visitors from all over the world. In 1979, Cape Coast was named a UNESCO World Heritage site, and rehabilitation efforts of the 1980s and 1990s aimed at creating a tourist site out of the tragedy that occurred there. Armed not only with its centuries-old cannon but also with museum-quality displays and artifacts, Cape Coast Castle has been transformed into an educational site, a home of international ethnic and heritage tourism, and a memorial to the hundreds of thousands of people lost through its "door of no return."

Though it was designated in the 1970s as a museum dedicated to the representation of West African history, by the 1990s it was clear that Cape Coast's primary role would be to encourage international visitors, particularly African Americans, to commemorate lives lost to the transatlantic slave trade, for it was within Cape Coast's walls that many African captives' dire fates were determined. Years of tense debate between museum experts, historians, funders from USAID, and delegates from the Smithsonian followed the UNESCO designation to determine the balance of content the museum would display. Even more acrimonious contestations developed between Ghanaian citizens and African American expatriates over the nature and implications of the renovations at Cape Coast Castle and its neighboring Elmina Castle. Many thought that converting the slave dungeons into a tourist attraction would diminish the gravity of the torture inflicted upon the slaves held captive there and would "whitewash" black history.[8]

Out of reverence for the historical and long-term suffering inflicted upon people of African descent in the diaspora, the inscription that was embedded into the wall of the castle as part of the renovations conveys a memorial tone that responds to many of the tensions that were evoked by the transformation of the castle into a museum:

In Everlasting Memory
Of the anguish of our ancestors
May those who died rest in peace
May those who return find their roots
May humanity never again perpetrate
Such injustice against humanity
We, the living, vow to uphold this.

Tens of thousands of tourists are welcomed each year to this monument, which has intentionally been transformed into what Pierre Nora calls a site of memory (*lieu de memoire*), a place where "memory crystallizes and secretes itself,"[9] where cultural memory is preserved, and where the past becomes activated in our contemporary lives. To ensure and augment the site's significance, museum curators constructed an official narrative regarding the life (and death) inside the walls of the castle that has been particularly meaningful for those who visit from overseas.

The castle itself plays a dual symbolic role in this elegy: It signifies the site from which Africans were expelled from their homes as well as the site at which, generations later, their descendants (both literal and symbolic) will finally find their ancestral home. At once, the castle is figured in the tourist literature as the site of the most extreme violence as well as the site of the warmest embrace for those lost long ago and now returned. It represents the commodification of human lives on the one hand, and the commodification of identity and heritage on the other. Its ambivalent metaphorization in the museum narratives works largely in the service of attracting African American visitors and encouraging emotional and financial investments in their African heritage.

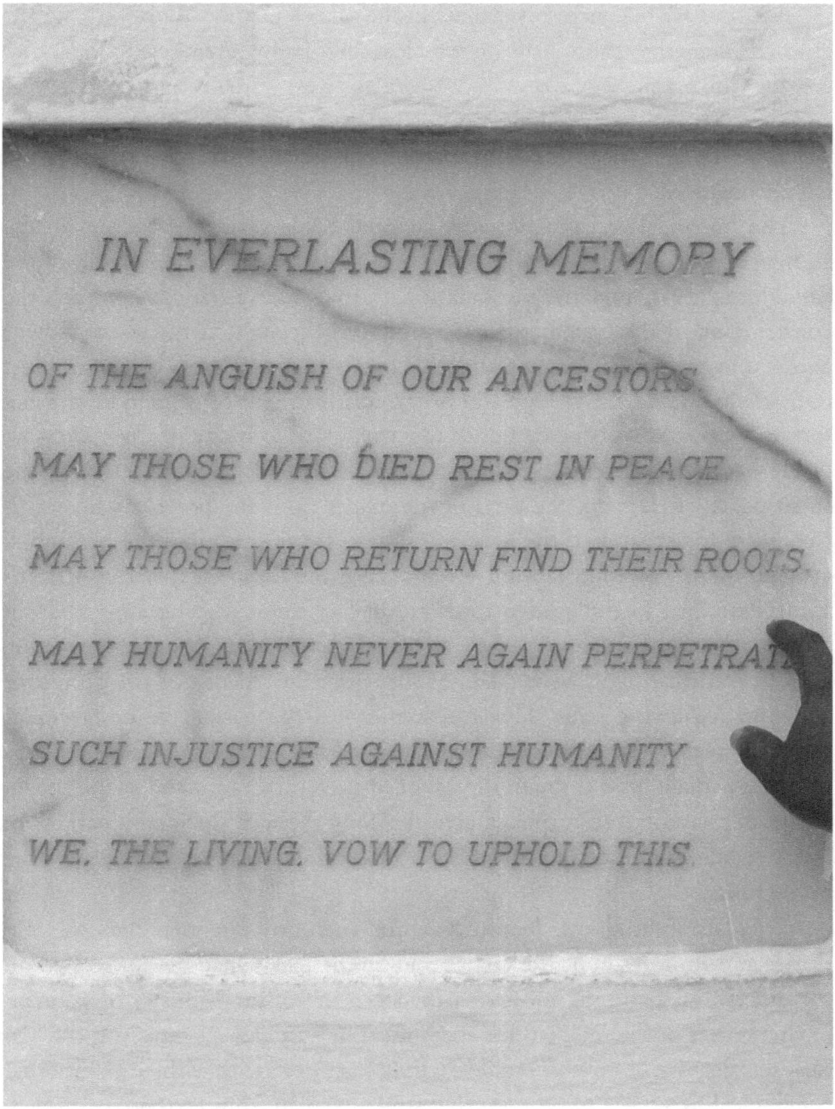

FIGURE 1.2 Cape Coast Castle Memorial Plaque. *Photo courtesy of Laura Murphy (2006).*

But who are the ancestors evoked in the castle's plaque? Who were the anguished? Were they those Africans who lost their family members to the trade? Or does the plaque evoke only those Africans who were sent to the Americas and now "return" to find their roots generations later? In the urgency of this welcome, those African losses that are not associated with the diaspora are largely obscured.

The historical account provided at each castle varies depending on the audience, the tour guide's particular interests, and the historical details of the site. Nonetheless, a relatively standard narrative of slave trade history and the construction of the forts has been reproduced throughout the coastal towns and is told to visitors, in some shape or form, at almost every remaining fort or castle in Ghana.[10] The rape and brutal mistreatment of women by the factors and governors of the castles is a fact repeated at many of these sites, no doubt because of its chilling effects. The so-called "door of no return"—the small portals that mark the exits of the castles onto the beaches where captives were forced aboard the awaiting ships—is a nearly ubiquitous symbol, evoked for its power to remind visitors from the diaspora that the Africans being described in the guided tours are in fact those who became slaves in the Americas. Official tour guides often lead visitors along the path departing African captives might have taken as they were forced out of the dungeons and into narrowing halls. This reenactment of the passage to enslavement serves to create a visceral experience of horror for the individual tourist. These routes eventually pass through the "door of no return," and end at the beach, where ships awaited the captives' arrival. Along the way, the guides narrate an affective tale of misery and torture that undergirds the typically solemn tone of the tours.

Circulating amid this institutionalized memory, however, there remain stories and rumors about the castles told by the locals that are not recited on the official tours and do not garner the attention of the Ministry of Tourism or the writers of the tour guides' speeches. They are not narratives of the historical trajectory of the slave trade on the coast, nor are they the romanticized teleological narratives of progress that students learn from textbooks. Instead, they are fragments of memories of a people's relationship to the slave trade that are secreted away in family stories and cautionary tales, "sequestered" from public view (as Bayo Holsey suggests[11]) but nonetheless privately shared all along the coast. For instance, Amissane Hackman, an official tour guide at Cape Coast Castle, confided that local people believed there was a tunnel under the sea connecting Cape Coast Castle and Elmina Castle. He had searched the entire structure but could not find evidence of such a tunnel, concluding that the story was merely "a lie" that people in the village had invented.

Perhaps it was not so much a lie as it was an explanation, via an architectural metaphor passed down through the generations, that rationalized how so many people could enter a building and never come back out.[12] The tunnel acts as a metaphor, which at one time provided a way of comprehending the seemingly inexplicable disappearance of people from the castle and now acts as a mnemonic device for remembering the devastating loss of people to the slave trade. Residents in the town of Cape Coast endured for centuries the intrusion of the slave trade in their lives, and in the intervening two centuries since the slave trade was abolished, they have passed down stories and images that have helped them comprehend the violence and suffering that took place there. The castles themselves, because of the stark contrast their forbidding edifices represent to the lifestyle and living quarters of those who live in their shadows, have come to be central to the symbolic networks of representation of the slave trade in this region.

Unofficial, unverifiable, and sometimes strictly incredible stories like the one about Cape Coast's tunnel abound at many of the sites of Ghana's trading forts and castles. As I travel around the coast of Ghana, I often ask tour guides if they know stories about the castles that are not included in the official narrative produced by the museum authorities. At Fort Amsterdam (also called Koramantin), the tour guide, Philip Atta-Yawson, mentioned that it was drunkenness that allowed the Koramantse people to be taken away on slave ships,[13] a story that Anne C. Bailey also heard from her informants in Anlo, Ghana,[14] and that the African slave Baquaqua reported as the source of his own demise in his slave narrative of 1854.[15] Another story that Atta-Yawson hears circulating among the older generation near Elmina is that early in the fort's history, Christopher Columbus found a map to the Americas in the castle.[16] At Fort Batenstein in Butre, a local tour guide provides a self-printed handout describing a time when Hitler supposedly came to hide in the fort during an exceedingly bloody battle of World War II. When asked if there is historical information regarding Fort Batenstein that the tour guides do not typically mention, an elder of Butre village explained that the hilltop fort was originally quite unstable, and it was only through sacrificing a young virgin and burying her under the foundation that the edifice was able to avoid crumbling. The Dutch, who were in charge of the construction of the building at the time, were reportedly grateful for the local intervention.[17] While it is certainly possible that some stories may be embellished for visitors (and researchers such as myself), remarkable stories such as these are told all along the coast by tour guides and locals alike, with little provocation. The stories, though they may not be accurate, help us to think about how people communicate the significance of the fort in the history of the region. These anecdotes and rumors may be clues to transgenerational memory transmission along the coast.

Most of the stories about the castles are not nearly as improbable as the ones reported above. Indeed, at almost all of the castles and forts, what people convey is a generalized cultural discourse of fear regarding these looming structures in their vicinity. Tour guide Atta-Yawson mentioned that his grandmother, who grew up near Elmina Castle, told him never to go into any of the castles because terrorizing spirits lurked there. He suggested that many older people held the same beliefs.[18] At Fort Metal Cross, an elderly tour guide mentioned that his mother did not like him to play around the fort as a child, though she worked as a domestic in the fort. He expressed a general childhood fear of the place, which he admitted defied any clear explanation and did not stem from his own personal experience with the building. The tour guide admitted that he also did not like sleeping there because he was afraid the place was haunted by the souls of captive Africans, but he did not typically mention that because the fort was used as a tourist guesthouse as well.[19] Other people along the coast express similar sentiments of fear and revulsion regarding the forts and their surroundings, echoes of the memory of slave trade violence, and also reminders that these forts were often renovated into places that represented a variety of forms of continued violence. Once they were no longer needed to house slaves, slave forts were often converted into prisons, insane asylums, military barracks, police stations, cramped refugee camps, oppressive governmental offices.

We can read these reiterations of violence within the walls of the slave castles as a reverberation of the slave trade's effects. The slave trade marked these buildings as sites of extraordinary brutality, which is repeated, both literally and figuratively, through the generations. As layer upon layer of violent history accretes onto these sites, they all too frequently become inextricably associated with memories of pain and suffering. Though the stories that people tell about the sites do not always explicitly name the earliest manifestations of the structures as trading posts for gold, ivory, or slaves, they reveal continued apprehension and terror associated with the structures.

Despite the fact that most people along the coast do not tell elaborate historical narratives of the trade, quietly kept stories regarding the nature of the trading forts that line the coast of Ghana proliferate because these ominous structures and the power they hold over the community beg explanation, even when people do not necessarily want to talk about the slave trade itself. Despite the relatively standardized historical narrative attached to the castles in official guided tours, the effects of the slave trade on individual and family lives have not been forgotten. People search for ways to understand the massive and intimidating buildings that dominate their landscapes, the proverbial elephant in the room, and they turn to family stories in order to comprehend the place these edifices have in their lives. Such stories reveal how the castles act as metaphors for the violence inflicted on communities for generations.

The metaphors associated with the castle and its mechanisms are the language through which West African people code their anxieties about power and exploitation, sacrifice and war, loss and suffering. "Lies" like the one the tour guide's grandmother told him regarding the tunnel from Cape Coast to Elmina are shared by people all along the coast—they are the secrets that are whispered near forts and castles spanning a distance of more than five hundred kilometers. The particular images of the tunnel or the sacrificed virgin are rarely if ever included in the official historical narratives of the tourist sites, but the fact that they are evoked repeatedly across a diverse geography to explain loss and fear can actually tell us more about the *effects* of the slave trade in West Africa than the histories disseminated in the tours themselves.

The significance of these stories, memories, and metaphors lies not so much in their veracity as in the realization that people in West Africa, for hundreds of years now, have sought and found mnemonic devices that serve to explain and explore the tragic realities and repercussions of the era of the slave trade. Even if we step away from the obvious and institutionalized "sites of memory" such as the slave castles, West African people have developed their own ways of explaining and describing the history of the transatlantic slave trade to help themselves and their descendants understand the devastating impact of the slave trade as well as African involvement and complicity in it. The nature of the discourse surrounding the slave trade in West Africa is varied, and in the last few decades, with the rising interest in African American genealogy and historical studies of the global trade that took place on Africa's shores, more (and no doubt new) explanations and images are in circulation. People in Ghana and all over West Africa have invented the means to explain and communicate how people could be made into commodities, how Africans could have been slave traders, how so many people could have disappeared from their shores, and how the repercussions of the slave trade continue to affect their lives.

Reading for Metaphor

Like most citizens of Cape Coast, the characters in West African fiction do not necessarily experience the slave trade as a part of their conscious, everyday lives. Nor is the slave trade usually the subject of extended narration in the common cultural discourse represented by the texts. Characters who populate the shores of a fictional West Africa, even those who dwell in the shadows of the looming slave castles, do not often brood over the historical injustice and violence of the slave trade. Instead, the slave trade typically appears in the literature in the forms of metaphors, fears, rumors, secrets, and even as misinformation, in much the same way as it appears all along the coast of Ghana.[20] Before the turn of the twenty-first century, few Anglophone West African writers made the transatlantic slave trade central to their narratives or wrote what we would call historical novels of the slave trade; indeed, in the twentieth century, they almost invariably avoided such narrativization.[21] And yet, like those anecdotes about the slave castles, which may seem largely insignificant to the people on Ghana's coast but are still being passed on and continue to affect people's behaviors and attitudes, memories of the slave trade lurk beneath the surface of many of West Africa's best-known novels and plays in the form of metaphors of capture, rebirth, suffering, and intimacy.

 Rereading West African literature in search of the metaphorization of the slave trade provides insight into the way West African authors (and people in general) explore the traumatic history of the slave trade on Africa's shores. This study focuses on some of the best-known and canonical West African works of literature because this choice makes clear that the slave trade is embedded even in the novels we most often read, teach, and discuss. As the book unfolds, many other canonical and noncanonical texts will briefly be discussed in terms of their incorporation and metaphorization of the trade as well. The objective for choosing to focus primarily on these high-profile works is to read them as representative of a larger literary trend in the late twentieth century. Furthermore, this study concentrates primarily on Anglophone Nigerian and Ghanaian fiction because those two countries are the most prolific nations in terms of literary production, but authors from Cameroon and Sierra Leone are briefly considered in this study as well.[22] Regardless of the genre or national origin, however, the slave trade plays a crucial role in the themes and concerns of West African literature. My central argument is that even when West African literary texts explicitly depict some later period or more contemporary concern, West African writers repeatedly return to the pervasive presence of the slave trade metaphorically encoded in the discourse of the region.

Metaphors of the slave trade are the unique means by which temporally distant and seemingly forgotten events are assigned to memory. Following Lakoff and Johnson, I understand metaphor to structure the very way we comprehend the world and to be "one of our most important tools for trying to comprehend partially what cannot be comprehended totally."[23] Metaphors provide insight into the way cultures—especially those that might seek to repress particular aspects of their history or to avoid historical narratives that might work in opposition to the interests of the collective memory—convey certain, very particular, aspects of their experience of the past. Ato Quayson points to a "symbolization compulsion" that is a latent and coded semiotic response to trauma that "is meant to highlight the threshold of an acute epistemological enigma signaled in the form of an insistent straying of the literal into the metaphorical, the metaphorical into the metonymic, and vice versa."[24] Metaphors package a traumatic past in a way that is digestible, communicable, and comprehensible. They turn literal pain into images that transmit the memory of suffering through the generations.

At the same time, metaphors structure the way people comprehend how the violence, corruption, and materialism of the slave trade inform their contemporary social and political lives. Because of their associations with unthinkable violence, metaphors of the slave trade can be mobilized to critique contemporary exploitation and brutality as well. As Nicolas Argenti and Katharina Schramm point out, remembering past violence can constitute a "constructive engagement with a fractured past and a moral judgment of its political significance."[25] As we will see throughout this study, West African authors layer images of slave trade violence onto scenes of contemporary political corruption, social tensions, and community cruelty to reinforce their pointed critique of contemporary Nigerian and Ghanaian societies. These metaphors are characterized by a flexibility that allows them to be transgenerationally communicated and appropriated according to changing cultural needs and interests, though they are not all necessarily passed down in an unbroken transmission from the era of the trade. Whether through mobilizing centuries-old images of the trade or through inventing new images altogether, West African authors express twentieth-century resonances of slave trade era violence through tropes that reflect the way people have come to comprehend the centuries of suffering inflicted upon Africa by the trade.

Because no living person harbors first-person memories of the slave trade, these metaphors often emerge in literary texts as if from a time beyond memory. They often *appear* to be fantastical, imaginary, fictional, or mythological, even when they can be traced to very real African experiences of the slave trade as it has been described by eighteenth- and nineteenth-century witnesses. This era of the slave trade is marginalized in history textbooks, and its effects on African coastal life and the personal suffering that resulted from it, in particular, have largely been erased from official histories as well. These metaphors often represent aspects of the African past that a community may seek to disown, but have nonetheless been contained and communicated in a more coded and less transparent form and continue to have an effect on the way people comprehend their personal experiences. Thus, when the past is actively recollected, it is through forms of what Rosalind Shaw calls "alternative history,"[26] which is not necessarily the language of narrative but takes shape in the forms of metaphors, allegories, fears, and rumors—tropes that are then passed down through generations. In the fiction of West Africa, these (sometimes cryptic) reminders of the slave trade interrupt scenes seemingly unrelated to the trade, indicating both the fragmented nature of the memory and the realistic ways people recall and experience those memories.

Though memories of the slave trade rarely take on a fully narrativized form, West African authors activate the memory of the slave trade in the shape of an image or trope, which reveals the past but is not typically explicitly historical. That trope can be an inexplicable fear of a slave castle or a physical pain that is summoned by any mention of the exchange of human lives. Though the images may function as active elements of contemporary discourse, they can often be traced back to a seed of memory planted during the era of the slave trade, connecting present concerns with the experiences of ancestors who died hundreds of years ago. When authors invent new images, not necessarily inherited from the era of the slave trade, they are suggestive of the experience of the slave trade, its violence, its physical effect on the body, its terror. Though the characters in West African fiction do not express clearly the relationship between their own suffering and the memory of the trade, the authors discussed here evoke these metaphors, through which they are able to explore the experience of the silent suffering associated with a transgenerational trauma. Though they utilize familiar historical contexts other than the slave trade and often depict characters in contemporary settings, the authors intentionally interrupt their texts with images associated with the era of the trade to indicate how their characters are indeed survivors of a long-term trauma.

Literary manifestations of the memory of the slave trade have been noted in the scholarly critical discourse as being unusual, if not entirely absent (a subject discussed at length later in this chapter); however, the slave trade is indeed referenced explicitly in several prominent West African novels. Sometimes mentioned in scholarship as exceptional cases in which West African authors atypically confront or at least mention the lasting effects of the slave trade, Achebe's *Things Fall Apart* (1959), Buchi Emecheta's *The Slave Girl* (1977), and Ayi Kwei Armah's *Two Thousand Seasons* (1973) have been treated as exemplary (if brief) in their depictions of the African relationship to the transatlantic slave trade, even as they are more substantively and explicitly exploring other concerns such as colonialism, domestic African slavery, or a more epic African history.[27]

Though the main goal of the present study is to reveal the persistent memory of the slave trade as it appears in novels where it has heretofore gone largely undiscussed, I want to begin with a short analysis of these three more prominent examples of the slave trade's appearance in West African literature, for even in these quite explicit treatments, we see secreted, metaphorized, and mythical modes of representing the trade. It is by understanding these phenomena that I will begin to frame the central work of this study: exploring and deciphering the language of slave trade memory in perhaps more surprising corners of West African literature.

Chinua Achebe's *Things Fall Apart* (1959), likely the most widely read West African novel, is focused largely on the moment when traditional Igbo culture came into contact with the missionary and colonial projects. Nonetheless, the novel contains a single instance in which the characters recognize the crucial importance of the slave trade as a foundation of the European expansion that they are witnessing at the time. In one brief reference, Obierika reminds Okonkwo of the role Europeans have played in their history. "We have heard stories about white men who made the powerful guns and the strong drinks and took slaves away across the seas, but no one thought the stories were true," Obierika recalls. The wise Uchendu replies, "There is no story that is not true."[28] The true story of European invaders who traded weapons for people was indeed recorded in the village of Umuahia, but not as part of the historical narrative of Umuahia's long and storied past. Like the "lies" told around Cape Coast Castle, the intrusion of the slave trade was not related in the oft-told tales of the great wrestlers in the village or in the recounting of the battles Umuahia had fought. Instead, the memory of the slave trade had been handed down in quietly kept rumors, and as such, the facts defy the belief of the people who hear them, even as they are being passed down through the generations.

Nevertheless, the incursion of the European slave trade did indeed affect the Umuahian culture, as it provided an entry for the violent religious and colonial conquests that take place in the novel. In this way, Achebe mobilizes the power of rumor to record a community's shared memory of a violent past—a past they would rather forget. The evidence of such a memory arises in the novel, not through long historical dramatization or through a narrative flashback, but instead in the midst of a situation that requires its recollection—it is a moment of oral transmission of memory in a literary text. Though they find it difficult to trust these stories, Obierika and his friends have access to a vital memory of a past injustice by which people were carried away as commodities in exchange for the very guns that lead Okonkwo into community punishment and exile later in the novel.

Thus, the "powerful guns" introduced by the Europeans not only embody the slave trade, but also come to stand as a metaphor for the corrupting influence that the slave trade wrought on the small African community. They are a metaphor of the violence associated with the trade, which continues to wreak its havoc on West African cultures and lives, and in particular, that of Okonkwo. Time and again in the novel, Okonkwo meets his downfall with a gun in his hand—he is severely punished for shooting at his wife during the traditional Week of Peace, and he is exiled from his home because his gun misfires and kills an innocent young boy. The gun is a constant reminder of the particularly tragic brand of violence that was introduced to the community through the trade. Achebe represents the lingering concerns regarding the slave trade's intrusion into Umuahia's narrative precisely through the provocative but muted and metaphorized nature of the telling.

Rumor also characterizes the presence of the transatlantic slave trade in Buchi Emecheta's novel *The Slave Girl* (1977). The novel depicts the story of a young girl who is the victim of an institution of domestic African slavery that postdates the era of the transatlantic slave trade by several generations. However, in the beginning of the novel, Emecheta reveals a belief widely held in the girl's village that the slave trade is the source of many of the problems that face them in 1916. In one scene based on a historical event, improbable rumors circulate that the widespread influenza outbreak of that year was conjured up as European revenge for the murder of colonial agents in Benin, an event that occurred in 1897, decades before the setting of the novel. The villagers mistakenly believe that the "Potokis" (Portuguese) had "shot" the disease into the air, and the response of "the people" is: "[The Potokis] came to places like Benin and Bonny, bought healthy slaves from our people and paid us well. And this is how they thank us."[29] Despite the fact that the Portuguese left the region many generations previous and the transatlantic slave trade had long before been eradicated, the dreadful memory of slave trading and raiding is invoked as a means to explain the unfortunate and inexplicable circumstances that befall the community.

References to the slave trade not only refer to the historical suffering associated with the commerce in human lives that no doubt affected the region in irrevocable ways. The evocation of the image of slave trading is also a vehicle that represents the inexplicable power slave-trading Europeans had to determine a community's fate even into the colonial period. These images symbolize the irrefutable exploitation of the community's resources and people. They refer to the lasting anxieties people have when they encounter sites of power. Though they clearly are misinformed about the continued presence of the Portuguese and slave trading, it is not the slave trade at all that the people are discussing by recalling the purchase of slaves on their coast. Instead, these images are indicative of a long-resident anxiety regarding the massive loss of life and large-scale bereavement brought on by mysterious causes. When disaster strikes the village, when disease takes its toll on the community, when inexplicable terror seems to be encroaching, the image of the slave trade is used to describe and understand the enormous gravity of a situation that has no discernible source. Contemporary pain is made communicable through the language of slave trade violence. The slave trade is thus woven into the subtext of Emecheta's text through the cultural discourse of fear in the community without being the actual subject of the action.

While Achebe and Emecheta have embedded the slave trade in their texts in rumor and whispers, Ayi Kwei Armah has explicitly confronted the slave trade in his fiction more than any other West African writer of the twentieth century. *Two Thousand Seasons*, perhaps his most historically driven novel, tells the story of a collective pan-African response to centuries of oppression at the hands of "white destroyers" who come from the desert and then from the ocean. Following an undeniably loose historical trajectory of African migrations that were at times threatened by and at times prompted by the trans-Saharan and the transatlantic slave trades, the novel utilizes the form of the written-oral epic to depict the heroic struggle of a small collective of Africans who refused to resign themselves to white power. A first-person plural "we" narrator strives to maintain a sense of "the way"—Armah's name for an African traditional culture and ethic that can guide African people out of domination by white destroyers and the tyranny of their "parasites," Africans who fed off the African community in order to access white power.

When Armah's narration turns to the slave trade past, the distinctively African experience is central. He concentrates on the raided villages, the wars in the interior sparked by increased slave raiding, the destruction of village life, African complicity in the trade, and African betrayals of trust by the corrupt African elite. His gaze settles on the coffles that led to the coast, life in the dungeons of the slave castle, even captivity upon the slave ship as it sailed along the African coast. Armah, invested in pursuing African memories of the trade, overtly mobilizes the text as a site of "heavy remembrance," which "should give greater force to the continuation of the beginning flow in search of our way."[30]

In confronting the slave trade directly, Armah stands out as a unique example among late twentieth-century West African writers. Indeed, he is one of the few creative writers invested in explicitly representing African precolonial history and its repercussions while other writers remain concerned with the glaring failures of contemporary African governance and other social inequalities that plague modern West African life. Armah describes the machinations of avaricious foreign invaders working hand in hand with a blind and covetous African elite, who together sought the destruction of the way of life of so many millions of Africans along the coast and well into the interior.

Nonetheless, the narrative does not constitute what we would technically call a historical novel. Unlike the typical historical novel, Armah's chronicle does not focus on recorded historical events or figures familiar to us from documentary accounts of the period. Nor does he write a neo-slave narrative like those we find in the Americas, which typically sets an extraordinary enslaved character against the background of slave history to examine the personal repercussions of the barbaric institution. Armah is not even particularly interested in an accurate depiction of those parts of the past he does represent.

What is particularly fascinating and telling about Armah's novel is that it describes slave trade history explicitly but also mythically, epically, allegorically. The setting of the novel is temporally diffuse, following undated moments along a mythical "two thousand seasons," in which it had been foretold that the people of Africa would be subjected to "fiery extinction, destruction among ashes and white, voracious conflagrations."[31] As the novel progresses, the unfortunate predictions come to pass, told through a hazy memory, bereft of details but rich in allegorical significance. Armah writes of

> [k]illers who from the desert brought us in the aftermath of Anoa's prophecy a choice of deaths: death of our spirit, the clogging destruction of our mind with their senseless religion of slavery. In answer to our refusal of this proffered death of our soul they brought our bodies slaughter. Killers who from the sea came holding death of the body in their right, the mind's annihilation in their left, shrieking fables of a white god and a son conceived, exemplar of their proffered, senseless suffering.[32]

Multiple forms of oppression coalesce as "killers" and later as "white destroyers," who visit upon Africa the most meaningless of miseries while posing in ever-changing guises. The differentiation between forms of oppression is minimized to highlight reiterations of cruelty. As the power of the white destroyers becomes more mesmerizing and infectious, African people turn from "the way" of the collective toward the temptation of self-interest. The slave trade is no longer really the central concern of the narrative, though its presence remains a motivating force in the text.

Instead, the extermination of a way of life, of a guiding ethic, becomes the real travesty of the novel, as African "parasites" adopt the blinding white path of destruction. Armah mocks the African tyrant's adoption of the white slave castle as his seat of power in a thinly veiled critique of contemporary Ghanaian politics and of the continued legacy of the slave trade in corrupt governance. In an attempt to convince the would-be African tyrant, Kamuzu, not to take the slave castle as a seat of power,

> we explained it was not power over our people we wanted, but the liberation of all of us from alien power; that if we were content, eager, in fact, to move into the seats of alien control ourselves, then we could not be liberators but traitors, another set of rotten chiefs taking advantage of our own people's immobilization to impose ourselves on them; that it might be easy enough to grasp such power at the moment, but once we succumbed to that traitorous temptation we would quickly find ourselves forced to keep faith not with our people—always the victims of this power—but with the white destroyers from the sea—the real establishers of this power.[33]

As a group of courageous initiates fights alone against shapeless and largely nameless, ever-changing forces of annihilation, the allegorical nature of the epic is explicit. Armah's sense of the uninterrupted replication of exploitative forms of power, instituted no doubt by the white destroyers, is nonetheless just as destructive in the hands of African despots.

Armah, while more explicit than any other writer in portraying the slave trade, is not attempting to write an authoritative or exhaustive or even accurate historical account of the past. Instead, he is exposing a narrative of palimpsestic oppressions that can act as a critique of the contemporary forms of conquest and subjugation that take shape in African guises. To accomplish this, he evokes the slave trade, not as a historically accurate chronicle, but as a metaphor that symbolizes the most extreme and unimaginable forms of exploitation and violence. In his call to remembrance, Armah intones,

> Certain it is decay runs exulting through our people, certain we have fallen into a grotesque dance of death, the dance of whites and kings and princes and other worms and parasites. But shall we call Idawa foolish urging us to remember even mortal bodies can destroy the lice infesting them? That our people will live, and will necessarily destroy the white destroyers infesting us together with their helpers the parasites? Shall we forget Isanusi's words: that left to ourselves our people would have the means and the will to destroy the parasites, but for thousands of seasons we have not been to ourselves, and if a path is to be found against the parasites that path must be laid deep enough to go against those bound to help the parasites against our living soul: the people of stone, the white destroyers?[34]

In employing the ambiguity and abstraction of the images of the "white destroyers" and "parasites" (as well as the positively valenced precolonial African "way") as the main focus of his pointedly critical appraisal of the last thousand years of African history, Armah releases the slave trade from its historical specificity and reduces it to the common denominator of exploitation in such a way that it becomes more readily available as a trope of the lingering reverberations of violence, cruelty, selfishness, and neglect that continue to afflict African societies into the twentieth century. The image of the slave trade itself then becomes a metaphor, as does "the way," allowing Armah the power to level a scathing critique on contemporary African forms of injustice and corrupt governance. Through this floating metaphoricity, Armah makes an optimistic plea for a social remembrance that might address crimes gone unpunished and lead Africa out of the recursive exploitation described in the novel.

These seemingly exceptional moments when African authors touch upon the history of the slave trade are actually an avenue into understanding how the transatlantic slave trade is fairly extensively figured throughout the canon. In order to examine how pervasively West African literature metaphorizes the slave trade, I turn to more oblique representations in the chapters that follow. Reading West African literature from this angle is significant, as the novels discussed in the rest of this study reveal that even in the seeming absence of explicit cultural transmission of slave trade histories, traces of the trade still survive in the metaphors, expressions, tropes, and figures that are handed down through the generations. Reading these texts through the lens of the slave trade recognizes the importance of those memories that may often go unspoken but continue to play a role in the community's discourse about itself. This method explores the potential of Ato Quayson's literary critical "calibrations," through which we can "wrest something from the aesthetic domain for the analysis and better understanding of the social."[35] By examining the metaphors of the slave trade, we can better examine the way the memory of the trade is experienced in West Africa and the effects it has had on the lives of individuals and the community.

Though many West African authors have subordinated the subject of the slave trade to other more pressing and contemporary concerns, it is fruitful for literary critics as well as historians and others interested in the legacy of the slave trade to locate the moments when authors do reveal an interest in the slave trade, to define a language through which we can understand the sometimes obscure ways the past of the slave trade is reflected in (and often interrupts) the narratives of West African literature, and to explore the implications of these moments for our understanding of how the slave trade has been remembered in West Africa. While historians and anthropologists often rely on the oral tradition to explore how the past becomes encoded in the experience of the present, the fictional and inventive nature of creative writing often leaves literature marginalized in the study of culture and the past. The metaphorical and sometimes cryptic nature of the devices used to represent the slave trade in fiction may obscure the potential use of reading this literature as a means to understanding the relationship between contemporary West African life and the history of the slave trade. However, African literature can provide significant indicators of the means of expression through which a culture transmits its past, perhaps precisely because of its inheritance of and experiments with the oral tradition. These fictional representations reveal how people package the past in a metaphor in such a way that even the most violent of memories can be passed on and even modified to serve contemporary purposes and critiques. Reading for metaphor can thus be instructive to those historians and anthropologists concerned with the historical and contemporary effects of the transatlantic slave trade.

Metaphor can accommodate meaning and memory that escapes narrative, and thus is an important site for examining how the memory of the slave trade is kept alive, even when it is not openly discussed. Jennifer Wenzel's description of the "afterlife" of the Xhosa cattle killing incident in South Africa provides an approach to memory that can be productively applied to the memory of the slave trade in the West African context. She writes that the collection of texts that represent the cattle killing, though "geographically and generically disparate," can collectively "demonstrate how narrative *form* can accommodate the presence of the dead and the haunting absence of their collective dreams."[36] Formal elements such as metaphor, images, and rumors do that same work of accommodating a past as well as the haunting *presence* of the collective memory of the slave trade. Reading the "afterlives" of slavery allows us to locate ways of understanding metaphor as an important conduit for translating the past into the present, for memorializing the transgenerational loss associated with the trade, and for critiquing how the legacy of the trade continues to have effects in the present. Furthermore, the exploration of metaphor as a site of memory can reveal the varied means by which West African people have produced a countermemory regarding the slave trade that competes with the dominant Eurocentric narrative of the trade.

The collection of metaphors discussed here is thus a potent reminder of the crucial importance of not only literary study of the trade but also the incorporation of metaphor and other figurative forms into the way we gather evidence of the past and the way the past is being recalled in the present. Paying attention to the centrality of metaphor in the coding of resistant messages and countermemory allows both the literary scholar and the social scientist access to temporalities that are not necessarily experienced linearly, and provides evidence, in fact, of how we experience the past through the way it is embedded and coded in our present. As Marcus Wood argues in his *Blind Memory*, "[T]he historic drama of transatlantic and plantation slavery must not be encapsulated in a history that appears to be stable, digested, and understood; this history is also *not over*, and is *evolving*."[37] Metaphors of the slave trade emphasize this undigested nature of the past as well as its unfortunate perpetual presence. Thus, the fluidity of metaphor, while unpredictable and multiply interpretable, embraces layered and nonlinear temporalities and reveals the "afterlife" of the past in our present. It also brings to light the very particular vehicles by which West African people transmit their most intimate and traumatizing memories.

Through the excavation of these images, it is clear that metaphors of the slave trade in West African fiction are not limited to the image of the slave castle that so many from the African diaspora hold so dearly in that paradoxical embrace discussed earlier. Instead, the metaphors for the slave trade move into the interior—into the homes of those who lost loved ones or hid from traders, into the landscapes surrounding their communities, even into their very bodies. The slave trade is not necessarily remembered as a political, cultural, or historical event. It is a personal, intimate, present experience embedded in memory and discursive forms that can survive the passing of time and that reveal the resonance of the past in the present.

Like Okonkwo's gun and the rumors about the slave castles make clear, the metaphors that emerge cannot be understood outside of the contemporary contexts in which they are used. Metaphors of the slave trade simultaneously signify the historical commodification of human life and its violent effects as well as a legacy of exploitation committed against and by people in West Africa over the last five centuries: domestic slave raiding, political violence, interethnic warfare, colonialism, resource extraction, prison abuse, alienation, poverty, and other forms of exploitation. Indeed, many West African authors use the slave trade itself as a metaphorical device that allows them to mobilize the historical violence of the era of the slave trade as a means to critique the corruption of contemporary governments and the violence and exploitation associated with contemporary life.

In Femi Osofisan's *The Oriki of a Grasshopper* (1995), for instance, Imaro accuses corrupt government officials of being modern-day slave traders, saying, "They continue to sell our people. Once it was for mirrors, for cheap jewelry, for cowries. The rich men raided the poor, captured them, and sold them off to the slave ships. . . . And the rich now have policemen. They have soldiers with numbers and uniforms. They make their numerous Luckys go down into the mines and bring out the ore. And then straight into the white ships. Always, always into the white ships. Into the insatiable white ships."[38]

The critique of the way in which state violence lends itself to global capitalist exploitation of both natural and human resources is made more radical by mobilizing the very gravity of the slave trade as a metaphor. These new "insatiable white ships" that transport the ore are personifications of the legacy of exploitation that West Africa has withstood. By relating that violence to the slave trade, Osofisan is able to amplify his critique of the corruption of contemporary politicians so that it can be condemned equally with the very worst form of exploitation Africans have encountered.

Similarly, F. Odun Balogun opens his short story collection *Adjusted Lives* (1995) with a tale of young initiates being captured and sold into the transatlantic trade,[39] and ends with a denunciation of the Structural Adjustment Programs of the 1980s as "enslavement" that was "worse than the 18th century slavery [because . . .] in the 18th century, only a portion of our population was physically enslaved, but now all of the population is enslaved."[40] In all of these texts, metaphors of the slave trade are utilized to represent the way West African people rehearse the abuses of slave traders when they replicate their paths to power. By linking the slave trade to contemporary societal and governmental failures, the authors of West African fiction utilize metaphor for its ability to highlight particular aspects of a referent and deemphasize others.[41] The use of mechanisms of the slave trade as metaphorical vehicles levels a scalding critique by focusing our attention on the violation of rights, the commodification of human life, and the exploitation of the weak that make a comparison between the slave trade and contemporary politics not only possible but politically necessary.

We can see, then, that reading these texts for metaphors of the slave trade does not limit them to one particular system of meaning or a singular interpretation. For instance, by reading Tutuola's trope of the body in the bag as a metaphor of the slave trade (as I do in chapter 1), we can better comprehend the means by which the slave trade can be metaphorized within fiction—but I want to emphasize that this is not the only way the body in the bag can be read, even within the very same text (and it is not the only way the text should be read either). The joy of metaphor is precisely this: that multiple readings, meanings, interpretations, and uses can be put to the very same image. Indeed, as we will see in chapter 2, when Okri appropriates Tutuola's image of the body in the bag, he provides new avenues for interpretation, avenues that provide useful critiques of the changing political and cultural landscape of Nigeria. It is this very flexibility that allows the metaphors to be employed over generations. It allows the authors to indicate the means by which memory can be activated in the present, as the metaphors continuously accrete meanings and values as the past and the system of images associated with it are reiterated. The multiple appropriations of the metaphor are evidence of its significance and resonance over time to describe both slavery and its legacy in West Africa.

Metaphors of the slave trade are characterized not only by their endurance over generations, but also by the shifting and accretion of meaning that accompanies such long usage. The images I will analyze in this study—the body in the bag, the *àbíkú*, the diseased body, the estranged mother, the impotent husband—are not only metaphors of the slave trade; they are also images of contemporary realities. This resemblance to contemporary reality does not undermine the slave trade valences of the metaphors so much as it underlines it. These images that become metaphors of the slave trade were not the sole invention of the slave trade; they did not disappear with the abolition of the slave trade; nor are they limited to representing the slave trade. Instead of masking the authenticity or intensity of experience in metaphor, metaphors of the slave trade expose the network of ways the slave trade has been mobilized to express African experiences of contemporary reality. As Ricoeur remarks, "Metaphor consists in obliterating the logical and established frontiers of language, in order to bring to light new resemblances the previous classification kept us from seeing."[42] Thus, the accretion of meaning on these metaphors not only demonstrates their shifting signification within the culture but represents a method of remembering the reiterations of violence that Africans have endured over the centuries.

On Amnesia in West African Literature

It is critical that we study these metaphorized representations of the slave trade in West African literature because for some time now there has been a growing popular, critical, and scholarly consensus that West African cultural memory is essentially devoid of traces of the slave trade. Although many Africanist anthropologists and historians have worked to uncover West African memories of the slave trade in their scholarship,[43] scholars who study the slave trade often lament the apparent absence of overt and explicit representation of the slave trade in cultural and literary expression. Achille Mbembe, in his article "African Modes of Self-Writing," mourns the fact that there is a dearth of investment in the history of the slave trade as it affected Africans in Africa. He claims, "There is, properly speaking, no African memory of slavery."[44]

His critique points to the deleterious repercussions on African modes of self-knowledge that result from intellectual neglect of the traumatic history of the slave trade and its contemporary effects on African life. Mbembe contends that African thinkers are blinded by both an attempt to reach toward a mythological African past that leads them to avoid the subject of slavery and a willingness to accept the illusion that "the temporalities of servitude and misery were the same on both sides of the Atlantic."[45]

Bogumil Jewsiewicki and Valetin Y. Mudimbe agree that the era of the slave trade has been erased by Afrocentric scholars, in particular, in a "colonial parenthesis" that erases the traumatic history of West Africa in favor of an essentialized, mythical African past.[46] They argue that many African historians adopt a Hegelian "conception of an interrupted time, where the intrusion of evil (a foreign invasion, but also the sins of the elite accomplices to a slave trade) breaks the original equilibrium" of a supposedly authentic Africa.[47] As a result, the drive for a redemptive and pure representation of a glorious and unified African past that can provide the basis for a triumphant future produces what they call a "black hole,"[48] which swallows any investment historians might have in representing the complicated history of European intervention and African complicity during the slave trade.

Similarly, Kwadwo Opoku-Agyemang, poet and professor at the University of Cape Coast, laments in his groundbreaking study of several brief examples of the slave trade in West African literature, that:

> what can be observed about modern African literature with regard to the range of its themes is that very few of Africa's writers have demonstrated commitment to the fullest exploration of the African experience. For the most part, our creative writers hug the bare shorelines of African history, touch the colonial experience, and report that to be all there is. The vastest depths and stretches of African history, slavery and the slave trade are never regarded in a sustained way or mined in any serious fashion for their lessons, their truths and their metaphors. . . . Modern African literature, then, is essentially a literature of forgetfulness, and the evidence is related to a gap in our history four hundred years long.[49]

Opoku-Agyemang observes that there are indeed traces of the slave trade in West African fiction, outlining a number of the most important and remarkable representations, just as Mbembe points to the methods of metaphorizing slavery in the form of witchcraft among the Temne uncovered by Shaw.[50] Nonetheless, both critics determine these literary and figurative interventions to be inadequate to the task of reminding a forgetful public of the past that informs their present. For these critics, the subordination of the slave trade to other themes and concerns undermines and undervalues the centrality of the slave trade in African history, culture, and memory.

Although as this study unfolds it will become increasingly clear that there are indeed a variety of ways West African authors have addressed the slave trade and its memory in literature without taking it on as their central historical context, it is imperative that we take these reported silences quite seriously. For, inasmuch as the metaphors of the slave trade taken up in this study speak to the way in which people do indeed memorialize that era of the past, the fact that the memory is metaphorized and therefore muted or whispered has enormous implications for understanding the West African response to the slave trade. This (suspected) literature of forgetfulness, which Opoku-Agyemang describes, speaks to a number of tensions regarding the slave trade that have relegated it to relative quiet, though not complete amnesia, as these scholars might contend.

Critics largely condemn the scholarly and intellectual community's avoidance of the slave trade in creating a narrative of Africa's past. Mudimbe and Jewsiewicki's concerns, in particular, focus on Afrocentric critics and their investment in a glorified vision of Africa that relies on the erasure of some of Africa's most painful and even embarrassing historical moments. But this attempt at repression is not solely academic. In part, the explanation for why the slave trade does not emerge as the primary theme or focus of literature and discourse in twentieth-century West African writing lies in the continued stigma attached to slavery and the slave trade in West African societies even today. Historian Emmanuel Akyeampong explains: "West Africans prefer not to discuss the legacy of slavery. Even successful and enterprising individuals do not easily shake off the social stigma of slave descent."[51] In his interviews with people who descended from slaves, Martin A. Klein makes a similar point: "Those of slave descent do not like to recognize their slave origins even where the person's origins are well-known."[52] Thus, because of the way local stigmas regarding slave status encourage people to remain hushed on the subject, the history of the transatlantic trade has not been the central impulse of narrative in West African cultures or, in turn, in its literatures.

This is due, in no small part, to the problem of African complicity in the slave trade as well. Elite African traders along the coast of West Africa trafficked in human beings in exchange for enormous personal material gain. African traders such as Antera Duke of Calabar were essential middlemen in the trade.[53] They had access to the vast human resources made available through warfare, kidnapping, and ritual sacrifice and to the vast material goods that the Europeans traded for those people. The inheritance of that trade is marked all along the coast, as families who were in control of the trade often continue to maintain both political and economic power in the region. For example, the descendants of Antera Duke remain an economically prominent and politically important family in Calabar. Robin Law chronicles the way the de Souza family of Ouidah has slowly obfuscated their ancestors' integral involvement in the slave trade in the family histories they publish.[54] Today's African elites might not want to make their ancestors' self-serving involvement in the slave trade public, nor highlight the relationship between their privileged positions and the slave-based economies that propelled many of their ancestors to power. Historian Martin A. Klein reminds us that the information passed on in African oral traditions is circumscribed by the desires of those in power. Memory and history are selective, and not everything can be stored; thus, those in power elect those moments in the past that "serve a legitimating function." Klein argues that we must understand official history as produced in this way, concerning ourselves with the question of "who and what they legitimate."[55]

The descendants of slave owners and traders have the institutional power to reject the significance of that era in West African history as it does not legitimate their role in the community. Thus, the shame of the slave trade past is one shared by both the descendants of slaves *and* slave traders. Neither community is particularly invested in reviving that past or investigating how the slave trade may have produced a disparity in wealth and power in the region that continues to play itself out in contemporary politics, social life, and kinship groups. For both groups, their legitimacy as citizens of relatively newly formed nations, free nations of free people, rests in the repudiation and delegitimation of that part of their past.

British colonial powers, too, played a role in deciding which histories of the slave trade would be legitimized, in order to solidify their role as rulers and later as cultural ambassadors in the postcolonial era. For the colonial powers to claim moral and political superiority, they could not activate a narrative of slavery that implicated them as perpetrators of a holocaust. Thus, African schoolchildren were not taught of the atrocities of the slave trade in school during the colonial period. Instead, colonial schools, in Ghana, for instance, taught children that it was domestic African slavery that presented an entrée for European interests in trafficking in humans, a curriculum that displaced European blame for the trade onto African cultures and implied a natural status as slave for African people. Students were also taught that the brutality of African warfare and conduct during the period of the slave trade required European colonization and civilization in order to provide an opportunity for Africans to achieve any participation in the global economy.[56] During the colonial period, then, the depiction of the slave trade in academic instruction was marked by a racist logic that legitimized the colonial presence and elided European violations of African sovereignty, along with the violence those encroachments entailed.

After independence, in Ghana at least, much of this same narrative was replicated in the school system, where students are often taught to avoid blaming Europeans for the slave trade and to interrogate instead how African traders could have sold other African people.[57] Furthermore, as Bayo Holsey convincingly argues, the pressure to focus on how Africa's glorious origins have inevitably led to its successful independence and bright future continues to dominate the discourse and marginalize the era of the slave trade in the romantic narrative of Ghana's past.[58] Whether given to Africans or Europeans, the privilege to author historical accounts of Africa's past has largely fallen to those who are invested in narratives that elide the era of the slave trade. In the end, many factors were, and indeed are, still working against the creation of an overt, explicit public narrative of the role the transatlantic slave trade played in West African history.

African critics such as Mbembe fear that for the African literary establishment (and for African communities in general), "coming to terms with the past," when it is so tainted by violence and even African complicity, might come to mean simply "wiping it from memory," just as Adorno feared following the Holocaust.[59] This is particularly dangerous, Adorno reminds us, when "the past one wishes to evade is still so intensely alive."[60] The critique of African scholars is meant to awaken attention to the era of the slave trade and to encourage African writers to explicitly attend to its effects on contemporary society. Mbembe maintains that "as long as continental Africans neglect to rethink slavery—not merely as a catastrophe of which they were but the victims, but as the product of a history they have played an active part in shaping—the appeal to race as the moral and political basis of solidarity will depend, to some extent, on a mirage of consciousness."[61] African discourse regarding the slave trade, according to Mbembe, must shape a narrative of incorporation and assimilation of the most sinister and most divisive aspects of that past, at least in part because it will help to provide a basis of truth upon which racial solidarity can stand. Wole Ogundele implores African authors to write about the slave trade because they "owe the exorcising narratives of these harrowing centuries to the victims of the trade and their descendants in the black diaspora, and above all to the continent."[62] For these critics, instead of avoiding the subject of the slave trade in the creation of a coherent national (and pan-African) narrative, it is precisely the explicit narrativization of the horrors inflicted by the slave trade as well as the admission of African participation in the trade that would provide the sought-after reconciliation for the suffering experienced on both sides of the Atlantic. This critical desire for and prescription of a particular form of representation (a form reminiscent, in fact, of African American representations of the trade) can sometimes challenge our ability to read the literature of West Africa as revelatory of the way metaphors of the slave trade are mobilized for memorial, historical, and political ends. This is not to argue, of course, that representing the slave trade in a metaphorized way is in some way preferable to historical novels. Indeed, as we will see in the epilogue, the twenty-first century has produced an intriguing new trend in historical novels in West Africa that deal directly with the trade and that are just as complex and compelling for scholars as the narratives in which the slave trade is structured as metaphor in the late twentieth century. However, critics who identify in African literature and discourse a silence regarding the slave trade past are not simply encountering an amnesia, but are actually encountering a particular form of representation that defies overt narrativization, for it is not the case that "silence necessarily represents a 'failure to deal with the past.'"[63]

The African critics' political goals, whether invested plainly in a more robust African memory or in pan-African reconciliation, require very specific forms of narrativization that respond directly to the political consequences of the past. As we shall see throughout this study, however, though they do not represent the slave trade in anything akin to the neo-slave narrative of African American literary tradition until the turn of the twenty-first century, it is precisely the West African writers' choice to metaphorize their memories of the slave trade that allows them to utilize literary representation as a means to address the political dimensions of the continuing legacy of violence engendered by the trade. As Rosalind Shaw argues, "'Common sense' notions of remembering and forgetting cannot encompass this instability [of transgenerational memory], or the work of sociocultural practices through which people produce and modify these processes."[64] The memory of the slave trade is "encrypted" in West African discourse, but as Argenti and Schramm suggest of traumatic memory, it is not "consigned to oblivion."[65]

The resolution to any anxiety we might have regarding whether the slave trade is adequately represented in African culture lies in our willingness to understand what constitutes representation in a more expansive light and in our investment in exploring the ways people actually convey their memories outside the confines of the (mythological though nonetheless tempting) historical "authenticity" that we find in historically situated narrative. This book seeks to address the questions Nicolas Argenti asked of slave trade memory in Cameroon: "If crimes, wars, acts of political violence, and various forms of political oppression are never spoken about, how are they remembered? To what extent is it possible to have a history of the unsaid?"[66] I argue that when we seek metaphorized forms of memory, we find that despite the near nonexistence of neo-slave narratives or protest fiction regarding the trade, West African literature is indeed brimming with traces of the slave trade and, thus, with depictions of the way in which people have expressed their historical and contemporary relationships with the trade for generations. In the case of the memory of the slave trade in West African fiction, however, those forms of violence do not go entirely unspoken. Much as Hayden White argues that annals and chronicles provide an alternative (and not an inadequate alternative) to fully narrativized histories, metaphorical representations of the slave trade express memories of the past in no less significant ways than the historical novel might.[67]

The Politics of Metaphor

Much of the desire to see literary and cultural representations of slave trade history no doubt arises from the vast proliferation of literary representations of slavery that developed in the Americas in the second half of the twentieth century. To best understand the African modes of representing the slave trade, it is useful to compare it to that of the African American literary movement that often took slavery as its central focus. To be sure, compared to their African American and Caribbean counterparts, West African writers in the twentieth century have indeed been less explicit and more figurative in the way they confront or engage the history of the slave trade. Toni Morrison considers the representation of slavery and the interior lives of slaves her responsibility as a black woman and her job as an African American writer,⁶⁸ while most West African authors tend to focus their primary attention on either the traditional past, the more recent colonial trauma, or present-day concerns like hunger, poverty, urban-rural tensions, intergenerational debates, gender relations, and government corruption.

In the wake of the civil rights movement in the United States, African American writers sought an end to the denial of extreme forms of racism and to the shame regarding slave ancestry, and in response, they produced a body of literature that made obvious the nightmare of slavery at the same time as it presented the black reading public with a usable past, filled with stories of survival, agency, and resistance.⁶⁹ In the 1960s, the genre of the neo-slave narrative clearly emerged, through which authors were able to explore the depths of slavery through historical reconstructions of the lives of fictional slaves.⁷⁰ Authors such as Toni Morrison, Charles Johnson, Robert Hayden, and Sherley Anne Williams brought slavery and the slave trade to the attention of readers across the United States and provided a countermemory to the institutionalized history of slavery. At the same time, the neo-slave narrative highlighted contemporary injustice against African Americans by emphasizing the way the history of slavery continued to inform American life well into the second half of the twentieth century.

Similar movements informed the "postslavery" literatures of the Caribbean and Latin America as well, spawning such authors, diverse in style and geographical origin, as Aimé Césaire, Edward Kamau Brathwaite, Alejo Carpentier, Miguel Barnet, Derek Walcott, and Maryse Condé,⁷¹ who directly address the history of the slave trade in their region, as well as its long-term repercussions, in contemporary life and discourse. Edouard Glissant described this writing as a "counterpoetics" that dwelled in the landscapes of an America that encourages a "tortured sense of time" that returns repeatedly to the "haunting nature of the past."⁷² As George B. Handley notes, "In form and content, [the neo-slave narratives] argue that slavery's persistent legacies are as much a result of how we choose to remember historical events as are the events themselves."⁷³ This transnational literary representation of slavery explicitly confronted, in form and content as Handley remarks, the undeniable presence of slavery in the construction of the past and present in the Americas.

In this powerful postslavery literature, the image of the slave ship has been read as the central "chronotope" of the experience of slavery in the "New World," according to Paul Gilroy.⁷⁴ In this figuration, the slave ship—the experience of seeing it for the first time, the life and death in its cargo hold, even the ship's very movement—becomes emblematic of the rupture, mobility, and transatlantic connections that have characterized the African diaspora for the last several centuries. From the standpoint of American historical and literary scholarship, critics tend to think of the Middle Passage as an origin of sorts for those who were enslaved in the Americas. The Middle Passage becomes a watershed moment or experience in the figuration and understanding of how Africans came to the Americas and as the nativity of the African diaspora. The Middle Passage, then, acts a focal point for imaginative expression of the crisis of Black Atlantic identity.

However, while Gilroy and Black Atlantic studies have spawned scholarship that seeks to connect the Atlantic world and the black diaspora to Africa, it often resorts to the image of the Middle Passage and reaches no further, revealing an American- and British-centered route to coming to terms with the African past, without ever touching Africa's shores or exploring African perspectives. Gilroy proposes to transcend the national boundaries inherent in British and American cultural studies by focusing on the slave ship as a chronotope, which is set "in motion across the spaces between Europe, America, Africa, and the Caribbean," but that motion focuses "attention on the middle passage, on the various projects for redemptive *return* to an African homeland, on the circulation of ideas and activists as well as the movement of key cultural and political artifacts."[75] It is no mistake that Gilroy uses the phrase "*return* to an African homeland," as much of his argument is focused on undermining a widely held misunderstanding of the dominant narrative of African retentions that would indicate a unilinear transmission of culture from Africa to America, which would end when the abolition of the slave trade cut off those direct connections. As a result, Gilroy's argument, despite his attempt to define and describe the crosscurrents of a black Atlantic culture, is written from the perspective of African American and Afro-British experience. In fact, Paul Zeleza goes so far as to criticize Gilroy's work as a "monument to American self-referential conceit and myopia in its obsession with the cultural inventions of the African American diaspora."[76] Gilroy's attempt to define a circum-Atlantic culture actually erases the participation of Africans in the contemporary period in the production of that discourse.

This erasure functions as if the slave ship hermetically seals the African context from the American. The African American is seemingly born on the slave ship. Though many scholars persistently and problematically refer to Patterson's notion of a "social death" suffered by captives held on slave ships,[77] within the literary and critical discourse on the slave trade, the slave ship also acts as a site of birth or reincarnation, a site of communication and transmission. It seems almost as if the slave ship is figured as a sort of womb for the African diaspora, and in Toni Morrison's *Beloved*, for instance, this relationship is explicit.[78] And as a result, the African origins—the African lives that were sacrificed for this reincarnation and the African people who were left behind to mourn and remember—are erased and silenced in the critical discourse.

Scholars searching West African fiction for the images of the slave ship or explicit narrative depictions of suffering and capture similar to those found in African American fiction could be led to believe, by its absence, that African people and writers are themselves silent on the subject. During the same period when African American authors were beginning to create a counter-memory to America's official histories of slavery, in West Africa, the advent of independence from colonial rule propelled scholars in a similar intellectual trajectory toward a usable past, but writers turned decidedly away from the era of the slave trade in their search for a historical narrative that would ground the seeming newness of their nations. In Nigeria, for instance, a lively literary community converged at the University of Ibadan, producing both creative writers and literary scholars. The continuing influence of *Negritude* and what later would be called Afrocentrism meant that much of the work (that was not directly an attack on colonialism) focused on unearthing a precolonial Africa untouched by the violence of slavery and colonialism.[79] At the University of Ghana at Legon, Kwame Nkrumah, in an effort to create a new society free from the specter of colonial histories that disparaged Africans as barbaric slaves, endorsed a history curriculum that would explicitly embrace the African past prior to the slave trade.[80]

Wole Ogundele argues that this future-myopia created a blindness to all aspects of the past that would highlight African pain, suffering, and division: "In the new Ghana," for instance, "there would be no more Ashante, Ewe, Fante, or Ga, only Ghanaians: new nation, new people, new language, new dawn: history abolished, history starting anew. This historical schizophrenia, common to all the newly independent nation-states, was not conducive to curiosity about the precolonial past beyond Negritudist celebration of culture and 'pride in our glorious past.'"[81] Seeking to highlight the elements of Africa's past that appeared unique, culturally rich, and politically positive, nationalist writings focused on the history of working communalism, the oral tradition, and African creativity and the arts. Achebe himself remarked that his own intended revolution was meant to "help my society regain belief in itself and put away the complexes of the years of denigration and self-abasement. And it is essentially a question of education, in the best sense of that word." He continues, "I would be quite satisfied if my novels (especially the ones I set in the past) did no more than teach my readers that their past—with all its imperfections—was not one long night of savagery from which the first Europeans acting on God's behalf delivered them."[82]

This archaeology of the African past—both literary and academic—sought to undermine the negative effects of the colonial mythology regarding Africa by reclaiming lost African traditions,[83] and many of the authors in this study—including Achebe and Tutuola—have been read as part of this recovery effort. Tim Woods argues that African literature responds to colonial trauma with an "obsessive return to history and the past."[84] He contends that "the choice for these African writers is not whether or not to have a past, but rather—what kind of past shall one have, and what shall be recollected and what forgotten? It is an issue of the control of memory: not only how to get a hold on the past, but also how to let it go."[85] In these early years of fervent African literary activity, there was an urge to turn away from the history of the slave trade and the trauma resulting from it by focusing efforts on the most inspiring aspects of the history of Africa and of African agency and invention. As Ayi Kwei Armah recalled, "I know, to this day, that Africans trained in literature the colonial way find it embarrassing to discuss such central issues, and seldom mention slavery in their works if writing is their profession."[86] Indeed, works that openly investigated the trade were not as typical of the African usable past renaissance as we find in the post–Civil Rights era in America.

By the end of the sixties, the first full decade of independence in Africa, both Nigeria and Ghana had ousted their newly elected governments, fallen into serious turmoil and even war, and were essentially considered failed states—if for no other reason than their failure to produce positive change in the lives of their citizens following years of foreign oppression. Thus, many authors felt compelled to turn to critiques of their current societies, producing what some critics call the "second generation" in West African writing, whose literary works focused on revealing the deep-seated disappointment and disillusionment young people felt in the decades after independence. As the earlier renaissance passed and authors began to write more critical and political works, the era of the slave trade still did not play a large role in the settings of novels and drama. As mentioned earlier there were exceptions, but even those exceptions did not constitute historical narratives of the kind produced in the Americas. For the most part the slave trade remained a subject marginalized in literature throughout the second half of the twentieth century—even as the subject permeates the subtext in the metaphorical guises we are discussing here, the slave trade is almost always subordinated to the pressing contemporary concerns of bad governance, corrupt politics, or conflicted traditional practices.

Literary critical approaches to the slave trade in African fiction have thus far emphasized this seeming lacuna, with a few exceptions that include brief discussions of the slave trade embedded in larger discussions of other issues. Critics have sometimes noted Ayi Kwei Armah's interest in the slave trade, for instance, but they typically do not analyze the formal aspects of the representation of the slave trade in a sustained way.[87] Maureen N. Eke has created a useful catalog of Ama Ata Aidoo's references to the slave trade,[88] while other critics (whom we shall discuss in chapter 5) tend to focus their energy on linking Aidoo's references to slavery to the diaspora and to the African American experience of the trade.[89] More recently, Adélékè Adéèkó has explored Yoruba-language drama for its portrayal of slavery, the slave trade, and the voice of the slave.[90] His work is particularly fascinating for his location of Yoruba *orikì* (praise poems) that praise prolific slave raiding, indicating the way literary genres continue to express and expose the values of the period of the slave trade well into the contemporary era. However, while Adéèkó's unique project addresses slave trade memory, it, too, situates itself from the perspective of the African American slave narrative and neo-slave fiction in that it focuses largely on African American literature and seeks out what Julia Sun-Joo Lee identifies as the "chronotope of the fugitive slave"[91] as its main means of identifying representations of the slave trade in West African fiction.

As a result of the political and social anxieties surrounding the slave trade as well as the dominance of African American representations in our imagination of slavery and the slave trade, critics have not typically concentrated on the figurative but nonetheless significant presence of the slave trade in the literature of West Africa. In many ways, the search for the slave trade in African literature continues to be dominated by the African American chronotope of the slave ship and a desire to see something of a protest literature or a neo-slave narrative emerge out of Africa against the atrocities committed during the era of the slave trade. Wole Ogundele condemns African authors for allowing it to be "the descendants of [slave trade] victims, in the Americas, who have been most concerned with trying to understand it at the other end, and with keeping its memory alive."[92] Ogundele's prescriptive insistence on an African authorial responsibility to represent the full history of the slave trade in literature stands as a clear example of how critics are seeking a representation of the slave trade that conforms to a preconceived notion of what constitutes significant engagement with that history. Critics who define representation of the slave trade within the terms of the historical novel or the neo-slave narrative will repeatedly find themselves disappointed by twentieth-century West African literature.

Perhaps it is possible, too, that critics have overlooked many of the manifestations of the slave trade that are outlined in the chapters that follow because they are often revealed in forms familiar to the African or Africanist reader, in figures and tropes that are so prevalent in the oral tradition that readers and critics have lost sight of the multitude of meanings the images might convey. As Paul Ricoeur notes, metaphors often recede from recognition and effect as the metaphor falls into more common usage within a culture.[93] When the literature is read against patterns of African representations of the slave trade over the last few centuries, however, it is clear that these images can be read as the structures through which West African writers and cultures express the memory of the trade.

It is politically and ethically crucial that scholars of West African literature acknowledge the alternative forms of memory that are being described by twentieth-century West African authors because when scholars declare an amnesia, the academy becomes complicit in the silencing of memory. Just as the memory of the slave trade continues to interrupt the narratives studied here, it also persists in the lives of those who continue to survive the trauma associated with it. The continued effects of the trade are expressed in gender inequalities, in the perpetuation of certain fears and anxieties, and in the commodification of human life and African cultures. If representations of the contemporary West African interaction with the past remain unrecognized or underemphasized, then they may continue to be suppressed and ignored, perpetuating the silences they themselves mourn. This is of particular importance as we try to recognize the particularity of African forms of collective memory, which are not guided or determined by European and American discourses regarding slavery. As Bayo Holsey reminds us, "The representation of the local specificity of collective memory embodies an important theoretical shift by de-universalizing European theories of historical consciousness."[94]

Thus, it must be toward the metaphors of the slave trade that we turn in order to understand how the trade is being memorialized in literature, instead of allowing the African American representation of the trade to influence our readings of literature from the other coast of the black Atlantic. By taking the metaphorical representation of the trade seriously, we embrace the African experience of the slave trade as it informs a larger understanding of the black Atlantic discourse of the trade. And then, as we turn to some recently emerging historical novels that were written at the turn of the twenty-first century in the epilogue of this book, we can better contextualize the development of the discourse regarding the trade within West Africa.

CHAPTER TWO

Magical Capture in a Landscape of Terror

The Trope of the Body in the Bag in Amos Tutuola's *My Life in the Bush of Ghosts*

We thus penetrate into the world of ghosts by means of a tragedy.

—Achille Mbembe

One afternoon while young Olaudah Equiano's parents worked in the fields, he spied an intruder kidnap the "stout" children of his neighbors two yards over. He shouted out to his friends, who caught the assailants and bound them, and together they waited for their parents to return home and punish the crime. This was no uncommon occurrence: attackers from other regions frequently raided Equiano's village to "carry off as many [children] as they could seize,"[1] a practice that was especially acute in times of famine. So common were these raids and other attacks on his village that Equiano's family and neighbors carried weapons to the fields when they worked. Young mothers were trained to wield broadswords, families fenced off their compounds with sharpened and poisoned stakes, and boys as young as Olaudah were trained in the art of warfare. As his mother's favorite child, Equiano recalls being particularly well-trained to defend himself from attack. Despite these protections and precautions, the people of Equiano's village were still not safe from invading bandits. In fact, on another morning while Equiano and his sister played alone in the house, kidnappers climbed the walls of the family compound, caught the two children unaware, and tied and gagged them before they could call out to their neighbors.

After two days of being dragged through the bush, Equiano managed to scream for help. He recalls in his autobiography of 1789 that his captors responded by tying him tighter and stowing him inside a large sack, in which they carried him for the rest of their journey through the woods. His time in the sack was a prelude, a foreshadowing, of the bondage he would experience for much of the rest of his life. Though he was born into a small sedentary village in what is now southern Nigeria, this bondage in a bag marked the beginning of his life in slavery, and it also inaugurated a life of almost constant escape, change, and movement that led him through practically all of the regions of what we now call the "Black Atlantic."

Equiano's experience was not uncommon in West Africa in the eighteenth and nineteenth centuries. The European slave trade encouraged slave raids in the interior where Equiano lived. The people of his community were oppressed by the constant "irruptions of one little state or district" (25) or another, which he later realized may have been "incited by those traders who brought the European goods . . . amongst us. Such a mode of obtaining slaves in Africa is common; and I believe more are procured [by war], and by kidnapping, than any other" (25). Philip D. Curtin remarks that "innumerable police records and criminal depositions" of the era record this kind of kidnapping, and "the dispersion of the compounds made such crimes easier to commit, and once such a child had been smuggled out of the territory of their own state, relatives could not easily follow them, as they were then in strange and hostile country and liable themselves to fall into ambushes."[2] The men, women, and children of the region could be enslaved through judicial ruling, as payment for debt, as a result of poverty and famine, and through raids and wars. By Joseph C. Miller's estimation, those weakest and youngest were often the most likely victims of the trade: "Though the buyers preferred strong adult males, the people actually captured in warfare, even in pitched battles between formal armies, included disproportionately high numbers of less-fit women and children, since the men could take flight and leave the less-mobile retinue of young and female dependents to the pursuers."[3] Equiano's narrative reveals the keen awareness that people in the interior had of imminent attack.

Fear of capture, then, was endemic and justified. Certain that at any moment they could be assaulted, bound, gagged, and carried away into the bush, people in many small unprotected villages were on their guard at all times. Sensitive to the constant danger that slave raids posed for him, Equiano's family prepared him at a young age for these raids to the extent that they could, and he remembered being able to warn others and deter the capture of his neighbors. Nonetheless, millions of West Africans, including Equiano himself, were not saved from enslavement. Raiders terrorized villages all throughout West Africa to feed the insatiable European trade. In response, the fear of random attack and captivity changed the way the people of the interior lived their lives and understood their environment. The threat of capture inscribed itself upon work habits, trade negotiations, even child-rearing. The terror inflicted by slave raiders impacted not only the traditions and habits of the people affected, but also the psychic lives of generations to come.

The Time of the Bush of Ghosts

This psychic wound is so deeply felt in the cultures of West Africa that the chaos and terror of the slave trade described by Equiano remain the backdrop, more than 150 years later, for Amos Tutuola's famous 1954 novel *My Life in the Bush of Ghosts*. The novel, which draws extensively on Yoruba folklore, follows the episodic journey of a young boy who is exiled in the "bush of ghosts," where he travels from town to town, encountering a wild variety of horrible ghosts and monsters who dwell in the dark hidden villages of the bush. There, the protagonist finds that no matter which village he travels to, no matter how nice life might seem there at first, his life in the bush of ghosts is plagued with "much trouble and severe punishment."[4]

Extensively reviewed and debated,[5] frequently examined in fiction courses, and even exploited as the subject of multiple popular cultural creations,[6] *My Life* seems to resonate with critical and popular audiences because of its fantastic depiction of what appears to be a timeless, untainted African life and culture. Harold R. Collins, for instance, appreciated Tutuola's novels for their "pristine, pagan, old African atmosphere."[7] Tutuola does set his novel in a kind of mythic time; however, it is not entirely pristine, not particularly pagan, and not precisely old Africa either. As Tutuola's protagonist travels through the bush, he also travels through time, encountering there some very specific forces in West African history—namely, the slave trade, colonialism, and the Christian mission project.

Attempting to locate the liminal space within which the narrative takes place, David Whittaker writes that the novel takes place "somewhere between the Nigeria of the 1950s and a contemporaneous spirit-realm."[8] Indeed, toward the end of the novel, on top of these palimpsestic historical impositions, Tutuola layers elements of his own mid-twentieth-century Nigerian culture, including television (161), Methodism (144), petrol and electric lights (99), and voyages to England for higher education (149). Oyekan Owomoyela is correct to conclude that Tutuola's own cultural and ideological position as a subject of British colonial rule is evident in much of his work.[9] Nonetheless, Tutuola's own contemporaneous 1950s culture clearly doesn't capture the depth of historical perspective that is implied by the novel's multiplicitous setting. Other critics, such as Ato Quayson, focus on the scene of domestic turmoil and rampant warfare that pervades the framing narrative without a particular investment in discerning the novel's specific temporal context. Quayson writes, "The opening section paints a picture of domestic strife arising from polygamous arrangements, the jealousy of rival wives, and the effect this has on the emotions of the children. This section finally ends depicting the ravages of war."[10] There is no question that it is family strife and war that compel the narrator to enter the bush of ghosts at the risk of his life, but it is more than an oblique reference to warfare that Tutuola intends to inscribe in the tumultuous setting as well as in the psychic life of his character.

In a style typical of a framing narrative (which is itself typical of many oral narratives that have been novelized), Tutuola introduces the main themes and settings that will guide the rest of his novel. The story does indeed begin with the protagonist's mother's struggle with her co-wives. By the third paragraph, however, the setting of the novel moves away from a domestic one to focus on the turmoil surrounding the village in which the narrator lives:

> In those days of unknown year . . . there were many kinds of African wars and some of them are as follows: general wars, tribal wars, burglary wars, and the slave wars which were very common in every town and village and particularly in famous markets and on main roads of big towns at any time in the day or night. These slave-wars were causing dead luck to both old and young of those days, because if one is captured, he or she would be sold into slavery for foreigners who would carry him or her to unknown destinations to be killed for the buyer's god or to be working for him. (17–18)

Tutuola reminds us later in the novel that "the slave trade was then still existing" (167) and that it was a "war of slavery" that "drove him into the bush" (151). Surely this is not Whittaker's Nigeria of the 1950s, even if inflected with the supernatural. Though later events in the bush reveal a layered temporality that allows for knowledge of mid-twentieth-century innovations, there is no mistaking from the very first page that the impetus for the narrator's journey into the bush is the slave trade itself. As time lines converge in the bush of ghosts, these specific historical references to the slave trade are crucial to comprehending the complexity of what Tutuola has contributed to the Yoruba folklore he has adapted for his novel.

These images of slave warfare may very well stem from the violent period of the Yoruba wars that took place in the early decades of the nineteenth century in the region we now call Nigeria. Slave raiding in Yorubaland reached its height relatively late, largely after 1790, in fact.[11] Despite British and US "abolition" of the transatlantic trade in 1807 and 1808 respectively, fifty thousand slaves left the shores of Lagos alone in the first decade of the nineteenth century, bound largely for Brazil, making Lagos West Africa's leading slave port in the transatlantic trade following the official abolition.[12] Lagos continued its dominance through the first half of the nineteenth century, as a series of events (including the fall of Oyo, jihads in the Sokoto caliphate, pressures from Dahomey's trade and its increased regional warfare, and regional conflicts among the Yoruba that ensued thereafter) led to the intensification of warfare and kidnapping in the Yoruba regions, feeding constantly increasing numbers of Yoruba captives into the slave trade. Much of this warfare was inspired itself by competition for stakes in the European trade,[13] and the Yoruba were among its most prevalent victims.[14] Furthermore, as Olatunji Ojo has argued, "With the rise of Lagos, Yorubaland became intimately drawn into the Atlantic trade. Its proximity to the Yoruba interior increased the violence associated with slaving, creating an expanding slaving frontier in the interior. Slave trading and violence were mutually reinforcing. Slaving operations intensified regional interstate rivalries; warfare weakened civilian chiefs, boosted soldiering, and pitted soldiers against their monarchs."[15]

This coincided with and encouraged what is known as "the Yoruba Wars," a long series of regional conflicts over control of access to slave-trading routes and to regional power. Those conflicts in and of themselves produced much-sought-after slaves for the transatlantic trade as well as encouraged increased domestic slave ownership, especially as the increased sale of slaves into the European trade required greater military strength that was supplied by domestic slaves.[16] During this period, rampant slave raiding threatened even the remotest of villages, and the city of Tutuola's birth, Abeokuta, was itself inhabited by refugees of the Yoruba territorial wars, who sought a safe haven in which they could hide from battles as well as slave raiders.[17] As slaves were kidnapped, taken as ransom, or taken as war captives, they were transported through the interior of Africa, often for months at a time, and sometimes they were hired out or sold as domestic slaves. Eventually, the majority of these captives were sold into the transatlantic slave trade.

Though the Yoruba wars no doubt increased the domestic trade and of course fed it, it was largely fueled by transatlantic needs and desires and economies. Patrick Manning notes that while there was indeed an increase in domestically held slaves in this region, the forces that fed into the transatlantic slave trade, including the Yoruba wars and the jihad of the Sokoto Caliphate, significantly reduced the Yoruba population residing on the continent in the early nineteenth century.[18] In this way, even after the official abolition of the slave trade, the transatlantic trade continued to flourish in the Yoruba region, and not coincidentally, increased slave raiding, slave wars, and slave labor on the continent as well. Though Tutuola does not name the precise conflicts to which he refers in the beginning of the novel, it appears that the Yoruba oral tradition from which he draws his narrative has kept a record of the lingering memory of the history of persistent conflict in the region and the "slave wars" that left people vulnerable to captivity and enslavement.

Tutuola's horrified description of being sold to foreigners in the framing narrative of *My Life* reveals emotively the terrifying effects the Yoruba wars and other slave-raiding conflicts had on the lives of those who lived in West Africa at the time, noting that both old and young could be captured and "sold into slavery for foreigners . . . to be working for him" (18). Though it is Africans who were the narrator's captors, his fear emerges from a cultural comprehension of captivity informed by the realities engendered by the transatlantic slave trade. Though no child would know for sure the destination of those who were made captive and certainly would not be able to imagine the suffering of forced labor in the Americas or in other parts of West Africa, the narrator's vivid recitation of a captive's possible fates allows Tutuola to effectively describe the fear inscribed on the imaginations of the victims of slave trade violence—whether they were taken away to another part of Africa to be "killed for the buyer's god" (18), taken far away to work for some other person, or left behind to ponder the terrifying fates of their lost loved ones, as the protagonist is left to do. Regardless of what time lines may converge in the liminal realm of the bush in the chapters that follow, the impetus for the action of the novel is firmly located in the chaos of these slave raids. The vivid descriptions in the framing narrative explore the imaginary realm of terror that the prospect of slavery and slave raiding represents for the narrator, a terror that must inform our reading of the mythic episodes that follow in the text.

It is in this setting of rampant slave raids and warfare, then, that the narrator of Tutuola's novel finds himself alone at home with his brother while his mother is away working. As in Equiano's narrative, this situation leaves the narrator and his sibling vulnerable to attack by slave raiders. The boys recognize that what he later calls a "war of slavery" (151) had broken out just outside their compound, so the boys decide to leave their home behind, run into the bush, and hide under a tree. Terrified and nearly paralyzed by their doomed fates, the two boys cannot take their eyes off each other as the older one flees and the younger is left helpless and alone in the woods. Minutes later, the narrator hears his brother call out for help, and he realizes, with some vague relief, that at least his brother had been "only captured as a slave and not killed" (21). Our young narrator is left alone at the edge of the bush, where "no brother, mother, father, or other defender could save me or direct me if and whenever any danger is imminent" (21). Even in this opening chapter, Tutuola reveals some of the most harrowing conditions the slave trade introduced to the people of West Africa. Their villages pillaged by people who often looked much like themselves, the Yoruba and so many other vulnerable groups were haunted by the specter of enslavement in their daily lives. The slave trade stripped uncountable men, women, and children of their closest relations and most intimate connections and left them vulnerable to death, disease, and extraordinary suffering. Knowing that he could not outrun this fate, the protagonist laments that "no doubt I would be easily captured or killed" (20). The young boy remains completely devastated by the overwhelming toll the slave raid took on his family and on any prospects he might have for protecting his own future as well. In fear that he, too, will be captured, he takes refuge in the forbidden bush of ghosts.

The overwhelming fear and sadness that Tutuola depicts in the framing narrative is evocative of the personal psychic devastation that took place all over West Africa during the era of the slave trade. More than twelve million people were made slaves and transported to the Americas to labor on plantations. However, those Africans who remained on the continent were no doubt affected by the destructive impact of the slave trade as well. Like the protagonist of *My Life in the Bush of Ghosts*, millions of people lost their mothers, brothers, and other family members to slave raids and slave warfare during the era of the slave trade. What remained in place of those intimate connections was dislocation, both physical and emotional. Like those people who founded Tutuola's own native village of Abeokuta after fleeing slave raiders, uncountable West African people were physically dislocated from their homes and any sense of geographical stability they might have enjoyed before this era of rampant warfare. Separated forever from their relations, their homes, and life as they knew it, refugees of the slave trade no doubt experienced an enormous sense of emotional dislocation as well.

When the young narrator's only escape from being captured by slave raiders is to enter the dark and forbidding bush, then, it is not solely some mythical time line that leads the protagonist into his innocent adventure. Instead, the bush is Tutuola's figuration of that physical and psychic dislocation, a portrait of exile in a landscape of terror.[19] Though the narrator is able to escape the actual slave raiders, he is never able to escape their lingering presence in his memory, his imagination, and even in his lived experience thereafter. This chapter explores the ways Tutuola employs the Yoruba oral tradition to represent the enduring legacy and memory of the slave trade in West African culture and psychology through his depiction of "life in the bush of ghosts" and the trope of the body in the bag that represents it.

The Cautionary Novel

An examination of the typical uses of the oral tradition from which Tutuola takes his narrative supports this new reading of the novel's historical complexity. *My Life* is Tutuola's refashioning of a series of familiar Yoruba tales, which he recalled listening to with his playmates in the evenings of his youth.[20] When the narrator of *My Life* is chased into the bush, he is chased into an unwitting performance of oral narratives, rehearsing time and again the fears and misadventures so familiar in Yoruba cultural discourse. His episodes in the bush are based on a number of different Yoruba oral sources, including hunters' tales and cautionary tales for children. In the oral tradition, each genre can serve multiple purposes within a community.

Cautionary tales, perhaps unsurprisingly, seek to caution people, old and young, to the dangers that might await them, and they present the audience with a model of behavior (and restrictions) that will help community members avoid such risks. For instance, cautionary tales often advise against travel in the woods alone by depicting the horrible fates of young people who dare cross into the evil realm of the forest. Moreover, simply by putting these dangers into language, oral narrators allow the silenced and unspoken fears of a community to be explored.[21] The stories allow audiences a means of escaping their fears by exploring them through the mode of the fantastic, in which the protagonist exceeds the limits of human life to defeat the forces that seek to destroy him, helping the community "come to terms with the world in which they live" and assert an identity that can aid them "in the face of the vicissitudes of history,"[22] as Isidore Okpewho has noted.

However, Tutuola's work is more than simply a recitation of the oft-told tales of the Yoruba. Though many of Tutuola's earliest Nigerian critics berated him for simply reiterating Yoruba folklore in his work,[23] Ato Quayson is correct in contending that we should understand Tutuola's work as a "strategic transformation" of literary genres, incorporating these elements of the oral tradition itself into a wholly new hybrid form.[24] The form Tutuola adopts is not strictly oral and not purely fiction but what F. Abiola Irele calls "a mythic novel," describing those African novels that "retain the essence" of the oral narrative in its allegorical and symbolic nature at the same time as they integrate the "dimension of a developed narrative form."[25] As such, Tutuola's work can be read as a collection of episodic oral tales or even as the picaresque,[26] but it is in his attention to the longer narrative arc, what Afolabi Afolayan calls the "single super-story,"[27] and to the formal qualities of the novel, that Tutuola reinvents the Yoruba oral tradition and manages to underline the ways the legacy of the slave trade in West African life has been represented for generations in the tales of his culture.

Reading *My Life* as a *cautionary novel* (as opposed to a series of cautionary tales) calls attention to the function of narrative and form in the work, and thereby calls attention to the more specific narrative setting and its historical implications, as well as to the use of literary figurative language and novelistic structures. As these cautionary traditions are translated into written form, they take on some of the dominant aspects of that form. The general "flatness" of the hero in the oral tradition, as described by Walter Ong,[28] is shed in Tutuola's move to the cautionary novel. The narrator of *My Life* is not the singular hero or hunter of the oral tradition; he is the child of the bildungsroman, the novel of growth and development. The structure of the novel affords Tutuola the opportunity to release the narrator from the static role of the archetype. Instead, the narrator's development (into one who knows good from bad, as he puts it) transforms a collection of Yoruba tales into a journey of psychological and moral development. The plot of this novel traces a narrator's narrow escapes from a horrifying fate only to find that the fate follows him nonetheless. Through the course of the narrative, he learns how to escape the haunting presence of his past and to use his acceptance of his fate as a way to return to the safety of his home. The narrator's return is not to his originary state of being, however; this narrative is one of a psychic journey from trauma to healing. It is the narrative of a personal quest for acceptance of one's fate, one's history, and one's experience.

With the added overt caution against slave raiders in the framing narrative, the rest of the seemingly episodic tale becomes a narrative that describes the long arc of a character emblematically working through the trauma of his encounter with the slave trade. By setting traditional oral narratives in an overtly historical framing narrative drawn from images of the slave trade, Tutuola historicizes and politicizes what might seem to be a series of generalized apolitical and ahistorical warnings to children. The written form allows Tutuola to turn a series of ghost stories into an allegorical reconstruction of past violence and alludes to a present fraught with the fear of repeating that trauma. Quayson argues that "what Tutuola elaborates are the more harrowing aspects of cautionary tales."[29] Indeed, Tutuola merges the implicit cautionary tales with the explicit landscapes, time frames, and metaphors of the slave trade to produce a novel that can provide context to the imaginative landscape represented in the folkloric tradition of the Yoruba. It is precisely through the migration of these stories from the world of the oral to the world of the written that Tutuola underlines the memory of the ghosts of slavery that is indeed alive in the West African imagination of the bush.

Magical Capture in a Landscape of Terror

In this proverbial bush, the narrator encounters the most terrorizing memories of all of Yoruba history: captivity and enslavement. When the young Yoruba boy enters the "dreadful bush" to escape the capture that befell his brother, he is unaware of its dangers and that it was "banned to be entered by any earthly person" (22). From the moment he enters the bush, however, he is surrounded by a whole host of terrors in ghostly forms—slavery is a constant risk in the bush, as are cannibalism, sacrifice, hunger, metamorphosis, murder, rape, and dismemberment. Tutuola evokes a panoply of fears of the bush to set the stage for the various forms of literal and figurative enslavement the narrator will meet while traveling in this haunted landscape. The threat of these bodily violations sets him on a path of almost constant motion, and the narrative arc of the larger novel is propelled by the protagonist's narrow escapes from capture in every corner of the bush, a resonant echoing of the near death experience he has just escaped by entering. In one episode, for instance, the narrator escapes being kept as the property of a cow-herding ghost only by his inability to eat grass, which leaves him starving and renders him useless to his owner, who then decides to kill him instead. He escapes his own murder only by being put on an auction block and sold to another woman who wants to sacrifice him to her god. The narrator finally runs away from the scene of sacrifice because he hears another man boast that he plans to eat the protagonist once he is sacrificed (44–48). The terrors fold in on themselves so that they all seem to be functions of one another—slavery requires dismemberment, hunger leads to human sacrifice, metamorphosis aids enslavement, cannibalism is undone by murderousness. The environment of the bush is one in which time lines and forms of violence merge, collapsing reiterations of slave trade captivity with images of all manner of hideous violence, revealing the way centuries of fears can be conflated in the imagination and can come to be associated with liminal spaces such as the bush.

Having only barely escaped the grip of the slave raiders in his home village, the protagonist is faced at every turn with an overwhelming number of reiterations of that captivity, indicating how the haunting memory of the threat of capture initiated during the slave wars has inscribed itself in the terrifying landscape of the bush. Fear of captivity in the bush of ghosts becomes the primary motivating force of the text and its protagonist's movements and emotions. As the narrative progresses, the landscape produces ever more frightening spirits, even those the narrator cannot see at all, all too many of whom plot his capture. In one episode, the narrator stops to take a rest in a tree he thinks will be safe for the evening. It appears that "every part of this bush was as clear as daytime," but when he looks again, he realizes that "there were uncountable . . . ghosts already surrounding the tree. They were waiting for me . . . they got ready to capture me" (66). Like his own childhood in his home village, although he believes himself to be safe, deep within this "landscape of terror,"[30] the narrator is faced with almost inevitable capture. "The whole of them seized me by violence or rape at the same time. . . . I thought they were going to eat me alive" (66–67).[31] Refusing the narrator any possibility of escape, the ghosts violate his body in the most violent ways; they "rape" him, they rub his body with sandpaper hands, they blind him, and they cut him with their razor-sharp fingernails (67). The landscape itself inflicts physical brutality and captivity upon the innocent narrator, elucidating how the bush surrounding villages has come to act as a metaphor for the lingering terror of capture and enslavement that permeates the cultures of the coast even into the middle of the twentieth century when Tutuola was writing. The threat of capture appears on nearly every page of the novel, reiterations of the originary violence that sent the child into the bush in the first place, reiterations of a historical violence that plagued the Yoruba culture for decades in the early nineteenth century.

The landscape's terrifying anthropomorphism becomes even more apparent later in the text, when, as the narrator tries to escape ghosts who are threatening to "catch and kill" him, the landscape "blows alarm" at his every step. The "talking land" reveals his location to his captors, as it attempts to aid his pursuers in his capture (85). The very landscape itself acts as a captor—there is nowhere in the bush that the protagonist is actually free from the threat of captivity. Tutuola's figuration of the bush as a landscape of captivity reveals the way in which memories and anxieties of slave raiding have become translated into narratives of ever-lurking captivity in the bush. Through his imaginary landscape filled with beasts and deception, Tutuola reveals the depth of anxiety experienced during the period of the slave trade but also lingering tenaciously even into the twentieth-century West African imagination. As Diana Mafe has noted, the bush is a representation of "conflict, specifically external conflict," through which the demarcation between self and other, danger and safety, home and exile is constantly being reiterated.[32] The discourse that links the bush landscape—ever-present on the periphery of a village and in a community's experience—to the violence of the slave trade reveals not only the extent to which geography played a role in the West African slave trade but also the temporal reach of the terror associated with it.

Derived from the folk traditions of the Yoruba, these tales of a haunted bush become particularly poignant as they reveal the lingering memory of captivity and degradation engendered by the slave trade. There is an essential conflation here of the two fears associated with the bush in the West African literary and oral tradition that illuminates the psychic power of terror. In Tutuola's narrative, the two most terrorizing inhabitants of the forest—slave raiders and the spirits/dead are superimposed on one another. Capture is the meeting point of these two assaults on the body and psyche. Even though the narrator seeks to escape the slave trade by entering the bush, the two are practically equated, for being in the bush of ghosts means certain enslavement. The bush becomes a metaphor for the terrors associated with the slave trade, and as such it haunts the African imagination. As we shall see played out even more explicitly in the readings that follow, through a sort of magical capture, the ghosts of the bush are able to lay complete claim upon the body of the protagonist, even to the point of creating him anew against his will. The body is no longer human in this economy but simply understood as the sum of its labor, as those enslaved were captives of a system from which they did not themselves profit. Gilles Deleuze and Felix Guattari understand capture to be a central capacity of the capitalist system. States capture labor to operate the machine of capitalism. Magical capture, in their formulation, is a power of the state, and in Tutuola's bush, it is ghoulishly transfigured.[33] Magical capture is mobilized by an extensive system of actors that sets in motion a global economy. For Tutuola and generations of storytellers all over the West African coast, magical capture is the means by which innocent villagers are brought into this vast system of exploitation and even consumption of African lives.

Even more vast and long-reaching, however, is the power that this enslavement has psychically. It is impossible in light of the framing narrative to avoid the implications of the narrator's being repeatedly bought and sold or traded in the novel. As we will see, the narrator of *My Life* is rarely ever captured without being forced to labor for his ghostly masters. His captivity leads to nearly inevitable enslavement. He is a representative of all the African victims of the slave trade, literally hunted and figuratively haunted by the slave trade. The slave trade not only captured bodies, but it captured minds and imaginations. Magical capture in the bush of ghosts, in this reformulation, becomes the way in which slave raiders continue to haunt the stories and also the lives of those living in West Africa. Magical capture, by necessity, must attempt to dehumanize its object in an effort to create from it precisely the kind of work animal that Tutuola's protagonist becomes. These metaphors of the slave trade reveal that imagination and memory have not been freed from the terror of the trade. In Tutuola's *My Life in the Bush of Ghosts*, this memory of dehumanization continues to haunt the landscape of West Africa and inspires the various literary guises that memorialize the atrocities of the violent past.

Dismembering Slavery

It is with this memory of pervasive fears of captivity and enslavement in mind that Tutuola himself writes, and in this landscape of persistent terror that Tutuola's narrator travels. The slave raiders in the land of the living compel him to escape into the forbidden forest, but as his journey through the bush of ghosts begins, the dislocated narrator is nonetheless haunted by the reminders of the trauma he just experienced. He remarks that "I could not stop in one place, as the noises of the guns were driving me farther and farther. . . .

After I had travelled sixteen miles [I] was still running further for the fearful noises" (22). Set in motion by the sounds and terrors of the slave trade, the protagonist delves deeper and deeper into forbidden territory, the only refuge he thinks he might have from being captured and made a slave. No matter how far he travels, however, he cannot escape the audible reminders of what happened during the slave raid.

In hopes of finding comfort from these terrors, the young boy enters an old house, which he imagines to be innocuous, but soon finds that it is inhabited by three very strange ghosts: one made of gold, one made of copper, and one made of silver. As he enters, he realizes that he is in a home of great luxury and wealth: everything in the house gleams because it is made of precious metals. He is lured in by the scent of delicious foods in the air. Like those who became vulnerable to the slave trade as a result of famines, droughts, and other community hardships, the narrator allows his stomach to decide which of these metallic ghosts he will follow when they beckon him to choose a master. The narrator's body itself begins to shimmer as the reflection of these ghostly metals shines upon him. "When I looked at myself I thought that I became gold as it was shining on my body, so at that time I preferred most to go to him because of his golden light" (24–25). His body is marked by their wealth, though he is not allowed the luxury of it. Dizzied by the light, he is made subject to them in both body and mind—the ghosts can hear and control his thoughts, through which they control his body and attempt to control his labor.

Ironically, because "every one of [the ghosts] wanted [the protagonist] to be his servant," the young boy has become the most precious and desired object in this room of extraordinary wealth (24). In a bizarre reversal of a slave auction, the three ghosts of precious metals—personifications of wealth themselves—compete to make the narrator their slave and inscribe or brand their marks of wealth upon his body, but only to the end that he must himself choose which of these ghoulish creatures he will serve. Though he is allowed a choice, he is nonetheless captive: the lights they shine upon the protagonist paralyze him, and his only choice is one of three all-too-similar fates of enslavement. Extreme hunger motivates his final decision, and he is tempted most to follow the scent of African cuisine offered by the copper ghost. He enters the copper ghost's home, unavoidably making a servant of himself for the first time in the novel, even as his foray into the bush itself was an attempt to escape the enslavement awaiting him at the hands of the raiders in his home village (27).

Unsatisfied with his decision, the three ghosts struggle over who should be master to their new captive. In the first in a series of physical bindings suffered by the protagonist, the young boy is held possessively by all three of the ghosts, multiply embraced until he "could not breathe in or out." Suffocating in the grasp of this spectacular bondage, the narrator is visited by "uncountable numbers" of ghosts who enter to settle the conflict. "It was at this time I noticed carefully all the ghosts who came to settle the matter that many of them had no hands and some had no fingers, some had no feet and arms but jumped instead of walking. Some had heads without eyes and ears" (27). All of the ghosts he encounters in this village seem to have an amputation of some kind: missing limbs, missing eyes, missing heads, or at the very least missing clothing. Though the three ghosts arguing for ownership of the new young visitor might enjoy golden and silver splendor, their neighbors all suffer from some bodily trauma or disability, and all run naked through the bush, representing the figurative dismemberment effected on communities through the slave trade and its attendant commodification of human life. Their bodies have all been devoured by the environment of human consumption engendered by the slave trade. The narrator's inverted auction turns into potential mayhem, then, as the negotiators propose to rip the young boy into three parts in order to share his labor (30), revealing the way the body in slavery is made other to such an extent that its integrity is no longer a priority. Indeed, equated as it is to its labor alone, the narrator's body can no longer justifiably be kept whole. Like the others in the community, his body pays the price of this inhuman trade; he, too, risks dismemberment as these ghosts attempt to force him into servitude. Within the economy of slavery, this unique division of labor is enacted on the body, through which all parties can benefit from that human commodity more precious than any gold, silver, or copper.

The Trope of the Body in the Bag

The narrator is saved and his body is left intact only when he is kidnapped by another more powerful (but "smelly") ghost, who engages the protagonist as his own personal slave. The narrator recounts his entrapment by the "Smelling-Ghost," who "gripped me with his big hands which were very hot and put me into the big bag which he hung on his left shoulder" (30). For three days, the Smelling-Ghost carries the young boy through the forest to his own village in a repulsive hunting sack, despite the protagonist's vocal protestations and anxious prayers that he be set free. The narrator depicts life inside the bag at length, depicting his own fears of the insects that lived inside the bag, the heavy items the ghost threw into the bag onto his prone and unprotected body, and his constant dread of the fate that might await him when the ghost finally opened the sack again (30). He plots his escape from the sack, hoping that he can trick the ghost, but he is held captive without any means of escape for the Smelling-Ghost's entire journey to his home village.

Childhood fear of capture emerges in the narrative here, in this most unlikely detail, what I am calling the "trope of the body in the bag." In *My Life in the Bush of Ghosts*, this trope is a means of metaphorizing the complete subordination of the slave's body. Later in the narrative, the protagonist is found at a crossroads by some ghosts who, again, "came to me and put me inside a bag which they brought" (72), in which they carried him to their town to serve their king. Throughout the novel, the narrator is made captive in other forms of bondage that are reminiscent of the bag. Mobility is necessarily circumscribed for "the body in the bag." In this form of capture, freedom is essentially eliminated, reminiscent of the life of enslavement that the narrator only narrowly escaped in the land of the living.

Regardless of whether this mode of capture and transport is feasible or efficient for the slave trader or whether this was a common or even historically accurate means of moving young captives, the fear that one might be kidnapped and carried away in a sack is clearly a meaningful trope in the African imagination of the slave trade. Stories of surprise kidnapping and captivity abound in West African folklore. A traditional Igbo tale tells a very similar story to the one told by Tutuola, in which the townspeople "live in terror of the beasts of the land and of the sea, for these beasts occasionally invaded them and carried many of their children away." Two young sisters defy their parents' orders to remain quiet to avoid capture and are thus carried away by these beasts. One is made a slave and the other a rich wife. When the two meet again, it is in the roles of slave and slave master.[34] This story records the persistent terror of slave raiders in the collective memory of the Igbo.

Some testimonies of enslaved people further confirm the existence of the fear of being made a captive in a sack in particular, and its significance for West African memories of the slave trade. Christian G. A. Oldendorp, for instance, interviewed a West African victim of the slave trade who had been displaced to the Caribbean and who described the methods by which people were being brought to the coast for sale: "Amina negroes were walking about and robbing [kidnapping] humans, especially children. They would put gags into their mouths, so that they would not be able to scream, and they put the children into sacks."[35] Naana Jane Opoku-Agyemang recorded a story in Gwollu, in northern Ghana, that recalled the "weird stories" that emerged at the onset of a period of slave raiding in the region of people "being trapped in nets and whisked away on the back of a huge animal."[36] Olaudah Equiano, as we recall, was held hostage in a sack and carried across the countryside to be sold into slavery (33), laying a foundation for the narrative reiterations in Tutuola's work.

This image is reinforced as a trope in literature as it comes to stand for violence and suffering when the slave trade itself is not necessarily conspicuous in the text. D. O. Fagunwa's *The Forest of a Thousand Daemons* describes a creature named Peril, "who fathered Loss who lived in the household of Starvation" and who seized the protagonist, confined him in a bag, and attempted to carry him away to his lair of mourning.[37] Tutuola's other work is persistently haunted by the specter of the sack. In Tutuola's *Simbi and the Satyr of the Dark Jungle*, for instance, the title character Simbi is kidnapped, taken to the "end of the world," and sold with other captives "as slaves for the foreigners." Simbi is eventually sold to a king who takes her as his slave in the expectation that he will sacrifice her. Throughout the novel, she is transferred from owner to owner and is carried in sacks along the way by her final owner, the Satyr.[38] In Tutuola's novels, characters who travel forbidden paths regularly encounter the terrorizing fear of being carried in a sack to a horrible fate. Ben Okri's *The Famished Road* signifies on this traditional trope of the body in the bag to create a sort of womb from which the enslaved captive rebirths himself into freedom, as will be discussed at length in the next chapter.[39]

These manifestations of the African body in the bag reflect the persistence of the memories of slave trade trauma recorded by Equiano and Oldendorp. As a mechanism of slave raiding, the sack acts as a metonym of the slave trade and of the slavery that people like Equiano suffered for decades after his capture. For Tutuola, the bag functions as a tool of the terrifying bush landscape, and in its juxtaposition to a slave raid and other forms of enslavement, acts as a reminder of the history of slave trade violence. The narrator's long episodic experience in the bush can be read, then, as an extension and reiteration of the attack on his life and his freedom in his home village. Once in the bush, capture seems inevitable, and the bag operates as a symbol of the inescapable strength of the mysterious powers of the slave trade that lurk in the shadows of the bush.

Held captive in the bag, the narrator of *My Life* is compelled to rehearse a situation reminiscent of the capture he thought he was escaping in the land of the living. The narrator, now trapped in a bag, must submit to being carried into the bush by the terrorizing and violent Smelling-Ghost. The monster threatens to cannibalize him—another fear common of those captured and enslaved for the European trade and another echo of Equiano, who wrote that he thought he was meant to be "eaten by those white men with horrible looks, red faces, and loose hair" (39). Instead of being cannibalized, however, the Smelling-Ghost transforms the narrator into a series of animals to extract entertainment as well as labor from the young captive. The narrator enumerates a long series of transformations he undergoes as a captive: "[M]y boss was changing me to some kind of creatures. First of all he changed me to a monkey, then I began to climb fruit trees and pluck fruits down for them. After that he changed me to a lion, then to a horse, to a camel, to a cow or bull with horns on its head" (36). Finally settling on the horse avatar, the Smelling-Ghost puts the narrator to work, transforming him into pure labor. "He put reins in my mouth . . . he mounted me and the two attendants were following him with whips in their hands and flogging me along in the bush" (37). The protagonist has not only been made a slave, but quite literally metamorphosed into a work animal. Children prod and inspect him, people look on him as a spectacle, he is forced to eat food fit only for an animal, and he is commanded to work day and night. Transformed again by his "boss" into a camel, he protests that he is unable to satisfy the desires of his masters:

> [H]e changed me again to the form of a camel and then his sons were using me as transport to carry heavy loads to long distances of about twenty or forty miles. But when the rest of the smelling-ghosts noticed that I was useful for such purpose then the whole of them were hiring me from my boss to carry loads to long distances and returning again in the evening with heavier loads. But as I could not satisfy all of them at a time so they shared me, half of them would use me from morning till night, then the rest would use me from the night till morning. At this stage I had no chance to rest for a minute for all the periods that I spent with them. (39–40)

Tutuola's ghastly antagonists transform the character into a beast of burden. Captive in this animal's body, the narrator is completely confined within the system of labor into which he has been abducted. He is thereby reduced to his labor alone. The animal's body is another iteration of the terrifying bag in that it is a form of inescapable physical bondage through which a specter of the slave trade captures and enslaves the narrator. The narrator's bondage itself transforms him into a slave; the narrator *becomes* chattel in his race to avoid it.

The Cycle of Enslavement

Episode after episode of the majority of *My Life* finds the narrator experiencing a three-part cycle: he is held captive by some ghost or monster, he is made the servant of his captor, and then he narrowly escapes the ghostly captivity. The cycle repeats when he is captured by another, often more disturbing, ghost. The narrator is constantly caught in this cycle of enslavement: in the twenty-four years during which he lives in the bush, he rarely experiences a moment when he is not either laboring for a ghost or plotting or enacting his escape, if not from a particular ghost then from the bush of ghosts itself. He is the figure of the perpetual runaway slave, but rendered through images that reflect the particularity of the West African experience of the trade.

As a captive of the Smelling-Ghost, the protagonist displays the entire complex of capture, enslavement, and escape. As we have seen, the narrator is kidnapped in a sack by a most wicked and powerful ghost. Even after he has been released from the sack for some time, he is forced back into the sack, for, as the narrator notes, the Smelling-Ghost "could not go anywhere without this bag, as it is a uniform for every king that reigns in this 7th town of ghosts" (41). This captor is no hunter or warrior; he is the king himself, and his power is marked by his ownership of that which he carries in this all-important sack—the living human he keeps there as his slave. When the narrator is finally allowed to emerge from the bag, the king Smelling-Ghost transforms him into a horse and "he would mount me mercilessly and both his attendants would start to flog me" (38). He is forced to work for the king, carrying him to all the villages of his realm, where the abuse and degradation continue. In this literal transformation into a work animal, his enslavement is clear—he is reduced to the labor as well as the status of chattel.

Eventually, the protagonist plots and accomplishes his escape, completing the cycle. Transformed briefly again into a human so that the monster can carry him inside his bag to another town for a meeting, the boy escapes, running as fast as he can into the bush. He is chased by the Smelling-Ghost, who threatens that if he catches the fugitive, he will permanently transform him into a horse for his own eternal use. However, the mobility required of such capture inspires a certain logic of movement in the narrator. As a captive of the slave trade, the narrator's mobility is dependent on the need of the trade to transport him to a new location. He is oppressed by this movement, which takes him far from his homeland, a mobility that he did not wish for himself, accustomed as he was to a calm, sedentary existence in his home village. At the same time, even forced movement teaches him the utility of mobility.

Thus, the protagonist uses the magic of his captor to escape; he uses the power of his juju to change himself into a cow and uses the power of his knowledge of mobility to move through the bush to escape (41–42). Captive, he is the slave to mobility; free, he utilizes the power of mobility to undermine the very system that instilled the notion in him. Transformed into chattel, his status as a captive is degradation; in freedom, the metamorphosis allows him to mask himself and assert his own subjectivity. Emmanuel N. Obiechina notes that Tutuola uses metamorphosis as a means to "demonstrate man's hope for survival even in the teeth of the hostile forces that surround him."[40] Almost immediately following, Obiechina remarks that Tutuola's narrators are forced to travel across and transgress boundaries in order to make their journeys possible.[41] Metamorphosis and movement, then, become a form of power that the narrators, often victimized by physical confinement through arbitrary borders and immobility, are able to take up as their own tools of resistance. The narrator of *My Life* remarks that he "remembered that I had taken the juju which [the ghost] would use before he could change me to any creature that he likes and at this time he has no power to change me to a horse again" (41). The narrator is unwilling to be held paralyzed and captive as a body in a bag—whether it be in a literal bag or in the form of an animal—and he is no longer willing to be subjected to transformations not only of body but also of spirit and status. As he learns that mobility and transformation are the nexus of the enslaving power of his captors, he manages to overturn the power binary of the trade. He crosses boundaries his captors dare not transgress and allows himself freedom through that movement.

In this metaphorical way, the cycle of enslavement emerges time and again in Tutuola's narrative. As we follow the narrator through his adventures in the bush, he is repeatedly caught in the bind of the body in the bag (in many shapes), is forced to labor, and then escapes. After escaping the land of the Smelling-Ghosts and their form of chattel slavery, the narrator is corked inside a log and forced to sing lamentations for the entertainment of his captor and his friends (50). He escapes the log and lives for a time with an *àbíkú* spirit and marries a beautiful ghost, but the minute he steps foot back on his path homeward, he encounters ghosts who want to "catch him," who seize him "by violence or rape at the same time," and who act as though they are going to cannibalize him (66–67). These horrible ghosts imprison the protagonist in a dungeon, where he is later held captive in a pitcher with only his head free (67). Again made captive as he was in the bag, with his mobility entirely stolen, he is forced to work for these ghosts as a "god" who serves them in their religious rites (70). His value as a captive "god" becomes known throughout the bush, and so he changes masters several times, because though he is a "god," he remains in bondage against his will. He remembers, "I was so frightened . . . so I tried to run away but the pitcher did not allow me at all" (79). He has no right to make his own decisions or to insist upon his own liberation. One of his captors even puts the pitcher god into a bag again to transport him to his town of the River-Ghosts (72).

The trope of the body in the bag recurs throughout the narrative to mark the way in which the haunting specter of bondage and enslavement travels with the narrator throughout his time in the bush. Even once the narrator is able to break free from the jar, his fearful escape sends him right into a giant spider's web, where he is held captive again, unable to loose himself from the sticky weblike substance that surrounds him completely (89). Wrapped in the spider's web, he is buried alive (92), again the captive of menacing ghosts who refuse to recognize his status as a free human being and who silence all his attempts at resistance. A grave robber accidentally frees him from his burial, but his escape leads him to the safety of what turns out to be an animal's pouch (95), where he is again transported to a town where he is held hostage and forced to work as a hunter for a horrible, greedy, multiheaded "flash-eyed mistress" who beats him and his companions any time they refuse to work as she desires (102).

The narrator eventually experiences a respite from a lifetime of enslavement when he marries a second time and, though he is disturbed by his own fears of being captured or somehow harmed even by his own wife (120), he is eventually able to forget his troubles for a time. But after being forced out of this short-lived luxury with his antelope wife, the narrator is again held captive. This time, he reports that a ghost "mounted me and rode me for about three days and nights before he released me" (136). Again treated as chattel and then later imprisoned again in a hard-labor camp (137), the narrator realizes that his life in the bush of ghosts is nothing but captivity, punishment, labor, and escape. Each time the protagonist is held captive in some form of corporeal bondage, the physical and psychological effects of the trade are reiterated and brand his very body with its ghostly powers of enslavement.

Working through Memories of Unlaid Ghosts

Despite these short-lived opportunities for escape, the cycle of enslavement persists as the narrator repeatedly, though unwittingly, flees into the grips of some other form of violence, some other psychological and physical terror resident in the bush. The narrator's journey through the bush exemplifies what Achille Mbembe describes as a kind of "threshold or specular experience," which indicates "extreme forms of human life, death worlds, forms of social existence in which vast populations are subjected to conditions of life that confer upon them the status of living dead (ghosts). In the contemporary African context, these extreme forms of human existence are experienced through the corruption of the senses as well as through the horror that accompanies wars and outbreaks of terror."[42] The terrorizing force of the slave trade transforms the narrator of *My Life* in such a way that he is a walking shell of himself, often literally morphed into unrecognizable creatures.

The narrator of the novel exists in a liminal territory, that of the bush, but he is also himself made liminal in it. He is both alive and dead, human and ghost, child and adult, slave and free, running and paralyzed, captive and fugitive. He escapes the literal slave traders only to be exiled in a constant state of slavery—in a world in which he is perpetually running from slavery and encountering new and more grotesque versions of it. Though Mbembe seems to be writing mainly of those ghosts in the bush and *their* specular power, his concept also describes Tutuola's narrator, who is made into a "wandering subject" by the transformative experience of the horrific human trade.

The implication of Tutuola's narrative, then, is that the violence and terror unleashed by the slave trade have had a powerful and enduring effect—not only on the young protagonist of the novel, but on generations of West African people as well. Indeed, as Geoffrey Parrinder remarks in the introduction to *My Life*: "Fear is present throughout. If anyone doubts that there is fear in African life Tutuola's story should convince them of its reality" (11). And Tutuola points to one (among many) very specific origin of this fear—the slave trade and the slave raiding it engendered. Through generations of storytelling, the slave trade continues to convey a haunting force, altering the psychic landscape and perpetuating a dramatic mourning as explored in Tutuola's novel. For his narrator, the memory of his original escape from slavery is inscribed on his body, which is constantly altered by its experience of enslavement. He is trapped, beaten, metamorphosed, worked, chased; his body is an image of slavery. But it is not merely these physical terrors that our narrator experiences; he also suffers a deep psychic terror. As a child, he is caught unaware by attackers who wish to enslave him. His mother is missing and his brother has been enslaved. Pursued as he is by the threat of enslavement, labor, and physical pain, the narrator seems generally forgetful of the events that led to his escape into the bush and is only occasionally reminded of his need to return to his home and family. However, the narrator does not precisely suffer amnesia. Instead, he lives out the terror of that moment of escape for the duration of his stay in the bush. The novel's cycle of entrapment, enslavement, and escape produces a kind of Freudian psychic repetition in which the subject actively repeats the very trauma that haunts him but that he does not necessarily recall consciously or understand to be the source of his bizarre experiences.

Tutuola's figuration of African memories of the transatlantic slave trade is, indeed, quite Freudian in its engagement with this traumatic repetition. The narrator of *My Life* has experienced a great loss that haunts him in his alternative life in the bush. In the moment when he loses his brother he is heartbroken and pained, for he is about to lose the innocent life of the child he once possessed. As soon as he is in the bush, he is transformed, becomes necessarily self-reliant but terrified at the same time, and is unable to shake his concern for the loss of his innocence, which he describes as being "too young to know 'bad' and 'good'" (23). A deep mourning haunts him as he aspires to find his way alone in the bush. Freud writes that "mourning is regularly the reaction to the loss of a loved person, or to the loss of some abstraction which has taken the place of one, such as a fatherland, liberty, an ideal, and so on."[43] In his narrow escape from the slave raiders, Tutuola's young narrator lost all of these intimate abstractions: his family, his homeland, his liberty, and his innocence, all in one traumatic moment.

In the drama of the terrifying dreamscape of the bush, the trauma of the slave trade and the narrator's escape are thus symbolically repeated. Repetition, as understood by Freud, is a means of "working through" a traumatic memory. Freud writes that "a thing that has not been understood inevitably reappears like an unlaid ghost, it cannot rest until the mystery has been solved and the spell broken."[44] The slave raid of the narrator's childhood, which by the end of the novel is now long past, has deeply harmed his psyche and has sent him into a state of confusion and unrest, in which he is haunted by a repetition of ghostly captures—by ghosts that actually are "unlaid." He is compelled to repeat the trauma of his escape from slavery, which will allow him to work through the psychic wound inflicted by the original trauma. As Alessia Ricciardi expresses it, "Mourning is not simply an emotion for Freud, but the performance of a work that, like interpretation, is a psychically transformative activity."[45] The repetition of the captivity, enslavement, and escape is the work required of the narrator to resolve the trauma he experienced at the hand of the slave raiders.

In fact, by the end of the text, the narrator has come to terms to some extent with the trauma and is not as likely to get caught in a trap or enslaved. Slowly, his episodes turn to questions of intimacy, which enable him to fall in love, create his own family, and rediscover dead family members; his adventures are less concerned with the trauma of capture. In select moments in the narrative, the protagonist admits that some small comfort in the bush allows him to begin to forget the trauma that sent him into the bush and his quest to find his way home. During his first marriage, he confesses that it was "three months and some days before I remembered my mother and brother again, because I did not remember them again when I married the lady" (63). Toward the end of his second marriage to the enchanting antelope woman, he comes to his senses, thinking, "I remembered to continue to be looking for the way to my home town as I had forgotten that for a while, because of love" (135). It is during these moments in his journey when he learns to be more ghostlike, "speaking the language of ghosts fluently as if I were born in the Bush of Ghosts" (136), and even learning their magic (157). Love allows him a respite, but the terror of the bush continues to loom and persistently interferes with his relationships, and he is invariably forced to return to the bush to seek a path that will allow him to escape from his psychic trauma.

Eventually resigned to his status as a captive in the bush of ghosts, a magical spell from the land of the living compels him to return to his homeward quest. In the end, the narrator meets a "television-handed ghostess" who tells him that he is "seeing the way every day, but [he does] not know it, because every earthly person gets eyes but cannot see" (162). Through the repetition of his near captivity and escape at the hands of slave raiders, the protagonist had in fact been acting out his journey homeward each day without realizing it. The psychic harm of the trade is slowly alleviated by the repetition of the trauma and his "working through" it. Working through the trauma inflicted by the slave raiders, and thereby psychically transformed, he is finally able to see the way out of the bush of repetition and back into his hometown, exiting exactly where he entered.

What Hatred Did

Ironically, Tutuola's narrator escapes the bush only to return to a similar scene of horror back in his home village. Once again, when he returns, he is bound with a rope and carried on the head of a man he recognizes as a slave trader. They walk through the bush for days until they reach a town far away, where he is literally enslaved. After twenty-four years in the bush, the narrator still has not escaped his fate. He labors like a horse again, clearly reminiscent of the scenes with the Smelling-Ghost, carrying heavy loads long distances, until he is nearly worked to death. Ill, he is taken to the auction block—reinforcing the slave trade implications of the auction block scene in the bush—and again there is no buyer willing to make such a poor investment. In exactly the same manner as he was finally disposed of in the bush, he is sold to a person (ironically, his long-lost brother who was previously captured by slave raiders) who seeks a slave to sacrifice. These events so clearly parallel those he experienced in the bush, it is impossible now not to see them as Tutuola's reminders that the narrator's life in the bush was one of enslavement as well. He mourns that "every slave buyer recognised slaves as non-living creatures" (170), echoing the crisis he encountered in the bush that those ghosts did not understand his humanity, nor did they think of him as equal or respectable. In the nonliving world a man could not receive humane treatment, nor could a slave in the living world.

While the novel enacts the narrator's confrontation with the real, living perpetrators of the slave trade, Tutuola's writing of the novel represents the conscious recollection of those events and the working through of the traumatic memory on the page. This novel, like others that reveal traces of the slave trade, allows for the dramatization of memory, which itself participates in opening discourse surrounding the history of the slave trade in West Africa. Tutuola parallels the narrator's life in the bush with that of his enslavement in the living world he escaped. The analogy reveals the implicit critique of the ubiquitous presence of slavery in the landscape of Nigeria's past and present— even when it is being repressed in a forbidden bush of ghosts. If the narrator of *My Life* is forced to repeat the traumatic memory of his encounter with slave traders, then the repetition of the story itself reinscribes that trauma into the collective memory of all those who hear or read the story.

In a conversation with students, Amos Tutuola once denied that his two early novels were allegories, claiming indifferently that ghosts are simply real.[46] Nonetheless, *My Life* depicts a series of episodes that represent the fear of the slave trade in their repetition of the concern with capture, bondage, servitude, and escape. This memory of captivity and enslavement is not limited to the particular time period of the Yoruba wars or even to the long period of the transatlantic slave trade. These memories transcend any singular time in that they continue to haunt the continent today. Indeed, *My Life* cannot be limited to any one allegory of a particular moment in Nigerian history as such, though many readers have tried to locate elements in the story that would encourage a reading of the novel as simply an allegory of colonialism. Tutuola manages to elude simple time constraints because the time of memory itself is layered. Tutuola aligns the space of the bush and that of the living world, just as he layers the time of the slave trade past with the present colonial world in which he lives, in a palimpsestic history of the memory of violence, a memory that no doubt is haunted by the specter of slave trade captivity, enslavement, and escapes.

Tutuola makes this explicit in his use of seemingly counterintuitive anachronism, allowing the presence of the present to reveal itself in the bush. Locating the text in an analogous present through the medium of the storytelling voice as well as through modern technologies, Tutuola also reminds his audience of the legacy of the slave trade in the present. When Tutuola mentions televisions, assize courts, crown agents, or the London metropole, he indicates the layered temporal space of the bush, a space in which the slave trade and the contemporary period exist simultaneously. The bush of Yoruba folklore provides a spatiotemporal distance that allows for the construction of a plausible realm outside our realist worldview, in which multiple time lines are allowed to overlap and converge. This temporal convergence of the era of the slave trade and Tutuola's modern world is characteristic of the folktale and indicates the importance of these seemingly mythical traces of the past to contemporary readers. Indeed, as Walter J. Ong points out, "in an oral economy of thought, matters from the past without any sort of present relevance commonly dropped into oblivion."[47] It is only insofar as the story remains relevant in the contemporary milieu that it is worth telling. Thus, the metaphorical space of the bush and the trope of the body in the bag become vehicles for memory, through which those most affected by the trade are able to package and transmit their most terrifying fears. These images persist in the literature because they remain relevant in the cultures. If critics want to claim that there is an amnesia regarding the slave trade in West African literature and culture, Tutuola seems to contend that there is no such amnesia, even if victims of the trade wish they could forget. Instead, we find that the memories of the trade have been located in a separate sphere, in a liminal space, in the chronotope of the bush of ghosts that renders human beings into bodies in bags, but nonetheless allows for the transmission and dissemination of those haunting memories.

The layered temporalities of the novel remind us that this is not simply a story of a boy running from slave raiders during the era of the transatlantic trade. Those moments of seeming anachronism, the palimpsestic time so characteristic of the oral narrative and storytelling, the return to contemporary indigenous forms of bondage at the end of the framing narrative, remind us that this terror, the trauma of the trade, is not short-lived, nor did it end with the abolition of the trade. In turn, the grief and loss that the protagonist experiences can be read as a transgenerational trauma, a tension that resides in the bush even for those not subjected to the terror of literal slave raiders. The sense of distance and belatedness this kind of "postmemory" (to use a term from Marianne Hirsch[48]) inflicts on surviving generations is revelatory of the sense of loss that West Africans experience, a loss of the ability to actively respond to the originary trauma, which from the distance at which they stand, they have no ability to prevent or alter. Despite their inability to intervene in the conflict, they are nonetheless sentenced to live with its aftermath. In *My Life in the Bush of Ghosts*, the postmemory of the slave trade, though seemingly lost or "forgotten," is expressed through Tutuola's use of tropes such as the haunted bush and the body in the bag, which he extracts from those Yoruba tales still told even a century after the slave trade was abolished. As Tutuola's revision of the cautionary tales of the Yoruba seems to attest, people do, indeed, experience the persistent residues of the distant past and unsuspectingly harbor memories of the most significant experiences of their ancestors, even when they are not explicitly describing those events.

Thus, it not surprising that it is a political and ethical statement that ends the novel. With an ending typical of a cautionary tale, Tutuola provides an abrupt moral to the story: "This is what hatred did" (174). For a narrator who claims to have no understanding of good and bad, Tutuola provides us with a remarkably strong ethical statement here. Reading the novel through the lens of the slave trade, it is clear that the hatred is far more widespread than the simple jealousies between women that left the narrator and his brother vulnerable to slave raiders. Instead, the hatred can be read as that between all people involved in the slave trade. It can be read as the legacy of suffering inflicted by the trade. The novel is an admonition against the kind of anger and anxiety that produces slave masters and slaves. It is a warning against the hatred that makes it possible for one man to be unable to see the humanity of another. Though, perhaps surprisingly, there may be no explicit condemnation, for instance, of his brother's life as a slave trader, the novel as a whole works as a moral compass, making any reference to servitude and bondage an uncomfortable one. By locating the origin of the painful enslavement of the brother and the narrator in "hatred," Tutuola's cryptic message rings out a political truth and a warning that remains important even in the twentieth century and beyond: The slave trade is what hatred did.

Tutuola is reported to have once remarked, "I don't condemn civilization. I simply don't want our people to forget the past."[49] *My Life in the Bush of Ghosts* may not be a historical realist novel that explicitly portrays the convoluted drama of the slave trade. However, as if to answer the contemporary critics who harbor an anxiety about the potential amnesia of Africans regarding the slave trade, Tutuola wove the oral tradition into his terrifying novel in a way that allows us to see the transatlantic slave trade's intrusion into the West African imagination of landscapes, memories, and bodies. In this, Tutuola is not alone. As we shall see in the following chapters, generations of writers follow Tutuola in metaphorizing the slave trade in ways that reveal reiterations of violence enacted upon the Western African coast, inventing and revising images that reveal a deep-seated cultural memory of the cyclical disruption of West African life that the slave trade has wrought over the last five centuries.

CHAPTER THREE

Geographies of Memory

Mapping Slavery's Recurrence in Ben Okri's *The Famished Road*

> To know who you are means knowing where you are.
>
> —James Clifford

Mahommah Gardo Baquaqua lived as a free man and a trusted servant in the court of the local king of Djougou,[1] in what is today called Benin.[2] As the king's most treasured servant, he sat at the foot of the royal throne and drew the envy of his avaricious colleagues. In his self-published narrative of 1854, Baquaqua informs us that a great "wickedness" was growing inside the king and among his counsel. Baquaqua, with other guards and soldiers "bent on mischief" (32), would lie in wait along the market road to steal the wine that women carried through the bush. Eventually, because of his enviable status as a member of the king's court and as a paid thief, Baquaqua himself fell prey to this immoral behavior and was "of course soon singled out as a fit object of vengeance by an envious class of [his] countrymen," who then "decoyed [him] away and sold [him] into slavery" (34). In order to lure him into their trap, his jealous companions flattered him with drumming and praise-singing and made him submissive by plying him with the strongest alcohol in the region. Like the Anlo musicians described by the historian Anne C. Bailey, who were drawn onto the decks and eventually into the holds of a slave ship because of their fondness for celebrations,[3] Baquaqua found himself enslaved the next morning when he awoke from his drunken revelries.

As a result of his enslavement, Baquaqua traveled through much of present-day Benin, only to arrive at the slave-trading post of Abomey, the regional center of powerful Dahomey. He then moved farther to the Atlantic shore, and finally across the ocean in a ship he describes as loathsome, filthy, and horrible (43). In the course of Baquaqua's narrative depiction of his enslavement and movement through the interior to the Dahomey coast, the author pays unusually close attention to the landscape and geography of the regions through which he travels. In its resolute concern with the precise details of the sites he visited en route to the coast, Baquaqua's story is, according to Allan D. Austin, "the only known description of that time by an African of his homeland and its neighbors."[4] Though several slave narrators do mention their lives in Africa, Baquaqua's attention to geography reveals his extraordinary ambition to thoroughly document his memory of Africa.

Before Baquaqua settles into the narration of his three-hundred-mile trek into enslavement, he describes the customs and practices of his culture, a detour that constitutes more than half of his autobiography. For the remainder of his narrative, Baquaqua describes his capture and enslavement. As he chronicles his transformation into a commodity within the transatlantic trade, he practically draws a map of the Dahomey hinterland and coast through which he traveled. His descriptions are so accurate and elaborate that Paul E. Lovejoy and Robin Law were able to trace his path through the interior of present-day Benin, all the way to the coastal port at Ouidah, for an edition of Baquaqua's narrative published in 2001.[5] Baquaqua describes his travels to Ar-oozoo, where he meets some sympathetic friends, then to Chir-a-chur-ee, where he was put in the stocks and surveilled at all times, and then to Chammah, where he was sold as a slave for the first time. He describes the route the coffle carved through the unpaved, hilly, shaded woods on the way to E-fau. He crosses rivers and streams, hears the singing of birds, looks upon the mountains with awe, and at night fears the wild animals that lurk in the dark wood. Eventually his coffle is driven toward what he calls "Dahoma" (probably present-day Abomey), where he appreciates the well-constructed roads and describes with interest the busyness of the populated city. Despite (or perhaps as a result of) his ability to chart his course all the way to the coast, Baquaqua realizes in Dahomey the futility of his dreams of escape, so far away in such an unknown land. He is marched to the coast at Gra-fe (a transliteration of the local name for Ouidah), where his days in Africa end. Baquaqua names each village through which he passes, remarking on its people, its flora and fauna, even the state of its infrastructure. His descriptions make it possible for him to chart his own journey to enslavement, a path very similar to the one that UNESCO has officially christened "the slave route."

There are many plausible explanations for Baquaqua's obsessive interest in geography. On the one hand, although he dictated and composed much of his narrative, Baquaqua did not physically write it himself. His amanuensis, Samuel Moore, certainly had his own motivations for the choice of subject matter in the narrative. Many slave narratives included an African geography lesson for the benefit of its largely American, Canadian, and British audiences who would know little of Africa's landscape and cultures. Indeed, these narratives were a primary source for understanding the terrain of the African interior, for few white slave traders could live on the coast and survive, much less write extensively about it. At the time of the publication of Baquaqua's narrative, in fact, there still were no white travelers, administrators, or traders who had made it as far inland as his home in Djougou. Moore applauds Baquaqua's project, writing: "Up to the time that Mohammah was 'forced from home and all its pleasures,' the foot of the white man had not made its first impress upon the soil; therefore the facts, matters, and things hereby related, will be the more interesting to all those whose hearts and souls are turned toward the wants and woes of that portion of the globe" (13–14). Moore's investment in mapping Africa would have been quite different from Baquaqua's, as slave narratives could serve as a source of knowledge that would lead to deeper European and American penetration into the interior. Moore himself urges Christians to help the "benighted people" of Africa, to raise Africans "to the standard of their fellow-men, and give all the countenance you can to their endeavors to usefulness and goodness" (28).

However, Baquaqua's own investment in describing these settings while narrating his story to Moore is of great value to our understanding of the African memory of the slave trade. There is a marked shift in Baquaqua's narrative—from the ethnographic third-person voice of Moore, which dominates the first six chapters of the text, to the autobiographical use of the first person in the middle of the seventh chapter—where Baquaqua begins to narrate his journey into slavery and then to freedom. In his first-person narrative, Baquaqua is concerned with the setting, which acts as the proof of his memory of life in West Africa. Baquaqua's nostalgia for his home produces a map of his memory, a record of West Africa that, though it existed ten years prior to the writing of the narrative, still remains present for him as he drafts his literary atlas. Even in the very moments when he describes his enslavement, he rhetorically creates an authority of himself through his effort to map the geography of Africa and utilize his memory as power. He describes the grasses and how it felt to walk on them (38–39), the wildlife in its aesthetic beauty and epicureal delight (37, 39), and the homes and their architectural differences across the region (39, 41), as well as the customs of the different peoples he encounters (37, 40, 41). Throughout, though he may not go into detail about every single aspect he records, the tone is of one who holds a knowledge inaccessible to all those with whom he communicates.

Meticulously documenting his journey into slavery, he utilizes mapping to mark his control over a landscape and a body of knowledge, when the narrative might otherwise appear simply to document his subordination and defeat. Baquaqua's text charts an alternative cartography, a map that no white person could make, through which he establishes the power to map as his own, a power generally reserved for white Europeans and Americans. He exploits the Western need for knowledge of Africa to expose African possession of an archive to which Europeans did not have access. The map of Dahomey and the interior that Baquaqua produces, then, is a layered reflection of his memory of the events he experienced, his new knowledge of the slavery he was destined for as he made that journey, his desperate desire to return home, and his knowledge of a world that was inaccessible to his would-be readers. The map acts not only to connect him emotively to his abolitionist audience, which it certainly does, but also to assert his own geography and impose his memory of the place upon the archive of knowledge of Africa. Baquaqua seems to utilize the power of the map to retain some little sovereignty for himself—the sovereignty of his own complex memory of Africa.

Baquaqua's last moments on the coast of Africa are spent on the water. His impressions are placed in a dissonant juxtaposition: just as he encounters the beautiful landscapes of the coastal lagoons and the wondrous and magnificent site of the slave ship, Baquaqua realizes (like Tutuola's narrator in chapter 1) that the landscape functions as a tool for collecting more slaves to be sold with him into slavery (42). He records that he then recognized, "All I knew was, that I was a slave, chained by the neck, and that I must readily and willingly submit, come what would, which I considered as much as I had any right to know" (43). Despite this knowledge, the focus of the narrative remains the geography of his imminent enslavement. As he describes the setting of his final entrapment into the trade, he writes, "I was destined for other parts; this town is situated on a large river. After breakfast I was taken down to the river and placed on board a boat; the river was very large and branched off in two different directions, previous to emptying itself into the sea" (41). This large slow river, which Baquaqua places on his map as the final African destination of his slave coffle, is the means by which he himself will be forced to relinquish his former life as an honored king's servant, and be emptied into the sea of global commerce.

Parallel Modernities

The mapping of Baquaqua's entry into the slave trade via a river helps us to navigate the unsteady terrain of Ben Okri's introduction to his Booker Prize–winning novel, *The Famished Road* (1991).[6] Written thirty years after Nigeria's independence, the novel is a scathing critique of the birth of postcolonial politics in the country. Okri tells the story of a young wanderer whose adventures repeatedly take him down the paths and roads and rivers of a newly independent Nigeria, but which persistently reveal a map of Nigeria's past and future as well. The novel's abstract opening lines provide the geopolitical setting of the story, compellingly echoing the journey taken by Baquaqua and so many others into slavery. Okri writes, "In the beginning there was a river. The river became a road and the road branched out to the whole world" (3). Okri's introduction seems at first to be mythical, falling in line with the standard reading of Okri's work as magical realism,[7] which is itself typical of the way people read the inclusion of metaphors and parables in West African literature. However, though Okri's work is clearly indebted to the magical realist tradition, these opening lines are more than simply an introduction to the supernatural qualities of Okri's work or to the nature of the narrator's spiritual life; they are a metaphor for the introduction of globalization to the coast of West Africa. Like Baquaqua's road that became a river that became a sea, Okri's road is conflated with water, with a river, which opens out to the world. And if Baquaqua's road leads him straight into Abomey and slavery, so Okri's road leads us back to the history of the slave trade, when the Niger River opened itself to those ships waiting at sea and thereby opened a route for the movement of Africans to the entire world.[8] This metaphor for globalized modernity is evocative of the movement and travel associated with Africa's early encounters with the West. Okri figures the river as a map of modernity, and, as Gilroy argues of DuBois, Douglass, and Wright, understands that our so-called "modernity" was "founded on the catastrophic rupture of the middle passage rather than on the dream of revolutionary transformation"[9] that was available only to those privileged Europeans who dreamed it.

The river Okri describes signifies on, but does not necessarily equate with, the Middle Passage here—indeed, the fact that it is a river itself tells us that this story begins long before people boarded ships on the Atlantic Ocean and left the coast of Africa. Nevertheless, the story of the river that becomes a road is a story of African connectedness, but a connectedness to the rest of the world that is marred by violence. The river that is a road to the rest of the world suggests the beginning of a shift in the narrative of West African history, the moment when slave-trading ships reached the coast and introduced a "New World" to unsuspecting and undesiring African people, not just along the coast but far into the interior, and negotiated with them there a "modernity," but only at the price of violence and brutality. "And because the road was once a river," Okri laments, "it was always hungry" (3). Thus, for hundreds of years, this river/road that pours into the sea insatiably consumed human lives, even long after the slave trade was abolished. Okri begins his novel with this metonymic image of the riverine networks that led to the Atlantic littoral and into slavery, but in the same moment at which he has called upon the memory of the slave trade, he shifts to the slave trade's afterlife—the era of independence in Nigeria.

In the midst of this environment is born a traveling figure, that of the child Azaro, who is a young spirit-child gifted with the *àbíkú*'s ability to die and come back to life, but who chooses a mortal life over ethereal existence with his spirit companions in the land of the dead. Azaro's picaresque adventures in his home village lead him to contend with the difficulties inherent in independence-era Nigerian society: hunger, unemployment, evangelical religion, violence, political corruption. He works for some time in a local bar, where he learns about the dark sides of human existence and Nigerian politics, which he tries to escape by wandering in the forest. There he finds another cast of characters and images that at turns haunt him and put him at ease. Still, everywhere he turns, in the bush as well as in town, Azaro encounters mythic visions of Nigeria's past, present, and future. Critics have focused much attention on Azaro's role as *àbíkú* and thereby as an allegory for Nigeria's future—a future in which Nigeria's dead past is "born" again, just as the *àbíkú* child dies and returns to life.[10] In the worst cases of reincarnation, Nigeria is doomed to repeat the past, only to die and be reborn again, in an infinite and violent cycle. By the end of the novel, the narrator asserts, perhaps Nigeria will choose, as Azaro did, to enjoy its life and stay alive: "One day it will decide to remain. It will become strong" (478). The book holds out a promise for Nigeria's future, if only it can recognize the power of rebirth.

However, Okri's novel is just as much about Nigeria's distant past as it is about its present and future. Just as it opens with this watery originary moment, Africa's entry into a supposed age of modernity and globalization, the narrative is concerned with the layered and recurrent significance of Nigeria's past in its present. The protagonist, Azaro, wanders through Nigeria's landscapes, and like Baquaqua, he maps the sites he sees along the road. The hungry river that becomes a road works as a metaphor for Okri's parallel modernities. At one and the same time, Azaro's journeys along that road reveal the hidden locations of that so-called "modernity" that was conceived between Europeans and West Africans in their interactions along the coast in the early days of the slave trade *and* of the self-fashioned modernity that was born at Nigeria's transition to independent, autonomous rule. Throughout *The Famished Road*, anachronistic irruptions of the slave trade in the narrative of independence-era Nigeria expose Okri's mapping of these two modernities upon each other to examine how memory of the past is always recurrent in the present and future. Through this, Okri critiques the violence inherent in both versions of modernity and explores the potential for Nigerians to take control of the archive of those memories to end this recurrent suffering.

The Shrine of Suffering: Nigeria's Remembered Past

Throughout *The Famished Road*, Okri focuses attention on the traces of slavery that lurk in contemporary African memory. Reminiscent of Tutuola's protagonist's adventures in the bush, Azaro's wandering in the mythical woods destabilizes any sense of narrative time, because it is in these woods that he encounters images of slavery and independence side by side. In one very brief instance of this juxtaposition, the slave trade's recurrence in Africa's present is made evident in the stories Azaro's mother recalls as she and Azaro walk along the forest's edge late one night. From the woods, Azaro and his mother hear the songs of the apocalyptic "new church" resonate "with a frightening vigour, with terrifying hope, great need, great sorrow" (282). But even louder and more haunting are the lamentations of "worshippers at the shrine of suffering," which was born of the "hunger, the wretchedness, of our condition" (282). Juxtaposed as the two places of worship are, Okri reveals the vivid presentness of a long-lived suffering.

In response to that lamentation and with that juxtaposition of ancient and modern lamentations in mind, Okri's young narrator makes a counterintuitive but revealing request of his mother: "I asked her to tell me a story about white people" (282). From the contemplation of suffering comes a desire for the memory of white intruders. Hesitantly, Azaro's mother recites the history that she has received through generations of storytellers: that African people taught white people about math and astronomy and freely shared their wisdom with their guests. But in an admonitory tone, she criticizes the white visitors: "They forgot many things. They forgot that we are all brothers and sisters and that black people are the ancestors of the human race" (282). In a declaration of their obligation to remember, she recounts the tragedies that can follow when a society refuses to remember such important lessons: "The second time they came they brought guns. They took our lands, burned our gods, and they carried away many of our people to become slaves across the sea" (282). Azaro has asked his mother to tell him about white men, and that story is not one of colonialism (as many narratives of Africa's history and the encounter with Europe tend to be) or of the more immediate neocolonial "development" schemes that litter the forest in which they travel with suburban homes. Instead, she tells a story that stretches all the way back to the earliest encounters with European culture and the transporting of Africans to become slaves.

Through the juxtaposition of the wretched and hungry lamentations heard in a local Christian church with the stories of conquest and kidnapping, Okri intertwines the slave trade and the current poverty, violence, and corruption that Azaro and his mother suffer in their small town. Azaro's mother evokes a memory of a violent past, in which people were stolen and forced into labor in foreign lands, and that cannot be erased because it is inextricably linked to the suffering of an apocalyptic present. If Tutuola's forest provides us a site of psychic repetition for the individual in *My Life in the Bush of Ghosts*, then Azaro's mother's stories and the communal lamentation of the worshippers that emerge from the bush reveal a kind of psychic repetition at the level of community, in the form of a collective memory that recalls the pain of the traumatic past and recognizes the way there lingers in the bush "an old pain, an ancient suffering, that has refused to leave, an old affliction renewed at night" (282).

What Okri is suggesting here is that the haunting past that began with the slave trade continues to have powerful, painful, and real effects on the present. Historian Toyin Falola outlines those effects on Nigerian life:

> The slave trade affected politics and state formation. Where states relied on revenues from it, the trade and its abolition affected their fortunes. . . . As more and more people acquired wealth from the

trade, social and political relations became more complex. The determinants of status changed from old age and family history to wealth and economic standing.[11]

The slave trade brought the decline of the Oyo Empire, the secession of provinces, attacks on villages, interruption of trade routes, and economic decline, eventually leading to the entry of the colonial enterprise. Today, its effects are still felt on the continent—"in the distribution of population, in marriage patterns, in continuing class distinctions, and in total population size, which remains relatively low despite its recent rapid growth."[12] These demographic and cultural changes feed a political imbalance in Nigeria that privileges those who hold wealth (which often may very well be a legacy of the slave trade itself) over the masses who suffer from lack of basic needs and services, and they produce hierarchical structures that allow for the continuation of extreme labor exploitation, which itself retains "important continuities with slave labor, including reliance on migration, on compulsion, on low pay, and on uneven sex ratios."[13] These are precisely the kinds of continuities that Okri is highlighting in his layered temporalities. Thus, the two churches in the forest are put beside each other and then juxtaposed with the story of European invasion and violation, revealing a palimpsestic history and a continuity of suffering that lies beneath the surface of contemporary Nigerian life.

The layering is complicated even more immediately thereafter when Azaro and his mother learn that his father has been attacked by politicians. Azaro and his mother find his father lying in the forest immediately after his mother's history lesson, and his father recites the "familiar" story of men who "asked who he was voting for," and when he did not answer, they "set upon him, took his money, [and] were about to do something worse" (284). This story is familiar not simply because postcolonial politics posed challenges to the stability of the region, but, as Azaro's mother suggests, because of the way people had forgotten what they learned from the histories of conquest and domination inaugurated in the slave trade. Okri seems to suggest that slave trade inequalities and political imbalances continue to repeat themselves in everyday life, making possible the continued oppression of the Nigerian people even after independence. The recurrence of violent histories is brought to the immediate present (and into the immediate family) with this brutal treatment of Azaro's father. This is but one brief encounter with slave trade memories that will continue to unfold as the narrative progresses, but in this section, we can see Okri's formalistic propensity for utilizing the space of the bush as a location for layering seemingly unrelated events (in both time and content) such that they produce a time line of painful continuities, thereby revealing the past's continued effects on the future. Throughout the novel, Okri will return to this method to reveal slavery's mark on the present.

The Àbíkú and the Unending Sorrow of Mothers

Even Azaro's status as an *àbíkú* evokes anxieties of suffering and loss that are connected to the history of the slave trade. Indeed, the image of the *àbíkú* is one of several ways Okri metaphorizes the effects of the slave trade on contemporary Nigerian life in *The Famished Road*. From the Yoruba language, *àbíkú* literally translates into English as "one who is born, dies" and has come to mean a child who is actually born to die.[14] *Àbíkú* children are born and then die, only to be reborn and die again repeatedly, tormenting their mothers, who beg them to remain in the world of the living. They can die an indefinite number of times and remain only once their family is able to spiritually "fetter" them to this world and to their home.[15] The notion of an *àbíkú* child is common to many West African cultures, especially where (and when) infant mortality is high. *Àbíkú* children are typically known by their names that signify the loss and suffering of their family members, such as Kòkúmọ́ọ́ ("he does not die anymore"), Máloọmọ́ ("don't go anymore"), Dúrójaye ("stay and enjoy life"), Dúrósinmi ("stay to bury me"), or Kúrunmí ("death ruined me").[16] (Among the Akan people of Ghana, similar children who die and return are sometimes named "Donkor," the word for slave in Twi, suggesting to the child perhaps that they should not go away from the mother again.)[17] The *àbíkú* child plays a most ambivalent role in West African cultures; he or she is a most prized possession that requires constant attention and material bribing to maintain a presence on earth, as well as the greatest tormentor of mothers as the child's death is a source of repeated grief and lamentation.

The *àbíkú* image has long engaged the imagination of West African authors. Both Wole Soyinka and John Pepper Clark-Bekederemo have written poems about *àbíkú*; Soyinka from the perspective of the disobedient and headstrong *àbíkú* child,[18] and Clark-Bekederemo from the position of a suppliant parent who wishes to entice the child to stay alive.[19] Achebe, in *Things Fall Apart*, famously focuses much of the central part of his narrative on Ezinma, the young *ògbánje* child (the Igbo equivalent of the *àbíkú*). The figure of the *àbíkú* has been understood as a liminal character, representative of both life and death, innocence and experience, good and evil, desire and loathing, spirit and human, thief and gift. As the *àbíkú*'s multiplicity allows it access to a variety of experiences, it is known as a wanderer, one who is able to be and see and do more than the average person, and thus is often gifted with a kind of unattainable insight. The *àbíkú* transgresses all spatial as well as temporal boundaries. This wandering figure has access to past, present, and future because of its status as a liminal being caught between the world of the living and the world of the spirits. Ever passing between these realms and ever aware of its access to multiple knowledges, the *àbíkú* maintains access to all realms—temporal and spatial—and thus represents that palimpsestic knowledge that allows access to the past in the present.[20]

As we have seen, those multiple knowledges are intimately linked with the history of the slave trade. Azaro's condition as a traveling soul links him to the painful geography of the slave trade era and gives him a visionary insight that allows him to see the repetition of injustices being enacted in contemporary West African politics. It is in this way that the *àbíkú*, particularly one who is both a perpetual wanderer and constantly at risk of being captured by so-called white traveling merchants as Azaro is, can be symbolic of the forced migrations, captivity, and enslavement associated with the trade. Indeed, as a representative of eternal wandering, the *àbíkú* can be read, as Chikwenye Ogunyemi has claimed, as "the trope of migrations. . . . The global implications *date back to slavery* and colonialism with their increase of forced, migratory patterns."[21] The *àbíkú* figure itself is a resilient trope by which people describe aspects of the slave trade that most intimately haunt them—forced wandering and captivity in an alternate and unknown world. This relationship to slavery and the slave trade is so powerful that Christopher N. Okonkwo argues that the African American neo-slave narrative was a fertile ground upon which such a transient and multiplicitous character could take shape and transform, suitable to the thematic interests of the "rivalry between oppressor/oppression and the oppressed, delimitation and revolt, and 'evil' and 'good,'" which is intimately linked to "the primordial tension between and interdependency of slavery and freedom."[22] The figure of the *àbíkú*, then, has been a productive image upon which writers can build a sort of postmodern and postcolonial discourse of slavery's multiplicity, liminality, and mobility.

Furthermore, the image of the *àbíkú* emphasizes repeated loss and the rupture of intimacy within families who endure those losses. Taken both literally and metaphorically, the *àbíkú* is a trope of loss and displacement for mothers.

Azaro represents a kind of perpetual loss as an *àbíkú* child. Azaro says that he and his *àbíkú* companions "caused much pain to mothers" (4), and that even the word *àbíkú* "spread horror amongst mothers" (8). Though Azaro has chosen to stay mortal on earth and not return to his spirit home, his constant wandering suggests to his parents that his *àbíkú* nature remains. As a result, the novel is scarred with mothers crying and fretting, or lavishing undue attention on their sons and the sons of their neighbors. Later, as Azaro's *àbíkú* nature is repeatedly conflated with his status as a victim of captivity, bondage, and sale, and his experience of captivity comes to signify that of an enslaved person, Azaro acts as a representation of the victimization of innocent Africans by the machinations of the slave trade and the sense of loss and mourning that resulted from it.

Surely his mother worries that she will lose the young wandering boy to the spirit world, but a more figurative loss is being described by the *àbíkú* figure. The power of the trope in Okri as well as in other evocations of the image is its resonance with the transgenerational loss of children who disappeared into the slave trade. In Buchi Emecheta's *The Slave Girl*, the slave's fetters are literalized. To convince her to stay in the world of the living, the parents of young Ogbanje Ojebeta use chains that are made of metal that was brought by the Portuguese to exchange for human slaves they purchased along the coast. Her *ògbánje* status and the charms that keep her bound to her home are intimately linked, then, to the slave trade, no doubt in part because her own grandfather participated in slave raids that aided the Portuguese in the trade. These unspoken links to the slave trade ultimately foreshadow the life of domestic slavery that she will suffer through her young life, linking the loss of African children into domestic slavery to the legacy of loss in the transatlantic trade.[23] Even John Pepper Clark-Bekederemo's poem makes oblique reference to the *àbíkú's* enslaved nature:

> We know the knife scars
> Serrating down your back and front
> Like the beak of the sword-fish,
> And both your ears, notched
> As a bondsman to this house,
> Are all relics of your first comings.[24]

The *àbíkú's* entrapment in the world of the living is a sort of figurative captivity and enslavement that permits escape from the fetters of his bonded life on earth only through his untimely and undesirable death.

As we historicize the trope, the *àbíkú* figure works as an anchor that connects present-day distress to the anguish of families long past, families who struggled with missing children who were made captive and sold during the slave trade. Misty Bastian has remarked on a similar connection, writing about the *ògbánje* that the child who dies and returns is a figure of unending *historical* loss: "If we think of *ogbaanje* children . . . as missing children—*much like children pawned to or stolen by distant and arbitrary powers* . . . then we also begin to historicise the entire *ogbaanje* religious phenomenon, situating it in a deeply temporal, southern Nigerian experience of fear, loss and mourning."[25] Furthermore, it is no mistake, according to Douglas McCabe, that the disappearance of *àbíkú* into the spirit world is explicitly, though ambivalently, aligned in Ifa discourse with both slavery and slave raiding of the nineteenth century. The *àbíkú*, understood here as a "thief from heaven," is in some ways complicit in disturbing the "stable rhythms of procreation, marriage, and lineage perpetuation"[26] when he or she chooses to die and leave the family behind, and thus must be fettered like "a thief or similar low-life, such as a goat or a slave."[27] The *àbíkú* is both the kidnapped and the kidnapper. The metaphor of the *àbíkú*, then, can be read as a vehicle for the transgenerational transmission of the experience of loss due to the slave trade. In Okri, the long-term effects of the slave trade can be located in the fear of having a child who is born *àbíkú*, and in the suffering, loss, and mourning exhibited by those who are compelled to live with the continual death and disappearance of their children. Okri employs the culturally persistent trope of fettered and captive *àbíkú* children as a reminder of the generations of suffering inflicted upon despairing mothers who have been forced to endure these losses associated with recurrent modernities.

The images that Okri relies upon to link the slave trade past to the present realities of Nigerian life—the river, the road, the *àbíkú*, the bag—are not merely metaphors, they are facts of the contemporary reality Okri is depicting in his novel. *Àbíkú* children continue to be born, feted, and mourned in West African cultures because people continue to suffer from poor nutrition, disease, and underdevelopment. People are kidnapped and children can still be taken away in sacks into slavery in twenty-first-century West Africa. Interestingly, the figure of the *àbíkú* points to the way many of the metaphors of the slave trade described in this study could be read as metonymic as well.[28] For instance, the sack in which slaves (and Azaro) are transported to the coast is a mechanism of the slave trade and thus a metonym. However, as time goes by and generations who haven't experienced the slave trade are born, the sack is distanced or separated from the system of which it was a part—distanced from the slave trade itself. Thus, the relationship between the bag and the slave trade becomes obscured over generations. Shaw reminds us that this is the nature of transgenerational memory: "When memories of violence are transmitted between generations, we often see . . . instability in which one form of memory transmutes into another, sometimes shifting back and forth between predominantly discursive and non-discursive forms, remembering and forgetting, commemoration and erasure."[29] The bag continues to bear meaning as a site of violence, as a metaphor, and even as a symbol of domestic slavery, or of corrupt local merchants, but sometimes is no longer overtly understood as a reference to the transatlantic slave trade.

Thus, the metonym, over time and as a result of changing contexts and uses of the vehicle and perhaps even a cultural desire to erase the memory of the system in which it was a part, actually becomes mobilized in cultural discourse as a metaphor. Often its original literal meaning can even be lost. In its metaphoric form, when put in the context of other mechanisms related to the slave trade, the metaphor then reflects the metonymic relationship or reminds us of it. It is only when a constellation of other evocations of the slave trade comes into contact with this metaphor that the metonymic relationship is revived and reconstituted. The figure of the àbíkú child, for instance, is explained away in contemporary discussions by a wide host of medical, psychological, or cultural rationalizations that threaten to erase any historical or figurative explanations for the concept. The metonymic aspect of the àbíkú as the captive child that is activated as a figure of one aspect of the slave trade is lost. If we read for metaphor, however, we see the historical resonance of the slave trade emerge in the discourse describing the experience of the àbíkú time and again, which serves to link contemporary suffering to a larger historical narrative of oppression.

Though the metaphors that Okri evokes are active elements of contemporary discourse in both literal and figurative, metaphorical and metonymic ways, Okri repeatedly traces their etymological lineages back to seeds of memory planted during the era of the slave trade. In so doing, he consistently juxtaposes and transposes present concerns with the experiences of ancestors who died hundreds of years ago. Though Okri takes some risk here in not fixing meaning in the metaphors he employs, the greater advantage of the signifier that *signifies too much* is that it allows him to reveal continuities between past and present. Thus the mapping of the slave trade past onto a metaphor associated with the present (say, the *àbíkú* or "politicians!") enacts a critique of contemporary African politics and the recurrent violence that seem to be endemic in West African history.

For Okri, the long-term effects of the slave trade can be located in the fear *and* possibility associated with becoming a body in a bag, in the anxiety and exhilaration of living as an *àbíkú*, or in the oppressive liberation of being born to wander—as well as in the suffering, loss, and mourning exhibited by those who are compelled to watch it happen to others. Azaro's life is marked by the ambivalence of the river with which he is associated in the beginning of the novel: the liminality of being between the spirit world and the human world, alive and dead, destined to follow a river that is also a road—all of which lend Azaro a sense of promise that is constantly tempered by loss. Thus, the ambiguous time represented on the map of Azaro's wanderings in the woods, the ambivalent relationship of families to the *àbíkú* child, the impossible exhilaration of wandering along time lines haunted by anachronism are all means by which Okri can contend with the painful and exhilarating recurrence of a tragic history.

From Enslavement Is Born a Wanderer

In a moment that again harkens to a past that continues to leave its mark on the present, Azaro becomes a victim of the lingering specter of the slave trade in much the same way we see Tutuola's narrator become trapped in a cycle of ghostly enslavement in *My Life in the Bush of Ghosts*. Okri evokes the trope of the body in the bag, which Tutuola so cleverly employed, to link contemporary politics to the slave trade when Azaro discovers that customers at the bar at which he works are not merely menacing, but quite clearly *captors*. Two "albino traveling merchants" conspire with a woman who "had a large sack on her back, which she gave to the albinos. The albinos unfurled the sack, shook it out, sending dust clouds into the air. They glanced at me furtively, and hid the sack under the table" (108). Clearly signifying on Tutuola's trope of the body in the bag, Okri resurrects the fear of being captured by men with sacks and evokes the history of the slave trade within the walls of Madame Koto's bar. Azaro even overhears two terrifying customers speak in what he thinks are "alien languages" and then ask his boss, Madame Koto, about him. They ask, "Will you sell him to us? . . . So we can take him with us" (109), overtly maneuvering to literally purchase the young boy. They offer as much money as Madame Koto desires if she will allow them to take Azaro away with them to "many places." When Madame Koto refuses, they threaten to take Azaro by force and manage to do just that, and again the sack emerges to suggest fears of the slave trade:

> The albinos twisted, shrugged, stood up, and spread out the sack. The woman distracted me with her smile. And then the albinos sprang at me and covered me with the sack. I struggled and fought, but they expertly bundled me in and tied up the sack as if I were an animal.... Overcome with fear, unable to move, surrounded by darkness and the death-smells of the sack, I cried: "Politicians! Politicians are taking me away!" (111)

Here, using Tutuola's language and imagery of capture and enslavement, Okri transposes the captivity that was prevalent during the slave trade onto twentieth-century Nigerian politics.

Clearly, when the two intimidating men offer to buy Azaro, Okri suggests the connection between these wealthy albino traveling merchants and the earlier white mobile merchants who stripped Nigeria's coast of its human resources. Madame Koto is a symbol of unrestrained commerce: Seemingly anything can be bought or sold in her shop by the unsavory characters she hosts, apparently even people. But instead of it being the uncontrollable capitalist project of global slavery that puts Azaro at risk, now it is "politicians" who are abusing the people of Nigeria, but that experience is always layered with the concerns of the earlier abuses of the slave trade. Azaro's exclamation that politicians are kidnapping him links parallel modernities: that of the introduction of the global trade in slaves and the new breed of indigenous politicians holding the people of Nigeria captive.

As if Okri is paying homage to Tutuola, Azaro is dragged deep into the forest while he is bound in the bag filled with "death-smells," and is held captive by the ghoulish traveling merchants as they travel to an unknown destination. Terrified that he will die, Azaro is immediately driven to break free of his captors. He finds a pocketknife, cuts his way out of the sack, and falls into a dark, raging river. The river he falls into, as is typical in the novel, turns into a road, and Azaro follows it: "The road was endless. One road led to a thousand others, which in turn fed into paths, which fed into dirt tracks, which became streets, which ended in avenues and cul-de-sacs. All around, a new world was being erected amidst the old" (113). In this symbolic act of self-birth—from captivity to independence, from the sack, into the water, and out onto the road—Azaro indicates his connection to both the past of the slave trade and the present state of Nigerian independence. Azaro is no longer a submissive victim, but instead becomes an independent soul, free to make his own path through the forest.

With his newfound freedom, Azaro becomes a traveler, a cartographer, even, for whom the forest becomes a map of how the past is alive in the present. The roads that he describes guide him out of captivity and lead also into the towns of the future, into a Nigerian suburbia-to-be. Old zinc shacks stand on new suburban culs-de-sac, a significant reminder to Azaro and the reader that the present and the future are neighbors of the past. Though the process of suburbanization seemingly destroys the forest and whatever else may lie in its path, still some remnants of the past remain. In this way, the present is laced with the memory of what once was, and the forest becomes a palimpsest that only Azaro recognizes. As Azaro attempts to understand how the past and the present are related and drawn upon each other, his mapping of the terrain helps us understand how memory functions.

By reading his maps of the road upon which he travels as indicators of the past in the present, we also read a geography of memory. For instance, Azaro attempts to describe the course of the road and the landscape that surrounds it: "The roads seemed to me then to have a cruel and infinite imagination. All the roads multiplied, reproducing themselves, subdividing themselves, turning in on themselves, like snakes, tails in their mouths, twisting themselves into labyrinths" (114). The image of the snake swallowing itself here seems to indicate a sort of self-referentiality or self-birth, which is clearly pertinent to Azaro's recent experiences. A typical Jungian reading of this snake image notes that "it is said of the oroborus [the snake that swallows its own tail] that he slays himself and brings himself to life, fertilizes himself and gives birth to himself."[30] In Yoruba cosmology, Oshunmare is the serpent deity that is associated with the rainbow and with regeneration and eternal life, as is the Dahomean *danh*.[31] Okri mobilizes this symbology, such that from the moment of his self-birth from the sack, Azaro is reborn, attaining his own liberation and utilizing the mobility granted him by his captivity to become a self-invested traveler. The image of the snake also seems to indicate a circular and repetitive path, reiterating Okri's interest in recurrence, but then Okri immediately renames the path labyrinthine. Indeed, Azaro's journey through the woods is not simply circular. Instead, Azaro characterizes the road as a "labyrinth" in its routes and logic, more tangled than a simple circle would suggest.

The trajectory of memory here is recurrent, but it is not merely cyclical. There are crossroads that populate this journey through the forest, but those crossroads double back on themselves and lead "towards home and then away from it without end, with too many signs, and no directions" (115). This is no simple circle that will lead him back home if he stays on it long enough. On his road through the present to the past, Azaro is lost in a maze of information, signs, and images that orient him both toward his unstable present and away from it. It is in this winding search for a destination that Azaro finds a mission, finds his own subjecthood. Cut from the womb by his own hand, Azaro does indeed find liberation but not a simple trajectory toward independence. As an analogy for Nigeria's own independence, this passage admits that independence is a sort of self-fashioning, like the snake that swallows its own tail, but the road is not well-worn or easy to follow, and it often requires a certain investment in the past. Indeed, the road may lead to some scenes of progress, but that development is always laden with the memory of the past.

The Map of the Wanderer

In his movement through time lines in the forest, Azaro is aligned with the wandering subject Mbembe describes in his discussion of Tutuola's novels. He enters a "ghostly sphere" where events never congeal entirely into a stable narrative because they are haunted by specters of the past. Past and future are undermined, memory is destabilized, and multiplication, fracture, and mutilation are ubiquitous. Mbembe argues that "one does not enter into the ghostly realm out of curiosity or because one wants to. Ultimately, a tragedy, indeed a loss is at the origin of everything."[32] A loss of human life through commerce launches this novel and a similar loss of freedom inaugurates Azaro's liberatory, visionary life of wandering in the bush.

Though his parents lament it, Azaro is indeed a traveler by his very nature. But his relationship to the road and to the bush is ambivalent in a way that Tutuola only hinted at with his journeying narrator. No longer simply compelled to wander, but now a savvy traveler with one eye looking backward, Azaro becomes a mapper of the terrain through which he travels and thereby gains a certain independence of its power of captivity as well as a certain control over the navigation of it. The road is both his torment and his salvation. At first, he is quick to notice the subtle and constant changes in the road: It recedes away from Madame Koto's bar, trees are being felled, large machines are lurking in the forest. But along the road, Azaro has visions that are not clearly images of the present or even glimpses of the future, but of some lingering past that has been left behind on the road. Like sacrifices left for the "King of the Road," memory has been sacrificed here, too, and it is only Azaro who is able to locate those moments and engage them. They have been crushed into the pavement of the road, they have been cemented together there, and they coexist, overlap, reinterpret each other, seeping into one another.

Later, when Azaro finds himself in the woods, it is again because of the threat of capture. In Madame Koto's bar, he realizes that spirits are her main customers and that they've come to the bar wearing borrowed human body parts, hoping to experience human reality (again reminiscent of Tutuola). Some of those ghastly human impostors were known to "abduct children to their realm" (136), another reference to those kidnapped by slave raiders to be taken to "the new world" as well as to Azaro's status as an *àbíkú*. Sensitive to the Tutuolan implications of such kidnapping, body-sharing, and slave-capturing spirits, then, when spirits shout out, "SEIZE THAT BOY!" another cycle of capture and escape seems imminent. Azaro does manage to escape his pursuers, but this time he enters a different realm of the forest's history. Here the spirits are everywhere, and, again reminiscent of Tutuola's bush, they call Azaro's name out so that he "felt everything was in conspiracy with the spirits to betray [his] hiding-places" (138). He runs until he is lost, where he finds relics of Africa's past awaiting him. "All around me were silent figures in great masks. All around me were ancestral statues. Wherever I rode I saw immemorial monoliths with solemn faces and beaded lapis lazuli eyes" (139). These monuments to the African precolonial, pre–slave trade past gather with a statue of Madame Koto to chase him through the woods. This layering of past and present provides Azaro access to that part of the past before the encounter with the West, before enslavement, before a call of "Seize that boy!" would evoke slave trade violence. This past, which his mother later ironically calls the "aquamarine beginnings" (183), follows Azaro relentlessly, refusing to allow him to ignore it. Azaro's two incidences of escape into landscapes laden with memories of the past refute the claims of critics such as Mbembe that memories of the slave trade have been forgotten. Okri seems to argue here that the past of the slave trade and the cultures that flourished before it are always lurking in the present, awaiting every opportunity to irrupt into memory.

However, what emerges is a past that figures both as "aquamarine" bliss and as "chaos and thunder" in the figure of Sango, the Yoruba god of thunder and lightning as well as a symbol of African resistance against the slave trade.

The images that overwhelm Azaro in the woods both haunt and lull Azaro. In his travel through the forest, Azaro is confronted with the traditional Yoruba culture and the history of the slave trade, but neither is allowed to have a particularly stable valence. In the forest of memory, every spirit is an ambivalent one. Is the pre–slave trade past "aquamarine" as his mother claims? Or is it a haunting ghoul that allows the forces of unrestrained commerce (in the figure of Madame Koto) to enter and corrupt? If Azaro is drawing a map of the memory of Nigeria's past, this map has no moral compass to guide us. Tutuola's narrator may claim that as a child he did not know what was good or bad, but he had yet to encounter the topsy-turvy world Okri evokes. Is the river a figure of birth or destruction? Are the foundations of Africa's past a figment of the imagination or part of an authentic previolence culture? Is the spirit world inviting or disconcerting in its pristine perfection? Is the *àbíkú* a symbol of hope or one of mourning and loss? Is the sack the source of enslavement or liberation? Is mortal life torture or love—or both? In Okri's postindependence novel, we find that the geography of this world has no true north; rather, it is a complex web of directions and misdirections that create a composite map of Nigeria's ambiguous and ambivalent past and present.

Locating Memory

At the same time as it critiques postcolonial Nigerian politics, the indeterminacy of Azaro's map undermines the very nature of mapping as it is defined in the Western world and provides a means by which Nigerians can contend with the legacy of the slave trade and colonialism. The logic of the colonial map was, according to Benedict Anderson, "a totalizing classificatory grid, which could be applied with endless flexibility to anything under the state's real or contemplated control: peoples, regions, religions, languages, products, monuments, and so forth. The effect of the grid was always to be able to say of anything that it was this, not that; that it belonged here, not there. It was bounded, determinate, and therefore—in principle—countable."[33] Azaro's map, in contrast, is one of ambiguity.

The wanderer's map is one of fleeting images and misdirection. It cannot fully name every site because each site comes to him as a flash of something left behind, something not quite there, but something always lingering. There is a sense of loss in being lost, in that there are places one seeks but can never find, but there is always something gained in the knowledge of uncharted territories and undiscovered monuments. As a result, Azaro is able to create a map of Nigeria's past that is not reflective of an institutionalized series of landmarks, but one that reflects a richer and more layered view that one can discover only by wandering. Many of the sites of memory on Azaro's map are conflations of more than one moment; they reveal recurrences and composite images. The wanderer's map is never stable, countable, delineable.

Mapping tends to be thought of as a means of charting space as if it were atemporal. In fact, however, all maps are essentially an event on a time line, a diagram of what existed at a very particular moment in history. After all, we cannot safely use a map of Lagos from 1970 to help us navigate the city today. What Azaro draws for us, however, is a map that cuts across time lines. The landscape that he encounters is geographically "labyrinthine" because it is temporally instead of spatially invested. When he travels into the forest, he travels through time, and the landmarks he encounters mark a path to times that are long past but still remain a part of Nigeria's present. He claims that he "walked on the dissolving streets and among the terrestrial bush.... I walked through books and months and forgotten histories" (307). The long-disremembered images of the past that he encounters in the forest speak to him, have an undeniable pull on him. If James Clifford has argued that "to know who you are is to know where you are,"[34] we might add that to know who you are is to know *when* you are as well—but that knowledge may not be as easy to ascertain.

The map generally functions (or at least purports to function) on at least two levels. On one hand, it provides a sense of orientation. It tells a person exactly where he is. On the other hand, it functions as a navigational device, showing how to get from point A to point B. At the orientation level, it designates landmarks, sites, and natural formations. Azaro's maps are filled with the rivers and roads that wind through his bush landscape. His maps also include sites of memory. He encounters monuments and monoliths; he describes sites of creation and of destruction. At the navigational level, Azaro delineates the routes of memory, how to move within that space representing time. What he draws is a map for moving between past and present, though he cannot sufficiently describe how to navigate directly *from* past to present. The road is too complicated to be certain. And yet Azaro moves fluidly between these temporal landscapes. Always stumbling upon crossroads and perpetually lost, Azaro plots the terrain of the past, which has previously seemed out of touch. The landmarks of the past lead him toward and away from the present at every turn.

Memory works like a map in this way: memories are layered and sometimes indistinguishable, such that we can feel transported through time and space merely as a result of one image from our past. We might begin in one part of our past and then wander over to some other connected yet seemingly unrelated moment in our memories. Like a woman who sees the portrait of her elderly husband but thinks he seems too wrinkled and gray because her memory reaches beyond his present countenance to the face of a younger man from an earlier time, Azaro sees his world with a composite view, remembering what it looked like before it was altered by time. His map recognizes newness at the same time as it is nostalgic for the way it appeared in the past. This is unlike recorded history in its linear, narrative structure. And it is unlike the rigidity of the colonial map in its determinacy in time and space. In his descriptions of the labyrinthine nature of the road, Azaro produces a countermemory. He both refutes the notion of the linear, atemporal, geographical nature of mapping, and, like Baquaqua, he also appropriates the right to mapping for himself—his own individual memories and the collective memory of the past—thereby authorizing those memories as legitimate landmarks of the past within the space of the present.

Indeed, if the map functions primarily for orientation and navigation, then its indirect function is to produce specialized, institutionalized knowledge and mastery. Mapping is a means of officially archiving space over time. However, by outlining the traces of a seemingly forgotten memory of the violent past of the slave trade, Azaro eludes the institutional drive to exclude elements of the past that might be less flattering to all those involved. Instead of being satisfied with the official narrative of Nigeria's past, the map Okri explores embraces the memory of the interior of Africa, which the slave trader, the colonist, and the suburb developer cannot see and will not see, despite their integral participation in its construction and destruction. At the same time, it may also be a map that many Nigerians would be hesitant to produce, as it reveals a past marred by perhaps the gravest genocide in human history, by which a few West African elites rose to prominence at the expense of millions who suffered. Azaro's map allows those repressed memories to take precedence over the official historical record. As Rosi Braidotti tells us, the nomadic person has a memory that "is activated against the stream; they enact a rebellion of knowledge."[35] By accessing these subjugated knowledges in his nomadic wanderings, Azaro becomes an archive of his own. The archive is generally the provenance of the colonizer; in fact, Derrida writes that "there is no political power without the power of the archive, if not memory."[36] Here, we see that Azaro has come to reappropriate the power of the archive. In his ability to map a past that still lingers in the forest, he gains the power to record those memories that were once denied his community.

Mapping Alternative Archives

Azaro does have one friend who seems to share his ability to record and affirm these memories of violence: the wildly abused local photographer. When we first meet the photographer, he is the "instant butt of jokes" (45), despite the fact that everyone wants him to photograph them and thereby make them a local celebrity. He appears throughout the novel, emerging from dark corners of the neighborhood each time there is a feast or a riot, to document the highs and lows of a community anxious to exceed its own poverty and despair. Unfortunately, he produces images his neighbors only half willingly recognize as themselves. Azaro remarks,

> When I looked closer at the pictures we all seemed strange. The pictures were grained, there were dots over our faces, smudges everywhere. Dad looked as if he had a patch over one eye, Mum was blurred in both eyes, the children were like squirrels, and I resembled a rabbit. We all looked like celebrating refugees. We were cramped, and hungry, and our smiles were fixed. The room appeared to be constructed out of garbage and together we seemed a people who had never known happiness. Those of us that smiled had our faces contorted into grimaces, like people who had been defeated but who smile when a camera is trained on them. (91)

The photographer's unique ability to capture the reflection of the community's true condition leaves them disturbed and belligerent. His crime is that he is able to see and reflect the reality they all wish they could deny—that they are poor, depraved refugees in their own country.

The photographer is also endangered because he captures a record of the exploitation of the community by the newly emerging independence politicians. His photos showed "thugs beating up market women. They showed the leader of the Party of Bad Milk from odd angles that made his face seem bloated, his eyes bulbous, his mouth greedy. He had pictures of politicians being stoned at a rally, he caught their panic, their cowardice, and their humiliation" (160). The power of the photographer was that he could "record the events . . . and make them real with his magic instrument" (182). His work is an archive of misery and exploitation that was available to everyone at every level; it is an indictment of both the community and those who oppress them; it is a democratic record of the recurrent violence fashioned by this new so-called independence.

The politicians retaliate against the photographer, the only other person who is aware of the subversive nature of taking control of the archive, by destroying his home, his equipment, and his photographs. As the photographer's home burned, Azaro "perceived, in the crack of a moment, the recurrence of things unresolved—histories, dreams, a vanished world of great old spirits, wild jungles, tigers with eyes of diamonds roaming the dense foliage. I saw beings who dragged clanking chains behind them, bleeding from their necks. I saw men and women without wings, sitting in rows, soaring through the empty air" (176–77). It is no mistake that here again, Azaro evokes recurrence, and that recurrence is marked by images of the slave trade: the slave coffle wearing chains and neck braces, and the Middle Passage in which Africans were "tight-packed" closely in rows to soar across the seas for sale in the Americas.

In that night of violence against the photographer, these images coalesce with the brutality of the politicians who seek to destroy the archive of images of contemporary suffering that the photographer seeks to create. Azaro mourns, "It was a night without memory. It was a night replaying its corrosive recurrence on the road of our lives, on the road which was hungry for great transformations" (180). On the one hand, Azaro is correct; the night seems to be one without memory in which violence is reenacted as if there were no knowledge of history that could prevent it. On the other hand, ironically, this is *not* a night without memory, and Azaro is the proof of it. In these very moments of destruction, he is a conduit of memory. He accesses visions of past violence—the coffle, the ship—which help him to contextualize and underscore the recurrence he describes. What's more, his parents do the same, and on this evening, they tell "stories of recurrence told down through generations of defiant mouths" (177). Even if the people do not have access to official archives, the memory of past violence does still live on. The memory of cruelty and abuse is resilient.

Nonetheless, Azaro's neighbors recognize the dysfunction of memory. Though powerful political thugs destroyed their town, the citizens begin to question their own memory of the events. It began to seem that "nothing significant had happened. Some of us began to distrust our memories. We began to think that we had collectively dreamt up the fevers of that night. It wouldn't be the first or the last time" (183). Okri contributes here to our understanding of the contested memory of violence in Nigeria. It is not simply that memory fails, but that we are all too aware of its fallibility and look to something to authenticate or authorize our memories. With the photographer gone, they have no one to confirm or document their experience. "It was as if the events were never real. They assumed the status of rumour" (183). The interaction of "history" and "memory" are important here. Pierre Nora's concept of history as those narratives that are condoned through institutionalized formats such as academic historical works[37] is in competition with the rumors and the stories that are the vessels for memories among those who have no access to these institutionalized forms of information. Their memories seem as though they are not to be trusted because stories shift; they change with the storyteller and with the perception of the listener. Azaro fears that all of the events of that night will dissolve "into a delirium of stories" (182). Their fear is that rumors and stories are tantamount to amnesia.

Still, the memory does survive because as a traveling subject, Azaro has a greater access to the locations of memory, the real *milieux de mémoire* that Nora claims hardly exist in the modern era. Nora argues, in his monumental study of French memory and commemoration, that modernity has left us with only "*lieux de mémoire*, sites of memory, because there are no longer *milieux de mémoire*, real environments of memory,"[38] by which he means that in contemporary culture, the drive to record the past has so overwhelmed us that memory—"true memory"—has been undermined and, indeed, destroyed by the urge to record the past in a material archive. The *milieux de mémoire* that have disappeared compose the record of the past that "has taken refuge in gestures and habits, in skills passed down by unspoken traditions, in the body's inherent self-knowledge, in unstudied reflexes and ingrained memories."[39] The basic premise of Nora's concept of "sites of memory" relies on the notion that modernity is structured in such a way that its attendant "disappearance of peasant culture, that quintessential repository of collective memory,"[40] has triggered the loss of those memories that are "retained as the secret of so-called primitive or archaic societies."[41] Nora's dichotomous system of history and memory matched against modernity and peasant/"primitive" cultures reveal the dangers of defining memory in the modern period through a reading dedicated to French historiography alone.

Nora's work convincingly indicts the memory industry and its corollary challenge to collective memory; however, in his rush to pronounce the death of *milieux de mémoire*, he excludes the possibility for the hybrid, parallel modernity that Okri envisions in *The Famished Road*. Nostalgic for the varieties of memory housed in oral cultures, Nora's formulation of contemporary memory loses sight of the way these forms of memory persist in contemporary societies such as the one Okri depicts, and are indeed *signs* of modernity rather than the absence or the failure of it. Okri's layering of slave trade history on the era of independence reveals precisely the "permanent evolution, open to the dialectic of remembering and forgetting, unconscious of its successive deformations, vulnerable to manipulation and appropriation, susceptible to being long dormant and periodically revived,"[42] which Nora claims is indicative of true memory. It is precisely in its ambivalent nature, in its ability to change and shift over time, in its recurrence in spaces marked out for development rather than nostalgia, that Okri's landscape (and the map Azaro makes of it) can function as a reflection of the modernity Okri both embraces and critiques in his novel. The forms of memory depicted in Okri's novel are not forms of so-called "primitive memory," and they are not remnants of a peasant culture in a premodern society. Instead, Okri's modern urban dwellers continue to live in a *milieux de mémoire* in which the past remains a lived experience that can be encountered in the dark creaking woods or along the path to the suburbs.

As such, Azaro's map is not one that is precisely documentary or material, nor could it be. It is figurative, metaphorical, and as a result, is constantly changing and labyrinthine. The map that Azaro draws for us represents the culture that has emerged, not simply out of the "aquamarine beginnings," but also from the violent rupture that accompanied the advent of the slave trade, and then again from the recurrent violence that accompanied Nigerian independence politics. The map associated with this temporally complicated space by necessity exceeds the material impulse of the archive. It relies on stories, metaphors, invisible monuments, and memories once forgotten.

Azaro's map, then, is revelatory of the process of modernity rather than the absence or ascendance of modernity. The modernity Okri describes is one in which the past and the present are lived inextricably, in which the present is undeniably aware of past injustices and abuses. In this way, Okri's characters, and Azaro in particular, are not subjected to modernity but are actually agents in the production of what it means to be modern. The alternative map engendered by this kind of thinking utilizes what Nora might consider traditional forms of memory in the service of a transgressive politics. Okri depicts a politics of memory, which recognizes the tools of the colonial regime—the power of the map to determine the nature of a people—but alters them in such a way that they can represent the memory of a citizenry born of the violence of both the trade and the emergence of a nation. The map allows them to transgress, refute, and deny the power of official histories by asserting a memory of violence at the same time as it critiques the rebirth of violence in contemporary Nigerian politics. Azaro's new cartography acts as both a critique of modernity and its attendant violences and an assertion of the way in which *milieux de mémoire* can persist and even are produced in the West African participation in modernity.

Nigeria's Memory Future

Toward the end of the novel, Azaro enters a dreamlike trance in which he travels through the narratives and past lives of Nigeria's memory. In this dream, he runs until he reaches the Atlantic, where he looks to the sky only to see clouds shaped like invading armies of ghosts, and "ghost ships of centuries arrived endlessly on the shores. . . . The white ones, ghost forms, on deep nights, stepped on our shores, and I heard the earth cry. . . . I witnessed the destruction of great shrines, the death of mighty trees that housed centuries of insurgent as well as soothing memories. . . . I saw the death of their many roads and ways and philosophies" (457). The slave trade here is overtly named as the end of an era of something sacred and the beginning of an era of violence and death. This disillusion is marked by an end of freedom. His memory stumbles through "slave alleys where innumerable souls had written their names on the walls with their flesh . . . [and] the garrisons of slave towns" (460). There, Azaro encounters former slaves who insist on the memory of their names and their demeaned conditions, people who record their trauma for posterity and activate the archive for Azaro. Eventually he is taken to the edge of the desert where a spirit threatens to take him away on a ship across the ocean of sand (461), reminding us of the way in which these events continue to threaten the narrator even in the present. It is not merely ghosts of the past who must record their suffering for us to remember, but Azaro and his neighbors as well. All these images of Africa's slave trade past surround and haunt him, like those statues and monoliths of Africa's early precolonial history that chased him earlier in the novel. Azaro cannot escape Africa's violent past, and it certainly cannot be erased.

However, Okri's novel is not simply about the recurrence of violence and the dread that it brings to Nigeria. Despite all that, it is a novel of hope. It is forward-looking, as memory tends to be, because the only place the past has to rest is in the future. In Azaro's reveries, he gains a vision into his best friend's past lives, which reveal the way the past can be understood as an anticipation for the future. In the vision of his friend's past, he sees multiple lives; some of which would be considered auspicious, others violent and destructive. In his vision, his friend Ade was even once a "one-eyed white ship captain who believed in God and wrote beautiful hymns and who made his fortune capturing slaves in the Gold Coast" (481), indicating an African embodiment of the complexity and even complicity in the wrongdoings of the past. The slave trade is a part of global memory. Responsibility for it is not the sole provenance of slave masters, nor are its repercussions strictly confined to the haunting of Africa's shores. Because the slave trade affected every part of the globe, its presence in our present cannot be denied. All past lives are a part of *humanity's* past, and simply remembering them is a movement toward a new New World. A future of recurrence, always, but also a future of remembrance. In his dreams, in distinct juxtaposition to the slave trade and the coups and wars that he envisions, Azaro also feels "old songs [begin] to stir. Old voices from the world of spirits. Songs of seductive purity" (477). This inflects recurrence with a new meaning. Recurrence seems primarily to be linked to violence and the slave trade throughout the novel, but here we can see the hopefulness of the recurrence of heroes and joy and the wisdom of past generations. Okri is not satisfied with a simple binary experience of memory that would posit recurrence as negative and some kind of creation as good. Instead, he allows us a sense that recurrence and memory provide hope and embody violence at the same time.

Azaro's father helps him to understand the maps he has been internalizing of this past landscape living in the present: "When you look around and see empty spaces, beware. In those spaces are cities, invisible civilizations, future histories, everything is HERE. . . . All roads lead to death, but some roads lead to things which can never be finished. Wonderful things" (498). In the end, Azaro responds, "I was not afraid of Time" (500). In this visionary moment, all the destruction and violence that Azaro has witnessed and recorded become a means of transcending that violence of the past and the fear it entails while still maintaining the archive of it. He is able to look toward the future, which can never be completed, and which is always populated by invisible pasts.

Conclusion: Things That Can Never Be Finished

If contemporary cultural critics have come to understand the map as the means by which Europeans grasped power and created a kind of amnesia of previous worldviews, then I am arguing that no such amnesia has ever existed, though there might be expressions of forgetting. As Okri depicts in *The Famished Road*, West Africans have created a counterdiscourse from the very same tools Europeans employed to attempt to destroy memory in Africa. Take, for instance, the naming of villages during the era of the slave trade. As slave raiders sought to destroy villages to gain personal wealth and status, they also engendered the resilience of memory and the drive for victims to encode their trauma for the future. In some places in West Africa, the effects of slave raiding are revealed through names describing the origin of a refuge born out of a community's escape from raiders in another region.[43] In the Senegambia region there are towns that are named "here where no one can reach them anymore" or "the village of free people."[44] An Igbo town that managed to fight off the infamous Aro invaders recalls their victory in the name of their town as well: "the town the Aro could not reach/capture" (Igbo Erughi).[45] The name of an island off the shore of Guinea-Bissau relates the opposite testimony; named Baducô or "one who stays," it articulates the fear that if one ventured as far as this island, they would never return home because they would be captured and enslaved.[46] The location of memory marked directly onto the map creates stark reminders of the way the slave trade shaped the lives and experiences of the people on the continent. These assertions of memory linger to remind those wandering travelers of an alternative narrative of history. Likewise, Okri's novel explores the resilience of memory and the imposition of a new structure of memory upon the landscape that expresses the experience of those who were left to suffer the legacy and consequences of the slave trade.

Critic Wole Ogundele argues that African authors have a responsibility to depict the precolonial past, the internecine conflict of African communities, and the violent past of the slave trade in historical fiction. He writes,

> Narratives of the factual precolonial past, which should complement and give reality to the fictions, are yet to emerge fully. With a genuine interest in the actual—as opposed to the mythical—past, the great wall separating pre- from postcolonial Africa can be breached. Historical novels about this immensely long and real past are still relevant, because that past remains relevant. The internal

economic, social-political, cultural, and psychological realities that made possible, and sustained for centuries, the inhumanity of slavery and the slave trade are still worth pondering over even in twenty-first-century Africa. How could this crime in which virtually all societies collaborated with alacrity, and the abolition of which some resisted to the bitter end, go on for so long on a continent reputed for her humane values? What were the fundamental changes in feelings, social values, organizations, and relationships that it wrought in the African universe?[47]

Ogundele prescribes the historical novel as a remedy for a perceived amnesia regarding the slave trade's effects on the social and political structures of contemporary Africa. The supposed myth-building that accompanies Okri's refuge in magical realism does not do justice to the memory of slavery and the slave trade in Ogundele's estimation.

Ogundele and other critics who lament a lack of overt historical narratives regarding the slave trade subscribe to what Nora would call "duty-memory," the cultural imperative that leads one to say, "[The] responsibility [to remember] is mine and it is I who must remember."[48] Nora critiques this form of cultural coercion to remember because it functions in the service of an official archive that would document so extensively and so obsessively that most memory would, in the end, be lost. This kind of obligatory duty-memory subverts the kind of authentic memory Nora desires. Even as we resist declaring memory authentic or inauthentic, mythological or historical, Nora's claims seem to be quite relevant. Because critics are so driven to see memory represented in ways that are narrativized, explicit, and historical, they are not able to read Okri's indictment of modernity as an exploration of the propensity to replicate the violence of the slave trade.

The insistence on narratives that would deal explicitly with the slave trade in its historical context actually makes it impossible for critics to recognize the varied ways in which the traumas associated with the slave trade and its effects are being documented—not through official channels or histories, but through the lived experiences of the people who continue to deal with its effects. The nights of memory, the photographer's countertestimony, Azaro's vision are all records of recurrent violence and its relationship to the slave trade—they simply are the means by which the oppressed manage to record those memories. Theirs is not the work of historians or even novelists, but their memories are evidence of the histories of violence they have endured.

The era of the slave trade is significant in the history of West Africa: an entry into a new form of violence and recurrence. If Valetin Y. Mudimbe is correct when he writes, "The metamorphosis of a memory, such as that found in an African colonial territory . . . takes place during a process of neutralization, re-creation, and rearrangement of a site, of its geography and of the values by which a tradition distinguished it,"[49] then what Okri does is to give life to a new realignment of memory that carries with it a new geography and a new ethic as well. Exploration of the effects of these memories works in the service of justice for those victims of the crime. Authors who choose to explore these irruptions of the past that impose themselves on our memory do not simply signal the possibility of alternate memory; instead, they activate a resistant and triumphant memory for the future. Amos Tutuola and Ben Okri recognize the correlation between forbidden spaces such as the bush and the forbidden memories of the trade. When their characters enter the bush, they activate memories rendered inaccessible by time, institutionalized history, and fear. Tutuola and Okri, like Azaro, look upon time without fear, and memorialize Africa's past in the service of liberating Africa's future.

CHAPTER FOUR

The Curse of Constant Remembrance

The Belated Trauma of the Slave Trade in Ayi Kwei Armah's *Fragments*

> In the early days our forebears sold their kinsmen into slavery for minor items such as beads, mirrors, alcohol, and tobacco. These days, the tune is the same, only the articles have changed into cars, transistor radios, and bank accounts. Nothing else has changed, and nothing will change in the foreseeable future.
>
> —Ken Saro-Wiwa

When European slave ships sailed into the port of Old Calabar in the late eighteenth century, Antera Duke, a wealthy local trader, welcomed them with a lengthy protocol that he and his merchant neighbors and family members had developed over generations of trading with Europeans. In a diary he kept of his daily life and labor, Duke depicts the elaborate ritual that took place as the ships pulled to shore and Duke and his people prepared a welcome. "I see Coffee Duke send his son to till mee news about new ship after Little time I hear 5 great guns firs in 7 fatherpoint so wee see ship come up his be John Cooper Tender arrive so wee firs 3 great guns for him."[1] The arrival of the ships required more than simply a military welcome; it also involved an elaborate costume change. "I go down for Landing to get all great guns Ready and wee have firs 28 great guns for ashor one one for every ship about wee shave head first and wer fine hatt & fine clothe & Hanschiff so all Captin and wee genllmen get Dinner for Esim house."[2] While Duke's main trade was selling slaves along the coast of present-day Nigeria, it was not merely an economic exchange that took place—it was also cultural. For the African traders on the coast, the interaction with sailors and ship captains involved a kind of pageantry that marked the trader as elite, and positioned him in direct contrast to those Africans he was in the business of selling. The African agents "dressed as white men,"[3] aware of the way their outfits had a rhetorical impact and a bearing on their transactions with the European merchants. The African dealer participated in the trade not only as a business venture, with a mind toward gaining individual material wealth, but with the awareness of establishing his status as a consumer and agent in a global economy. Donning European attire revealed a certain ostentatious consumption that their everyday clothes might fail to communicate to their European counterparts. The elaborate protocol and displays of wealth announced the entry of these African traders into a global network not only of slavery, but of capitalism, commercialism, and consumerism.

In exchange for the nearly seventy-one hundred enslaved people Duke saw leave the coast between January 18, 1785, and January 31, 1788, Duke and other agents in Old Calabar were afforded luxuries to which they previously had no access. Grandy King George, a contemporary of Duke's, wrote a wish list of the items he hoped to secure through trade with Europe. He wrote to his liaison, "Marchant Lace[,] when you Send a ship[,] send drinking horns for Coomey and sum fine white mugs and sum glass tanckards with Leds to them[.] Send Pleanty of ships guns[,] the same as Sharp had[.] I dount care if there was 2 or 3 on a Slave[.]" He continued by asking for goods suitable for decorating the home of a gentleman: "Send me one table and six Chears for my house and one two arm Schere for my Salf to sat in and 12 Puter plates and 4 dishes 12 Nifes and 12 forcks and 2 Large table spoons and a trowen and one Pear of Ballonses 2 brass Juggs with their Cisers to lift the same as a tanckard and two Copr ones." And he added requests for his own attire and maintenance: "Send me one red and one blue coat with gould Lace for to fit a Large man[.] Send buttr and Suger for to trade[.] Send sum green[,] sum red[,] sum blue Velvet caps with small Leace[.] and Send Sum files for trade, So no more at Preasant from your best friend. GRANDY KING GEORGE"[4]

These are merely short excerpts from the overwhelming list of goods Grandy King George requested his "best friend" bring from Europe on his return. His language clearly reveals a lack of concern for costs—even though the costs are measured in human lives—as he is willing to buy guns even if one slave can purchase only two or three weapons, in part because those weapons could themselves produce so many more captives. The concern for very particular, high-quality materials such as pewter and velvet indicates a man who is extremely knowledgeable about the most expensive of European wares, and his concern for furnishing his own home suggests that he had an imagination for European domestic fashions at the time as well. It has always been clear that the export of African lives was a lucrative business that supplied Europeans with the human commodities necessary to maintain their plantation systems around the Atlantic littoral. However, the sale of Africans also provided African traders with their own luxuries, which showcased, for Europeans and Africans alike, their connection to an international market signified by the values of consumption encouraged by the trade itself.

Though it is certainly the case that some African elites indulged in ostentatious displays of wealth long before this era, the slave trade introduced a radical transformation in African consumer culture on the coast. With the introduction of the transatlantic slave trade, which consumed the lives of more than twelve million African people, European fashions and culture were consumed as well. Material culture was irreversibly altered in this intervention. Many African elites began to represent their wealth not through the people with whom they associated, not through reserves of indigenously produced goods, but through the display of their ill-gotten gains reaped from their participation in the global slave trade. If we accept the notion that status in African society before and during the slave trade was determined largely by "wealth-in-people"—the idea that the people for whom a person acts as patron determine his personal status and indicate his level of prosperity—then we must investigate the ideological implications of the way in which material goods came to a greater prominence as status markers alongside the value of human beings.[5]

For even if a model of wealth-in-people persisted in West African societies, the demand for consumable wealth dominated much of the transactions of the period and determined the extent of the "unholy partnership"[6] between the European ship captains and the traders on the coast. Indeed, the distinguished African historian J. D. Fage contends that it was early trade with Europeans that encouraged the devastating consumer culture that dominated West African economies in the fifteenth and sixteenth centuries, thus making continued participation in the slave trade tremendously desirable and an easy shift from other so-called "legitimate" trade. "The prime reason for the concentration of slave-trading forts on the Gold Coast would seem to be that from the earlier trade, the natives of the Gold Coast had developed a growing taste for European imports and had evolved a competent commercial organization for dealing with these imports and distributing them in the hinterland."[7] By the seventeenth and eighteenth centuries, Stephen D. Behrendt contends, "African demand for Atlantic goods transformed fishing communities along the Calabar River into the entrepôt 'Old Calabar,' trading European, Asian, and African commodities."[8] As we have seen through the diaries and letters of Antera Duke and Grandy King George, by the end of the eighteenth century, the people of the region of Old Calabar were very particular and ostentatious in their desires for material goods produced in Europe. It was the drive toward consumable European goods that, at least in part, encouraged the traders on the coast to barter with the lives of people. Though slavery and slave trading existed in Africa before Europeans arrived, we can see that the contact with European traders radically altered African cultural dispositions toward manufactured and foreign goods, which in turn supported the expansion of the slave trade on the coast of West Africa.

For Africa's coastal elite, the desirability of the cargo being brought into Africa came to exceed the worth of the human lives being shipped out as cargo to the West. These early encounters continue to result in the commodification of human life, such that today in Africa (as in much of the world touched by this early global trade), a person's status as a "modern" individual can be measured largely by the person's ability to exhibit a certain kind of commodified wealth. Jane Parish argues that among the modern-day Akan, for instance, "conspicuous consumption of Western goods is one of the ways in which contradictory ideas associated with modern identities are constructed. . . . It is the way in which local Akan consumers express their participation in 'modernity' as a distancing from the past."[9] They little suspect that they are participating in a very particular "modernity" introduced by the transatlantic slave trade in the fifteenth century that has been inherited over the centuries thereafter.

The Been-To and the Malady of the Past

Ayi Kwei Armah's second novel, *Fragments* (1970), is an exploration of the twentieth-century effects of rampant consumerism that were initiated during the era of the slave trade through access to Western goods. Written a little more than a decade after Ghana claimed independence from Britain, the novel critiques the nation's bankrupt postcolonial governance and culture. The work followed right upon the heels of Armah's first novel, *The Beautyful Ones Are Not Yet Born*, which allegorically excoriated Kwame Nkrumah and the corrupt politicians who took Ghana under their control after the British were excused from power. In that short time, Ghana saw Nkrumah rise to the stature of a hero, winning the Lenin Peace Prize in 1963, but by 1966 he was deposed by a military coup after changing the constitution to allow himself status as president for life and single-party rule. In *Fragments*, Armah illustrates his disdain for the corrupt, lazy, and anti-intellectual behaviors that he believed led to the squandering of opportunities opened to Ghanaian society by self-rule. Underneath the surface of this postcolonial disappointment, I will argue, the novel also constitutes Armah's exploration of the way these twentieth-century tribulations are an effect of the transatlantic slave trade. Armah depicts the way the materialism so central to contemporary Ghana's crises is but a symptom of long-standing economic and social misappropriations of values that grow out of seeds planted during the transatlantic slave trade.

Fragments, set in 1960s postindependence Ghana, is centered on the protagonist, Baako, who returns to his hometown after living for some time in the United States. He represents the classic "been-to" character of West African literature: as a Ghanaian who has *been to* America and has returned to his family after several years' absence, he is expected to return wealthy and overwhelmingly generous.[10] However, Baako finds that he has not made the return—either emotional or financial—expected of the "been-to." He returns home only to find that he feels completely alienated and that he cannot be employed. His family hopes he will resign himself to a life as a wealthy and successful corporate or government drone, thereby producing the funds to build a house, maintain a car, and display the level of unambiguous, overt consumerism that will place him in high regard in their society. Struggling to understand what is expected of him, Baako stumbles from family member to family member, disappointing nearly everyone's expectations and hopes. Unable to fulfill his own dreams or those of his family, he falls into what is characterized—by his family and critics alike—as an insane depression.[11]

Many critics attribute Baako's mental and physical illness and his inability to function within Ghanaian society to the disturbing materialism that has altered West African values, urged on by Western standards of living. Certainly, Baako's disorientation in confronting this materialism is much the same experience Armah had when he returned from America: "With the dawn of independence in Ghana, Armah, returning to his country, was shocked to realize that independence was the fellow-traveler of both materialism and Westernization and that political corruption also followed in their trail."[12] The realities of postcolonial life had been an overwhelming disappointment to Armah, as Ghanaian society appeared to be obsessed with material wealth—certainly not the culture Armah had hoped would be ushered in by the previously promising change in Africa's governance.

Armah turned to writing to express his anxiety over the materialistic corruption that seemed to be endemic to this stage in Africa's long history and to explore what he thought were its causes. In *The Western Scar*, William Lawson argues, "Baako's emotional disorder is in large measure a reaction to a more widespread social disorder that Armah demonstrates in many aspects of Ghanaian life. A central core of spiritual or ethical value has almost died. Families, communities, religion, art, and politics are all affected by a pervasive obsession with commodity."[13] Baako cannot produce a car or a home for his family after his return, nor can he even buy fancy cigarettes or liquors like his acquaintance on the plane, Brempong. Ojong Ayuk claims that materialism in Armah's novel is like a "sea threatening to engulf everybody."[14] Indeed, according to most critics, Armah's writing is focused on a westernized West Africa that produced distorted traditions and psychologically disturbed characters whose identities were replaced with mere markers of consumption.

I argue that these readings only touch the surface of Armah's compelling critique of contemporary West African culture and consumerism in *Fragments*. Critics locate Armah's first level of critique regarding the materialist culture of contemporary Ghana, but beyond that initial critique, Armah is also exploring the gap in historical consciousness that allows for this materialism to persist.[15] Demonstrating the belated traumatic effects of the slave trade as they are made manifest in contemporary relationships, practices, and memories, Armah delves into his character's distress by tracing this contemporary materialism back to the history of the slave trade. Baako's failure to produce wealth satisfactorily is only the immediate cause of the problems he encounters at home, including the debilitating illness that eventually results in his ostracism and institutionalization. Instead, the more central and compelling source of Baako's pain is repeatedly located in his recollection of and desire to represent the traumatizing effects of the slave trade. Throughout the novel, Armah links Baako's stress and existential nausea to his psychic and physical acting out of the memories of human trafficking and the Middle Passage, making explicit links between the materialism of postcolonial Ghana and the earlier vicious and deadly consumption of human lives exemplified by Antera Duke and Grandy King George. Linking Baako's illness to the return of the repressed memory of the slave trade is integral to understanding Armah's larger critique of West African history as it informs and engenders the contemporary anxieties of Ghanaian politics and family life.

The Curse of Constant Remembrance

The first time Baako experiences the malady that forms the core concern of the novel, he is in the United States. We learn of his illness from Efua, his mother, who is awaiting his return to Ghana. She tells Juana, a woman she meets on the beach: "It has been confusing. They say there was nothing wrong with his body. The prophet says it was a sickness of the soul" (35). This introduction to the unusual nature of Baako's illness occurs, not coincidentally, as his mother stands with Juana under the looming "white form, very small at this distance, of the old slave castle which had now become the proud seat of the new rulers, the blind children of slavery themselves" (30). The two women stand beside Christiansborg Castle, built by the Danish in 1661 as an early trading post, where they exchanged European goods for slaves and gold from the interior of the Gold Coast. Ironically, the castle was made the seat of Ghana's government when independence was wrested from the British in 1957. The significance of housing the seat of the newly formed independent government in an edifice built by those who sought to exploit the African continent for their own material gain is explicit here, even as Armah dubs the government "the blind children of slavery themselves" (30) and Juana expresses her concern that the correlation between the European rulers of the castle and the newly installed Ghanaian leaders is not so obvious to those who pass by the castle as part of their daily routine.

The denial of the castle's implications is representative of the collective refusal to remember that Juana describes as the affliction of all of Africa: "The real crime now was the ignorance of past crime, and that, it seemed, would be a permanent sort of ignorance in places like this" (30). The Christiansborg Castle stands as a monument to a historical past that is marked by pain and suffering and might act as a site of memory for West Africa. Remembrance of such suffering might even preclude the possibility for repetition of similar forms of corruption and oppression in that location. Despite its potential as a memorial, the castle awakens in Juana what she calls a "curse" of "constant remembrance" (30), which is double-edged in that she regards the memory of the slave trade as critical to African consciousness but feels nonetheless a constant discomfort as a result of those memories. Despite Juana's remembrance, however, Armah indicates that the history of the trading castle has been elided through the replacement of its previous incarnations with a new Ghanaian institutional power, which seeks to ignore the traumatizing memories associated with the site, and, Armah implies, to replicate, to some extent, the crimes of the past. The monument's power over the representation of the country's past and its present erases recognition of the corruption of both.

As Juana and Efua contemplate Ghana's lapse in historical memory under the shadow of the castle, the mention of Baako's "soul sickness" takes on a new dimension as it is immediately and intimately juxtaposed with Juana's musings about the double bind of the "curse" of the memory of destruction and the destructiveness of forgetting. The reference to Baako's illness at the foot of the slave castle thus implies a possible physical relationship to the memory of the slave trade, the kind of memory that Nora describes as "the body's inherent self-knowledge, unstudied reflexes and ingrained memories."[16] Throughout the novel, Baako psychically and physically experiences the memory of the slave trade as the "curse" that Juana describes, as he exhibits a bodily rehearsal or acting out of the pain of the slave trade, which becomes more evident as the novel proceeds. This early connection between Baako's illness and the image of the slave fort marks the trade as a germ of disease in the novel, uncovering the historical context of a problem of contemporary life and creating a lens through which to read Baako's later disturbance.

When the reader finally meets Baako as he travels around Paris on his way home to Ghana, his illness again is linked to his need to remember. As he walks to the Trocadéro, watching children skate and musing over the unintelligible prayers of an old man, he reads the inscription of a poem by Valéry, which is on the top of the west wing of the Palais de Chaillot:

TOUT HOMME CRÉE SANS LE SAVOIR
COMME IL RESPIRE
MAIS L'ARTISTE SE SENT CRÉER
SON ACTE ENGAGE TOUT SON ÊTRE
SA PEINE BIEN-AIMÉE LE FORTIFIE (51)[17]

Housed inside the Palais' walls are both the French Musée National de Marine and the Musée de l'Homme. The ironic juxtaposition of a museum that celebrates the long maritime history of a country that prospered through its participation in the transatlantic slave trade and a museum that celebrates the cultures of the world including those cultures that were endangered by the trade does not seem to escape Armah here, as he integrates it into Baako's return Middle Passage from the new world back to Africa. The inscription reminds Baako that he has a mission as a writer. Indeed, this vocation to which he is called engages his entire being, as he begins to feel inexplicably ill almost immediately.

Baako physically experiences this need to create, and in a dizzying confusion, he turns to read the sign on the other wing of the Palais, but he "could not remember it afterward" (51). Though Armah intentionally does not include it in the text in order to signify Baako's repression of its message, the inscription there reads:

IL DÉPEND DE CELUI QUI PASSE
QUE JE SUIS TOMBE OU TRÉSOR
QUE JE PARLE OU JE ME TAISE
CE CI NE TIENT QU'À TOI
AMI N'ENTRE PAS SANS DÉSIR[18]

Baako represses the memory of this inscription that acts as a reminder to him of how artists are silenced. As the inscription reminds him, Baako's art depends on who is listening to him, and as his mother later chides, he seems to write only to himself. And though Armah writes that "there was nothing outside that he had seen to raise in him such a feeling" (51), it is immediately following this poetic reminder of the importance of an audience for the artist's concerns that Baako's illness, a "weak feeling," returns to him. Recognizing that the production of art is not limited strictly by its creation but also by its audience's reception leaves him paralyzed, wondering who would "desire" to hear his message.

Baako turns inward and finds that his illness is associated with a kind of vague disgust, but whether that is with himself or with the world around him or both is unclear. "Within himself what he was aware of was vague: an unpleasant but not at all sharp sensation that everything he had done in about the last half year had been intended as a postponement, a pushing away of things to which he felt necessarily called" (51). Baako's repulsion from the postponement he has been living in the United States urges him to return to Ghana as soon as possible, and he cancels the remainder of his sojourn in Paris. The inscriptions on the Trocadéro are like a command to him, which we later realize compels him to write about the episodes of Ghanaian history to which only he seems to have access or interest.

Baako realizes that, as Sartre's protagonist Roquentin (who could be Baako's psychological compatriot and was certainly an influence on Armah) puts it, "the past is a landlord's luxury. Where shall I keep mine? I have only my body: a man entirely alone, with his lonely body, cannot indulge in memories; they pass through him."[19] Like Roquentin, Baako has only his body to house his memories, and that body is constantly reflecting his experience of those memories. As memories pass through him, he can only hope that there is someone there to receive the message and to process this memory his body seems to be rejecting. Baako's nausea, then, is brought on not by his anger with consumer culture precisely, but by a feeling of artistic helplessness in the face of a history that has been silenced.

Though Baako does not consciously recognize that his illness is in any way connected with this movement toward the past, when he is on the plane, he begins to zero in on his problem. His illness returns, again triggered by his interest in history—this time specifically by histories of criminal violation. "He had had thoughts, very clear and sharp, of the enormity of things here and of the sameness of what was below, and also these strange thoughts, peopled with the living aftermath of amazing crimes still unable to discover what it was that had happened not so very long ago, totally dazed by the present's continuation" (44). Even from his place on the plane high above the city and seemingly removed from any history, Baako is disoriented by his recognition of the uniform refusal of memory on the part of the people on the ground in Ghana, which allows them to ignore those "amazing crimes" that left their mark on Africa through the centuries since European contact. It is this identification of Africa's potential for collective forgetting, linked with his vocation in Paris, that leads Baako to attempt to record those criminal histories through his own art when he returns to Ghana.

A Language No One Can Hear

On his return to his home in Ghana, Baako believes he may be able to find some constructive way to alleviate the communal forgetting regarding the violence of the past, which he, like Juana, abhors in Ghanaian culture, by conveying that past to other Ghanaians. Through this intervention, Baako seeks to diminish the dread and unease he suffers but has not as yet fully comprehended. His desire to communicate the history of the slave trade represents an attempt to assimilate the trauma of the trade, both for himself and within the narrative of the Ghanaian past. It is clear that Baako is not alone in the knowledge of the past and present corruption that he is trying to communicate. He recognizes that others in the community "could not help but see the things he'd seen and more. But they accepted it" (131). In his effort to avoid accepting the deplorable status quo as well as the knowledge of generations of suffering that resulted from it, he seeks out a form of communication that he thinks will touch the largest segment of Ghana's population.

To accomplish this, Baako (like Armah himself) optimistically explores his opportunities for expression through writing for television. Acknowledging the centrality of the transatlantic slave trade to the development of West Africa's contemporary cultures, Baako produces unorthodox and dramatic television treatments that both explicitly and metaphorically depict images of the haunting presence of the slave trade. One of his screenplays opens with the towering image of the slave castle, with its "sharp-edged pillars, shafts, all white, superimposed on recipients of violence" (146). The evocation of a violent racialized past bursts into the drama of immediate and present violence staged under the ghostly and threatening figure of the slave castle in the background:

> LS: OVERVIEW, COASTAL VILLAGE, QUIET, CIRCULAR, DARK.
> NIGHT.
> ON HILL IN DISTANCE, MASSIVE WHITE STRUCTURE OF SLAVE CASTLE.
> MS: SECTION OF CASTLE,
> GUNS POINTING OVER VILLAGE,
> PILES OF CANNON BALLS BESIDE THEM.
> SENTRY PACING.
> CUT TO VILLAGE.
> HOUSE WITH ROUND WINDOW OPENING TO A SMALL VIEW OF CASTLE.
> THREE WOMEN AND TWO MEN SITTING, STARING MUTE AT FLOOR.
> CHILD LOOKING OUT THROUGH WINDOW. (146)

Just as Juana stands in the shadows of the slave castle at the beginning of the novel, in Baako's scripts, the villagers cower below the sights of slavery's weaponry. The script, which depicts the lives of the people who work in a slave castle during the era of the trade, juxtaposes the ominous symbol of violence and the eclipsed and silenced villagers below. Mute, the villagers signify the way in which Ghanaian voices and memories have been silenced by the domination of the castle.

The form of the television drama itself allows Baako the opportunity to present episodes from the Ghanaian past dramatically, whereby the event becomes real, human, and immediate. It crosses time lines so that the historical is presented in live action, performatively exploring the relationship between the present and the slave trade era. He chooses this medium because he is particularly concerned that his messages should reach everyone in Ghana, even the people in the villages, people who might be illiterate or otherwise unable to access knowledge of Ghana's past. He contends that television is "a much clearer way of saying things to people here" (80) because it would be a "matter of images not words" (81). Baako recognizes the difficulty of communicating historical trauma: audiences eager to discuss this aspect of Ghana's history are few, and most people are openly resistant. He refuses to accept, however, the idea that this history must remain silenced or that the people of Ghana will not or cannot accept their history. Thus, as Baako intends to face the painful past directly by inserting a record of the era of the slave trade into the narrative of Ghana's history, he responds to both the repression of the memory of the trade in Ghanaian culture and to the anguish he has felt as he is compelled to remember it himself.

Baako utilizes the visual juxtaposition that television provides him to metaphorically illustrate the existence of the slave trade past within the present landscape, articulating in this way his critique of contemporary consumer society. He recognizes that the slave trade sowed the seeds of materialism, introducing a wealth of foreign goods that were bought at the hideously high price of human life—an exchange that he continues to witness in his community, as the worth of individuals in the postindependence era is regularly determined by the value of foreign goods they are able to supply. Baako's compulsion to write about historical encounters with the West, including the era of the slave trade, seems to his colleagues and family to be disconnected from the concerns of contemporary society.

Armah himself once claimed that "Creative Writing engages the reader in a constant interactive process between the past, the present, and the future, calculated to make educated persons not passive endurers of present conditions, but active protagonists aware of past causes, and willing to use their awareness to help shape future results."[20] As Armah points out here, the role of the artist is that of an educator who "opens our vision" to those aspects of the past that might have been forgotten or overlooked, events that continue to have an effect on present-day life whether people are aware of them or not. Clearly, Baako is precisely one of those creative writers who take it as their responsibility to interact with the past in their work. He is particularly invested in revealing those parts of the Ghanaian past that most people dare not mention, as they are either too painful to remember or too traumatic to recount. In order to do this most effectively, Baako attempts to find an alternative method of communication that is more likely to be transmitted, and, even more important, more likely to be received.

Baako's increased attention to the medium of television and his search for an alternative language in which to communicate with Ghana's citizens reveals implicitly that without a receptive audience, all communication is essentially impossible. Baako's teacher recognizes that he has something of the "missionary" in him, and Baako confirms this label, suggesting that he thought of writing as a "way of making my life mean something to me" (80). He wants to avoid the possibility of writing only to himself, which he says he does not think is possible, and he even suggests that he "wouldn't want to" because it would not satisfy his desire to make meaning out of his training as a writer. The decision to write for television changes all of that. If his family's myopic desires were disappointing, he still "saw more possibilities of hope in the larger society" (102).

So long as he has hope that his television screenplays will communicate to a larger Ghanaian audience, Baako's nausea seems to be something of a remission, and he becomes more confident and sure of the importance of his work. Briefly relieved of his illness, he feels none of the pains of memory because he is producing work that will give voice to the history that he believes is plaguing Africa in its very silence. When asked what his work is about, he answers flatly, "Slavery," and his boss interrogates him:

> "Why such a choice of topic?"
> "How do you mean, why?"
> "You understand me, Mr. Onipa," said Asante-Smith, with a small yawn. "Look, we're a free, independent people. We're engaged in a gigantic task of nation building. We have inherited a glorious culture, and that's what we're here to deal with." (146–47)

Baako's superiors actively refuse to disseminate the narrative of the past that Baako considers so essential to the vitality of the nation. They seek to replace that past instead with an essentialized, sanitized, positive narrative of the African past.

Regardless of their insistence, it becomes increasingly necessary for Baako, as he feels it is for the nation, to confront the gruesome history of the slave trade. However, at every turn, he is silenced or reprimanded for his desire to expose his "free, independent people" to a narrative of their country's history that includes the most disturbing aspects of the slave trade. Baako's boss goes so far as to refute any impact the slave trade might have had on Ghana's culture, asserting, "What you've just said has nothing to do with our people's culture—all this slavery, survival, the brand" (147). It is in these responses to Baako's work regarding the slave trade that we see the critical erasure of memory that Armah believes haunts life in contemporary Ghanaian society. In fact, however, through Baako's work as well as his illness, Armah indicates the way surviving the transatlantic slave trade has altered African lives and perceptions, despite all pressure to ignore and erase its impact.

Jonathan A. Peters argues that the rejection of Baako's work results from the fact that his writing requires "attention and reflection."[21] This is absolutely the case, but Baako's colleagues are not merely lazy or unthoughtful: They have a particular aversion to the *content* of Baako's scripts. They actively refuse to disseminate the information Baako considers so essential to the narrative of the nation. Moreover, they are unable or unwilling to hear it themselves. He critiques society's refusal to understand the past at the same time as he insists through his writing that the past persists in his memory and has had a significant effect on his life. When Baako finds that no one is interested in the work he is trying to produce, his illness returns and he becomes physically and psychically overwhelmed by the past. Without a receptive audience for this exploration of the past, activation and assimilation of the traumatic memory is undermined, repressed so that the past can continue to exert its deleterious power upon the present. It is as if, even in his attempts to find an alternative language for his communication, Baako is speaking a language—the language of a traumatic and violent past—that no one is willing to hear or understand.

Purging Slave Trade Memory

Recognizing the futility of his attempts to communicate a history that he feels is traumatic both at the level of his own personal life and at that of his nation, Baako quits his job, burns his manuscripts with the titles "Slavery," "The Brand," and "Survival," and immediately falls seriously ill: "open or closed his eyes hurt, his head, his whole body hurt, his eyes were not steady. . . . He wanted sleep for a body bruised all over from the fever within, . . . three days already in bed, too ill and too weak to get up when he wanted to. He turned on his belly to lessen the discomfort. That hurt too, and the sheet under him felt wet and clammy from his sweat" (155). Physically exhausted from the effort to communicate, and purging from every orifice, Baako's body is made the site of a metaphorical illness—his disease is a representation of his being silenced and Ghana's history being erased. He admits that a "whirling torture" had "filled his mind" (131) and that he "found no way to get away from the mixed uncertainty" (155) he was experiencing.

Critics repeatedly attribute Baako's illness to his feeling of impotence in his inability to provide materially for his family and his repulsion against the corrupt, money-obsessed elite classes. His concerns are certainly piqued by the corruption he encounters in his family and among the people with whom he works. Indeed, Baako seems to contract a unique form of homesickness in which he is actually made sick by the interactions he experiences on his return home. However, he is not nostalgic for some bygone era of preconsumeristic Ghanaian society. He has no delusion that it has ever existed. Instead, at the heart of his homesickness is his comprehension of how that materialistic mentality is linked to the tragic past of the slave trade, and the forced recognition of his inability to represent that part of Ghana's history in a meaningful, communicative way.

By the time Baako quits his job at Ghanavision, he has nearly been convinced of the futility of his efforts to participate in conversations regarding Ghana's history, but his mind obsessively returns to the manuscripts he wrote and the way they were overlooked or sanitized for popular viewing. Again, he attempts to produce creative work regarding the slave trade, and he begins to vomit profusely, dredging up, through this excrement, the history his community is attempting to repress. Just after being interrogated by his mother regarding his writings and writhings, Baako's illness resurfaces:

> His mouth filled up as if his saliva were flowing to escape some pressure from below, and it would never stop. His eyes felt out of the sockets, floating detached in a steady blast of warm air getting hotter every moment. There was one sharp needlepoint of pain boring into his skull from the top of his head, and the cold line along his neck was spreading. There was no more room in his mouth, and the moisture was in his throat, threatening to choke him. He ran, forgetting every pain and weakness, straight to the bathroom . . . before the huge vomiting fever came draining out of him, tearing itself out of a body too weak to help or resist it, dropping in waves that left him shivering, tasting all through his head the thick bitterness of his own closed-up bile. (159)

Baako's purgation of his "closed-up bile" is an alternative means of releasing the repressed history he is attempting to impart to his community, and it (not coincidentally) resembles the vile sickness that enslaved people experienced on the Middle Passage.

As Baako's literary representations of Ghanaian historical trauma have failed to reach an audience, Armah finds another location through which to express this painful memory. If Baako cannot effectively communicate a past that seems to defy *reception* (if not representation), then his body comes to affect a space through which that information can take shape in a sort of *body language*. This body language cannot be refused or ignored by his family and friends. His physical illness reveals itself in a way that is evident to all those who encounter him and communicates that which his scripts could not: it expresses the radical alteration of the African body and psyche by the encounter with the slave trade.

Baako's body itself has become a site of memory; his malady is a metaphor of the slave trade and the realm of the abject that it has been relegated to in Ghanaian culture. If trauma is the belated experience of an event so violent that it cannot be processed, then Baako's body conveys a doubled enactment of the trauma associated with the unassimilated violence of the distant slave trade past—his body articulates belatedly both the physical violence of the Middle Passage and the narrative violence committed in the drive to shed the memory of the slave trade. Just as Geneviève Fabre describes the embodiment of the memory of slavery that exists in contemporary African American dance—"the body, that was so central to the lived and felt Middle Passage experience, is entrusted with the task of representation and figuration"[22]—so

Baako's body becomes a vessel of memory, and he purges that memory in order to survive the pains it induces in him. If that purging cannot come through the communicative act, it afflicts his very body.

The history of the slave trade has returned to Baako in the form of the abject, as Julia Kristeva describes it: "There looms within abjection, one of those violent dark revolts of being, directed against a threat that seems to emanate from an exorbitant outside or inside, ejected beyond the scope of the possible, the tolerable, the thinkable. It lies there quite close, but it cannot be assimilated."[23] Baako is faced with the challenge of the memory of the slave trade; that it is, at once, both unthinkable and yet always in thought, as the repeated image of the slave castle reminds us. Though he attempts to create representations of this history, his body reacts intuitively against the memory of men in chains and the commodification of human life. He is unable to make complete sense of this era of Ghana's past in his writing, and is drawn "toward the place where meaning collapses."[24] There he is face-to-face with the abject, with that which is "discharged like thunder,"[25] "disturbs identity, system, order,"[26] and which is "constantly remembered,"[27] like Juana's curse of constant remembrance. Engaging the slave trade is to look upon the utmost of grotesque horrors. The slave trade turned a global enterprise into death for millions; it reversed generations of legitimate trade relationships into centuries of deplorable human exchanges; it transformed an internationally developed system of capital and credit into an impetus for warfare and terror. Thus, the slave trade is the worst kind of abjection: "immoral, sinister, and shady: a terror that dissembles, a hatred that smiles, a passion that uses the body for barter instead of inflaming it, a debtor who sets you up, a friend who stabs you . . ."[28] The abject events of Ghana's terrorizing past haunt Baako, and it is only through writing that he seems to be able to assimilate these most offensive of memories that have come to him across generations.

The Human Cost of Cargo

As he suffers his memories alone in bed, Baako once more feels a compulsion to write, and his writing takes the form of a fractured play, which again delves into the enduring effects of the slave trade on Ghanaian culture. Aware that the slave trade's commodification of human life and his family's vision of him as the deliverer of consumable "cargo" are intimately connected through a layered temporality, he writes a short diaristic treatise on the relationship between the so-called cargo cults of Melanesia and his own post–slave trade culture. The cargo cults are a ritualistic religious expression of the fetishization of material goods introduced to Melanesia by Europeans. Purportedly, when the Melanesians first saw the wealth that colonists (and later, soldiers) brought with them, they believed that Europeans had some spiritual connection that entitled them to the extravagant goods. Melanesians began to build ports, in the hopes that ships would come to the shore to bring them riches. Generations later, Melanesian millenarian groups await a savior who will bring them goods that will usher them into modernity and into a status superior to that of those Europeans who oppressed them.[29] Baako fears that he is supposed to be the savior who returns home with the Western goods so long denied the African people. As he had complained earlier to Juana (who, over the course of the novel, becomes his girlfriend), "there is the family, and the hero comes and turns its poverty into sudden wealth. And the external enemy isn't the one at whose expense the hero gets his victory; he's supposed to get rich, mainly at the expense of the community" (103).

Baako then expands his claim beyond the immediacy of the contemporary postcolonial Ghanaian culture by evoking, through a parallel with the Melanesians, the historical era of the slave trade in Ghana, and the way in which, in Ghanaian history, it was *people* who were exchanged for that cargo. He asks himself how close Ghanaian culture might be to the Melanesian cargo worship, and he responds with images of an African exchange with a distant continent that occurred hundreds of years previous: "Two distinct worlds, one here, one out there, one known, the other unknown except in legend and dream. But the twilight area between the two is also an area of knowledge, twisted knowledge perhaps, but knowledge resulting from real information in the form of incoming goods, *outgoing people. The main export to the other world is people*" (156–57, my emphasis). The trade Baako evokes in this passage is not the Melanesian one, but once again that of the slave trade in West Africa. The commodities being traded are human lives, and as he extends the historical effects of that exchange to the present, Baako correlates the desires and messianic expectations of contemporary society with the historical ships that carried material goods to the shore in exchange for human cargo during the era of the slave trade. And again, in the contemporary period, outgoing "been-tos" like Baako are exchanged for incoming goods.

This commitment to material wealth in contemporary Ghanaian culture is figured as a human sacrifice, which becomes quite literal when his infant nephew dies later in the novel as a result of his family's extraordinary greed. It is no mistake that Baako's family is often represented as exhibiting a "slavish consumption of things"[30] and as being "slavishly worshipful in their attitudes toward white values,"[31] as their contemporary consumer desires are inextricably bound to the history of African participation in the transatlantic slave trade. The novel asks, as Wole Soyinka is still asking more than forty years later, how the culpability of the African participants in the slave trade continues to infect the politics and economies of West Africa. Soyinka writes,

> Since then, for reasons which must be clear to all observers of Africa's ongoing travails, that dark reality of the African past has become a political reference point, a quasi metaphor, in addressing the many ills of the continent—from the most benign forms of leadership alienation to crude despotism, genocide, internal colonialism and, indeed, even racism within the acknowledged homeland of the black race. The enthronement of governance by disdain, of unapologetic conduct and policies of condescension, threadbare tolerance and worse by leaders toward our own peoples, inevitably results in questions such as: What is the difference between then and now? Between them and us?[32]

Baako's metaphor of the cargo cults reinforces his insight that this materialism is no modern, postindependence malady. In fact, the disturbing Ghanaian consumer mentality is the result of hundreds of years of cargo exchanges, which worked to lower the value of human life while increasing the value of "wealth-in-things." Though their ancestors survived the transatlantic slave trade safe on Africa's shores, some of them were no doubt responsible for those horrific exchanges of human life. Postindependence Ghanaians are, in Armah's estimation, still haunted by a fate of enslavement and enslaver even two hundred years later, as they reenact the tragic sacrifices of human life that were characteristic of the slave trade.

Incorporating Abjection

By articulating the unfortunate legacy of the slave trade either through writing or through his body, Baako incorporates the abjection of the slave trade and thereby assimilates it into his understanding of himself and his culture. His purging of history into some legible, communicative format is a viable alternative to the physical incorporation of the abject, which caused Baako to physically purge himself of the memory. Thus Baako realizes he is able to relieve some of his pain through writing about Ghana's past, as his "urge to trap it [in writing] before it disappeared made him forget the general pain of his body" (156). As a result of this reprieve from his illness, his life becomes one of complete reflection, a kind of reflection that his mother, who wishes to help him, can neither penetrate nor understand. Robert Fraser appropriately identifies Baako's problem as one of "self-communion," which his family can understand only as a dementia resulting from "committing thoughts to paper apparently for no eyes but his own."[33] The silence that this entails, and the lack of a correspondent audience for his writing, is construed by his family as a kind of lunacy that must be treated. Baako's illness is associated with the thwarted act of communication and the closed system in which he is attempting to effect that communication.

Communication is at its most basic both the production of a message and the process of its reception. Discussions of pain such as that by Elaine Scarry indicate that certain experiences resist our ability to process them through language.[34] In representing the history of slavery, there is a sense in which the trauma of the past, too, exceeds the bounds of human language and, as a result, that trauma is nearly impossible to communicate. William Wells Brown, an American slave narrator, expressed his inability to describe his experiences of enslavement by claiming that there was either no way to explain the pain or, if there were, that it would be inappropriate to express it to an audience.[35] Likewise, many West African authors have avoided the direct historical treatment of the slave trade in their works. This seeming "amnesia" might similarly indicate some impediment to naming the trauma and to iterating the resulting pain, or, alternatively, it might result from the possible impropriety of such a representation for any number of reasons, such as the political implications of speaking of such a topic, the lingering discomfort with the experience of enslavement, or the immediate necessity of writing about more recent traumas on the continent including colonialism or contemporary forms of oppression and corruption.

However, as Tim Woods astutely defines it, "trauma can be experienced in at least two ways: first, as an experience that cannot be integrated into one's own experience; and, second, as a catastrophic knowledge that cannot be communicated to others."[36] Baako does not appear to encounter any obstacle to *integrating* the horrors of colonialism into his own narrative, nor does he seem to struggle with *articulating* the trauma that seems to possess him; in fact, he explicitly depicts the slave trade and its effects in his writing. Perhaps, then, it is more useful to consider the second part of the transaction of communication: reception. Without a receptive audience, any speech act is rendered meaningless. When an author manages to find the language through which to situate his pain or the pain of generations, the communicative project is still not completed. In order for a speaker or writer to have communicated, *an audience* must be receptive to his or her language.

Though the history Baako invokes in his writing is hundreds of years past, he elicits in his audience the same reaction as contemporary survivors of trauma evoke from their listeners: "Insofar as they remind us of a horrible traumatic past, insofar as they bear witness to our own historical disfiguration, survivors frighten us. They pose for us a riddle and a threat from which we cannot turn away. We are indeed profoundly terrified to truly face the traumas of our history."[37] As Felman and Laub describe, audiences to the narrative of survivors are limited—few people want to confront their greatest terror. Similarly, Baako's friends and family are repulsed by the narrative he is trying to communicate. Indeed, for those who are aware of his contemplations, he appears to be exhibiting signs of madness. As far as the community is concerned, Baako, in his literary and physical incorporation and representation of Ghana's abject past, *becomes the abject himself.*

The community's refusal to comprehend the narrative Baako is attempting to construct thus leads to tragic results. Just as Baako recovers from his illness and his revelation regarding the cargo mentality of Ghanaian society, he encounters his uncle and other family members, who corral him and take him to the insane asylum without explanation. The members of the posse shout:

> "Stay far from him. His bite will make you also maaaaad!"
> To this another, closer voice added in sage, quiet tones, "The same thing happens if he should scratch you." (170)

Baako's family violently expels him from their midst in sheer terror, treating him like an innocent but rabid dog Baako saw brutally murdered in the street at the beginning of the novel. His sister resigns herself to the notion that she must treat Baako as if he were inhuman as she enlists countless, nameless members of the community to participate in the effort to subdue Baako, whom they see as a force of terror in their midst: "Now the others were quick with the speed of fearful men about to be released from their fear" (170). His family and neighbors seek to distance themselves from his alleged madness, exonerating themselves from its claim upon them, terrified by what they consider to be its literal power of infection.

Instead of attempting to hear Baako's message, the community makes Baako himself into the form of the abject, that part of the community its members wish to expel because it so reminds them of their most disturbing memories. When a bystander asks what happened to Baako that he needs to be put down in this way, someone suggests that it might be a curse of an enemy, and the response is:

> "It was himself, they say."
> "Books."
> "Ah, yes. Books."
> "Books." (172)

The community's unwillingness to reconcile themselves with the past and to accept the narrative that Baako is attempting to write leads them to exile Baako to the depths of an insane asylum rather than come to terms with their own symptoms of that tainted past. It is almost as if *there is no audience* for Baako's work and words, though it is clear he is attempting to make his work as accessible as possible. His role as a communicator is radically and universally refused. Again, his language, though accessible, is not accessed. The past, though narrativized, is not heard.

Pathologizing Memory

The question of Baako's "madness" guides the action throughout the rest of the novel, and critics have attempted to understand it since the novel's first publication. Ayo Mamadu claims that "Baako . . . broods his way literally into the asylum,"[38] and William Lawson attributes his insanity to intense alienation.[39] D. S. Izevbaye claims that "there are hints within the novel that Baako had neurotic tendencies before his return to Ghana," which lead to "full madness" by the end of the narrative.[40] In Derek Wright's configuration, the "neurotic" Baako is "hounded by his family into the mental exile of madness,"[41] which exhibits itself, "finally, as clinical insanity."[42] Baako is by turns diagnosed as schizophrenic,[43] regarded as having an "emotional disorder,"[44] and compared to Hamlet in his madness.[45] If this rehearsal of the critical discourse surrounding Baako's illness is overwhelming, it is strictly because the consensus regarding Baako's condition is nearly unanimous.

Armah's critics unintentionally align themselves with the position of Baako's family in the text, equally unresponsive to the way Baako's problems are related to history (and in particular to the history of the slave trade). They are all too willing to believe his family's unprofessional diagnosis of Baako as mentally ill. Despite the fact that Juana—the only professional psychiatrist in the text able to diagnose Baako's dis-ease—is not convinced that Baako is mad, critics are generally willing to accept his family's verdict in their own critical reception of the novel. Throughout the text, Armah reveals that the madness, instead, is in the culture that has developed in Ghana, which makes it possible for rich administrators to fight one another to steal televisions from the poor, for families to allow their children to die for an opportunity to increase their wealth, and for a community to beat a man to the ground because he quietly writes alone in his room. Armah potentially commits a greater injustice here by essentially pathologizing Ghanaian contemporary culture, a Eurocentric position that many scholars have criticized. Nonetheless, as Kofi Owusu puts it: "Society's unreasoning 'reason' condemns Baako's reasoned 'unreason' as 'madness.'"[46] In Armah's reformulation of reason and abjection here, the community's rabidly violent treatment of the harmless Baako reverses the critical diagnosis, allowing us to recognize the reason in Baako's illness and the lack of reason in a society that would censure him.

Despite Armah's explicit contempt for the society that condemns Baako to the insane asylum, Baako, in his role as the abject in his community, is read as "hysterical" when his body manifests the anxieties about which his society dares not speak. It is indeed true that each time Baako's desire to express the repressed history of the trade is silenced, his body manifests that abject history. However, Armah's negative depiction of Ghanaian society reveals that Baako's condition should be read as pathological only insofar as this diagnosis is understood as a construct of those who wish to excise that which stands outside their own system of order and control. The label of hysteria or madness is a means to exorcise those who speak "in the mode of a paralyzed gestural faculty, of an impossible and almost forbidden speech . . . and the drama of hysteria is that it is inserted schizotically between that gestural system, that desire paralyzed and enclosed within its body, and a language that it has learned in the family, in school, in society, which is in no way continuous with . . . the 'movements of its desire.'"[47] Baako is forced to write to himself, which he explicitly tried to avoid. He appears to be "having a conversation with no one, talking alone to [himself]" (158), as his mother puts it, because for those on the outside, his language and ideas are repulsive and disorderly: they appear "somewhat mad from the standpoint of reason,"[48] and they are, indeed, nearly inaudible to those to whom he is speaking. His pain, fostered by his inability to communicate, is manifested bodily, and read by others as a sign of their propriety in diagnosing him as hysterical, insane, mad. However, Baako's writings are representative of the way the slave trade continues to resonate in the minds of contemporary African people in much the same way that Maria Diedrich, Henry Louis Gates Jr., and Carl Pedersen describe the memory of the Middle Passage, in that it "emerges not as a clear break with the past and present but as a spatial continuum . . . Submerged beneath the surface of the dominant language, it constantly seeps through and inevitably affects it."[49]

If Baako appears to be mad, it is only in the *reception* of his message, or in the mis-reception of his communication, that we can come to understand the madness inherent in the exchange. Baako's problem is not an inability to find a language for that painful past he wants to communicate and assimilate, but the inability to find an audience that is receptive to his message. The madness does not lie so much in Baako's language or the lack thereof, but in the conditions of society that make his message and his radical revision of history unacceptable and unheard. Armah's critique, then, is not of consumer culture itself, nor is it of the difficulty of articulating the history of a disconcerting past, but it is of the unwillingness of the community to receive the transmission of information regarding the slave trade and its effects on contemporary life and culture.

Yet Something Hidden

Baako, though confined within his own society, represents for Armah a possibility for African people to refuse the materialism that has been inscribed on them by the lingering effects of the slave trade. By making contact with the past, Baako works to transform the curse of constant remembrance into a narrative that can accommodate and incorporate the effects of the traumatic era of the slave trade and thus potentially overcomes the experience of memory as a curse. Reiterating his investment in the memory of the slave trade, Armah ends the book with Naana, Baako's blind, elderly, traditional grandmother, who contemplates her life, Ghana's past, and Baako's future. In that reflection, she asserts that it was the slave trade that brought materialistic and destructive conditions to West Africa. She refers to the child of Baako's sister, who died at his own birthing ceremony because the family was more interested in collecting monetary gifts from their guests than tending to the child. Naana links this contemptible behavior to the sacrifice of human lives exacted by the slave trade. She claims that "the baby was a sacrifice they killed, to satisfy perhaps a new god they have found much like the one that began the same long destruction of our people" (199). She continues, refusing to forgive those in her community, past and present, who "split their own seed and raised half against half, part selling part to hard-eyed buyers from beyond the horizon, breaking, buying, selling, gaining, spending, till the last of our men sells the last woman to any passing white buyer and himself waits to be destroyed by this great haste to consume things we have taken no care nor trouble to produce" (199). Again past and present are conflated here, as Naana critiques the way the slave trade has created a contemporary obsession with materialism.

Baako's mother and sister and all those who participate in this murderous consumerism are not a new invention of postindependence modernity. They are the ideological descendants of slave raiders and elite slave traders who valued their own wealth over the lives of their fellow human beings. Naana is the only one able, then, to see what Baako has seen. And she is the only one who has hope for Baako—that he can continue to fight this corruption born of the slave trade. She admits that "in all that noise I thought he would surely die," but she leaves us with a more hopeful (if uncertain) outlook for Baako's ability to finally communicate successfully: "Happy event if in his future there is yet something hidden that will reveal itself with time" (199). There is a last hope that Baako will rise above the pathologization that haunts him to find an audience who will allow him to reveal a silenced, traumatic past.

The practice of sacrificing human lives for the sake of material gain is a legacy of the devastating devaluation of human life that was integral to the workings of the slave trade. Engaging these historical legacies allows us to examine contemporary politics, community, and memory. Indeed, as Paul Gilroy reminds us, "the history of the black Atlantic since [1492] continually crisscrossed by the movements of black people—not only as commodities, but engaged in various struggles towards emancipation, autonomy, and citizenship—provides a means to reexamine the problems of nationality, locality, identity, and historical memory."[50] This critical ability is often devastating for Baako, but the novel's exploration of Baako's Atlantic return draws on his experience of the crossing to evoke a historical memory and to resist the silencing of it.

Cathy Caruth claims that trauma is experienced "solely in the *structure of its experience* or reception: the event is not assimilated or experienced fully at the time, but only belatedly in its repeated *possession* of the one who experiences it. To be traumatized is precisely to be possessed by an image or event."[51] If this is how we define trauma, then Baako has indeed experienced a form of trauma. Despite the fact that Baako experiences trauma nearly two hundred years after the transatlantic slave trade was legally abolished, the apparently unassimilated past returns to possess him, both psychically and physically. His active attempts to work through these memories are thwarted by his family and community, who pathologize his process of narrativizing and assimilating the trauma of Ghana's past. It is his community's refusal of knowledge, as he puts it, "in the form of incoming goods, outgoing people" (157), that makes him appear to be not simply someone who is struggling with the past, but someone who needs to be expelled because of his relationship to the past. For Armah, it is precisely the diagnosis of this return as pathological that marks a debilitating disengagement with the past that corrupts Ghanaian culture in the postindependence era. Through this indictment of Ghana's blind embrace of the materialistic legacy of the slave trade, Armah indicates that the "curse of constant remembrance" that Baako experiences is also liberatory in that it can release him from the contemporary enslavement of materialism, greed, and corruption. Thus, the physical and psychological upheaval that Baako experiences, in and of itself, is not at all pathological but merely a part of the process of an active and positive engagement with and incorporation of the traumatic past.

By depicting the long-term effects of trauma, Armah alters the discourse of psychoanalysis to include not only the African historical context, but also the "memory traces of the experiences of former generations" to which Freud referred in his later work.[52] In his transgenerational extension of the process of trauma, Armah still holds out hope for the transformative effects of working through trauma. In his ambiguous and uncertain ending, he forces us to consider whether it is possible that exploring the distant traumatic past could lead, not to the pathologization of memory, but to a change on the continent, to a successful communicative act that might be received by society and digested without the need to continually purge it. We are left to wonder whether the abject slave trade can be processed in narrative form such that it might produce a shift in African culture away from the devaluation of human life, which Armah claims is endemic. Kristeva astutely asks us a similar (though possibly rhetorical) question: "Does one write under any other condition than being possessed by abjection, in an indefinite catharsis?"[53] Indeed, Baako's possession by the abject of the slave trade works as a sort of catharsis for him, which he hopes will be equally cathartic for his community. Just as each moment of remembrance of the slave trade for Baako is a moment of purging, it works for the audience as an opportunity for catharsis and healing—but only if we are willing to listen.

CHAPTER FIVE

Childless Mothers and Dead Husbands

The Enslavement of Intimacy and Ama Ata Aidoo's Secret Language of Memory

> From the fragments of the myth of male dominion, we seek to structure a new way of saying things, one apposite and graceful to the new situation. The urgency is to acquire a language which expresses the woman's grasp of reality as present and immediate; even in love, such urgency must not be suspended.
>
> —Hortense Spillers

Though the transatlantic slave trade was outlawed in Denmark in 1802, in England in 1807, in the United States in 1808, in Sweden and Norway in 1813, in the Netherlands in 1814, and in France both in 1794 and again in 1817 (after Napoleon reinstated the trade in 1802), the illicit trade in human lives was still a lucrative enterprise on the west coast of Africa by the 1830s and '40s. Historians of West Africa disagree on the degree of impact that abolition had on the sale of slaves, both domestic and transatlantic, but all agree that the legal abolition of the slave trade did not coincide with an end to trading in practice. The competition for increasingly scarce clients and resources that resulted from abolitionist policies helped to inflame a new phase of regional conflicts, which ironically seemed to escalate slave capture and trade along the coast. The effects of the trade rippled through the coastal communities of West Africa—and even much farther into the interior—decades after it was officially outlawed. Domestic servitude increased, but illicit transatlantic trade remained a viable enough business to continue to influence significantly the politics of the region.

In the first quarter of the nineteenth century, in what was then called the Gold Coast, the Asante and Fante were in a nearly constant struggle for dominance, as the Asante of the interior vied for a position on the coast from which they could manage their own Atlantic trade, while the coastal Fante fought to maintain their commercial and political bonds with the British as traders of goods and people at coastal forts such as Cape Coast. Though by the 1820s the slave trade had been in steep decline along the Gold Coast for decades, European sources show that the slave trade was increasing in 1827.[1] Paul E. Lovejoy and David Richardson have argued that though Gold Coast suppliers seem to have been hit harder by the abolition of the trade than the dealers located at some of their rival export centers, slave prices along the Gold Coast actually rose after 1820 as a result of both continued (though decreased) demand for exports and a possible increase in domestic demand after abolition,[2] thus continuing to make slave trading a sustainable business. In the interior, though the end of the legalized transatlantic slave trade certainly impacted the Asante, there were numerous expansions and infrastructure projects under way that indicated the economy had by no means collapsed as a result of the abolition.[3]

Alternating periods of war and peace were characteristic of Asante-British relations in the 1820s, as large factions of the Asante vehemently opposed the expansion of British control to the south and sought their own expansion in the region, while other factions sought to negotiate peacefully.[4] Though the Asante claimed never to go to war solely for the purpose of obtaining slaves, warfare continued, and as a result, war captives continued to be produced.[5] Thus, while the Asante struggled to sell these captives along the coast, the numbers of domestic slaves increased dramatically, lowering their value such that exchanges and tribute previously paid in slaves were expected in ivory and gold.[6] This shift in commodity payments most likely prevented the Fante from paying tribute in the Asante region, which was just as well for many anti-Asante Fante communities, and as Mary McCarthy claims, it might have even encouraged Fante resistance against Asante power on the coast.[7] Thus, it is clear that decisions regarding the transatlantic slave trade not only continued to have a ripple effect in Gold Coast politics and conflict, but perhaps highlighted the tensions in the region as well as allowed for the continued production of enslaved captives and domestic slaves. Though the West African transatlantic slave trade had largely shifted eastward, slaves were reportedly being sold along the Gold Coast and were certainly in large supply throughout the region.

Nearby in Yoruba country in what is now called Nigeria, warfare was becoming a way of life. During the early 1820s, Dahomey and Oyo engaged in a war, which, though it slowed Oyo's trade in slaves with the port at Ouidah, had the effect of allowing King Ghezo of Dahomey to decimate or annex whole villages, feeding war captives into his already thriving slave market in coastal Ouidah.[8] When the Oyo Empire, renowned as it was for its power as an exporter of slaves, fell, new centers of Yoruba power emerged and vied for control of the slave trade in the region.[9] The civil wars that erupted as a result pitted neighboring communities against one another. Vulnerable small villages caught in the midst of these struggles were often sacked and their people sold into slavery in order to supply arms and other goods to the warring parties. The resultant instability allowed Islamic jihadists from the north to conquer parts of northern Yorubaland. Simultaneously, the trade of slaves in Lagos increased significantly, overtaking Ouidah in predominance, and demanded a regular supply of captive coffles from those wars. Because of the rampant warfare, the transatlantic trade actually flourished. Yoruba country was being squeezed from practically all directions, at least in part because of the inhuman pursuit of human capital.

It was in 1821, during this period in which West Africa was being ravaged by warfare, that the Yoruba village of Osogun was unexpectedly attacked by Fulani raiders from the north. Unprepared for the onslaught, women and children fled into the bush while the few men who were not in the fields attempted to protect the village and their families with whatever weapons they could lay their hands on. Those who attempted to escape were swiftly followed by Fulani horsemen, who threw lassos over their heads and herded them as if they were animals. In this crowd of human captives was a young boy named Ajayi, who has come to be known as Samuel Ajayi Crowther, the first African Anglican bishop and a prolific linguist. He remembered the day he was captured in this way: "sometime about the commencement of the year 1821, I was in my native country, enjoying the comfort of father and mother, and the affectionate love of brothers and sisters. From this period I must date the unhappy, but which I am ever taught in other respects to call blessed day, which I shall never forget in my life. I call it unhappy day, because it was the day in which I was violently turned out of my father's house, and separated from my relatives, and in which I was made to experience what is called to be in slavery."[10] A conflicted Crowther considered his abduction from Africa an ordeal as well as a deliverance, because in his mind, it was the work of God that allowed him this painful but unique opportunity to experience salvation through this unhappy separation from his family.[11] However, his enslavement is nonetheless a torment, as he remembers that it was this day that kept him from knowing the comforts and affection of his family for twenty-five years before he managed to become reacquainted with them by chance.

This familial separation was not uncommon in the slave trade, and in fact it was often a calculated decision on the part of the European slave traders on the coast, who, in their attempts to make their business most efficient, frequently chose to sever any bonds between parents and their children in order to increase the likelihood of selling each one to the highest bidder. In his anthropological research about Africans enslaved in the Caribbean, Christian G. A. Oldendorp found that "it is a normal occurrence in this trade that husbands are separated from wives, and parents from their children. No captain likes to buy a mother with a small child, for the simple reason that she is thus bound to take up more room on his ship than if she were alone."[12] Thus the economy of the slave trade was calculated in such a way that family bonds and human relationships could be considered a risk that was to be avoided at all costs. As a result, twelve-year-old Ajayi was separated from his family, put on a Portuguese slave ship, and taken from the coast without knowledge of what would happen to him next.

What did happen over the rest of his life has earned him the honor of being one of the most famous men in nineteenth-century African history. Young Ajayi was briefly held as a captive on a slave ship before he was rescued by a British naval patrol and resettled in Sierra Leone. Over the next twenty-five years, Ajayi, renamed Samuel Crowther, briefly went to school in England, earned a degree from and taught at the newly established Fourah Bay College in Freetown, Sierra Leone, and was ordained a minister in the Anglican Church. He returned to the Niger region to become a missionary and to establish regional Anglican churches. He spent much time in Abeokuta, where he established the mission that would later be the pulpit from which the Reverend Ransome Kuti would preach and the church that Wole Soyinka and his family would attend in his youth. As it turned out, Crowther's new hometown of Abeokuta was not far from Osogun, his natal village.

After living in Abeokuta for some time without any news of his family, Crowther was finally reunited with his mother in 1846, and recorded the following entry in his journal for that day:

> August 21. The text for this day in the Christian Almanac is "Thou art the helper of the fatherless." Is. 10:14. I have never felt the force of this text more than I did this day, as I have to relate this pleasing fact, that my mother from whom I was torn away about five and twenty years ago, came with my brother in quest of me this day. When my mother saw me she trembled, she could not believe her own eyes. We grasped one another, looking at each other with silence and great astonishment, but big tears rolled down her emaciated cheeks. [. . .] We could not say much, but sat still, and cast now and then an affectionate look at one another, a look which violence and oppression have long checked, and affection which has nearly been extinguished by the long space of five and twenty years.[13]

The experience of grief that must have consumed families during the period of the slave trade is rarely remarked upon in the African record. There are few moments when an African writer encountered the opportunity to divulge the intense emotions that accompanied the great loss that so many people along the coast must have experienced at one time or another during the era of the slave trade. This moment of reunion in Crowther's journal reveals that throughout his entire life he had defined himself as "fatherless" because of his estrangement from his family at such a young age. Moreover, it suggests the emotional devastation that separation caused those mothers whose families were disrupted by slave raiders. "Thus," Crowther mourns, "my poor mother has been suffering since I left the country. This is only one instance out of many of persons who have been robbed and oppressed by the cruel hand of the slave trader."[14] Crowther indicates not only the unbearable pain of mourning that his own mother experienced, but also the endemic suffering that must have pervaded the region as a result of the loss of so many human lives to slavery.

However, though his family had reportedly searched for him for two or three years, they were compelled to give up their search as a failure.[15] And as Crowther remarks, when he met his mother again, he cast her an affectionate glance, which he describes as "a look which violence and oppression have long checked, and affection which has nearly been extinguished by the long space of five and twenty years." As this grown man finds himself reunited with his estranged mother, he experiences not only the relief and joy that he had long decided would not be his privilege in his lifetime; he also feels a hesitation, a remnant of that earlier recognition that he would no longer be able to experience familial love. In this moment, which might otherwise have been entirely joyous, Crowther is reminded of violence and oppression in the recognition of his unfamiliarity with maternal affection. He is forced to recall the fact that his union with his mother was severed and his possibility for familial love "checked" and "nearly extinguished." Thus, though this entry in Crowther's journal is notable for its expression of suffering and loss, it is also remarkable because it depicts the near complete loss of emotion, the decimation of familial bonds, and the destruction of affection and love that the slave trade wrought and this reunion can barely heal.

Frederick Douglass makes a similar remark regarding the effects of slavery in the context of the United States. In his depiction of the day when his mother was sold away from him, Douglass comments, "For what this separation is done, I do not know, unless it be to hinder the development of the child's affection towards its mother, and to blunt and destroy the natural affection of the mother for the child. This is the inevitable result."[16] Douglass adds that his sale was not only remarkable in that his hope for a mother-child relationship was severed at this moment, but that it resulted as well in the dissolution of any bond he felt between himself and his siblings. This scenario of Frederick Douglass's childhood (a familiar scene in much African American abolitionist literature) echoes the diabolical calculus of slavery that Crowther experienced and that determined the possibilities for intimacy between people of African descent across the expansive geography of the Atlantic world during the era of the slave trade.

However, the African experience of this loss, even in its similarity with that of the African American slave, has a certain particularity, as the loss was almost always permanent. Unlike Crowther, most Africans who were separated from their families were met with an interminable loss, which no searching or hope could bridge. Crowther records the Yoruba proverb that states: "When a slave dies, his mother hears nothing of it: but when a child dies, there is lamentation; yet the slave was once a child in his mother's house."[17] Though stories survive of enslaved African American families who were reunited in the United States, the African experience of loss was often complete, in that the loved ones who were captured into the trade were so often sold to another continent, never to be seen again. In the case of the African experience of the transatlantic slave trade, children not only disappeared forever without hope for eventual return, but mourning was restricted because there were likely few ritualized outlets to mourn those who were merely missing. Any consolation provided to enslaved African Americans by the hope that they might join their lost family members in the afterlife would have evaded African families as well, for they were unable to perform the rituals of death and mourning that would initiate their lost children into the realm of the ancestors. As Crowther points out, using his own family as an example, with systems of mourning constricted within communities confronted by such continual trauma, death, and disappearance, the result was a widespread rupture in even the most intimate of bonds.

Staging Domestic Slavery in the Transatlantic Context

By 1846, when Crowther wrote of his reunion with his mother, the transatlantic slave trade was still very much alive and had not yet been relegated to the space of memory. Slowly over the course of the century, the illegal ships stopped coming to Africa's shores to purchase human labor. By the end of the nineteenth century, the British had prohibited slavery within the Gold Coast as well. Nonetheless, the internal trade in humans, which found its zenith during the era of the transatlantic slave trade, continued to thrive in some parts of West Africa well into the 1870s. Domestic slaveholders and traders continued, despite all ordinances to the contrary, to buy and sell laborers for domestic and agricultural labor. Slaveholders petitioned the British government to suspend colonial policies that would mandate the renunciation of ownership of slaves and pawns.[18] Men purchased women in place of marrying wives; women bought children for domestic help; invalids invested in slaves to aid them in their daily lives. Children and women were especially sought after in this economy. In fact, Peter Haenger claims that "almost everyone who had succeeded in saving up a small sum of money was in a position to purchase a slave child."[19] As was true of the 1820s when Crowther was captured, the transatlantic slave trade and the domestic slave trade were intertwined. As the British sought to end slavery throughout its colonies and the colonies of Spain and France, domestic slavery in Africa increased.

The relationship between the global transatlantic trade and the increase in domestic slavery is not lost on West African writers. Similar to Ayi Kwei Armah but with much less venom, Ghanaian author Ama Ata Aidoo explores the historical antecedents to Ghana's complicated postcolonial existence. Two of Aidoo's works, *Anowa* (1965) and *Our Sister Killjoy* (1977), explore the frightening and personal repercussions of the transatlantic slave trade as its effects extend for generations after abolition. *Anowa*, set in the 1870s, dramatizes the life of a young African woman who is tormented by the fact that her beloved husband owns slaves and whose every experience of intimacy is scarred by what she sees as an inhumane and unethical trade in human lives. *Our Sister Killjoy* tells of the adventures of a young Ghanaian woman studying abroad in Germany a century later, in the 1970s. She finds that every encounter with love and sexuality is haunted and interrupted by a past that most people prefer to forget. Both works return repeatedly to images and metaphors of the transatlantic slave trade as a way to articulate the irrepressible nature of the bodily and personal legacies of the slave trade affecting the intimate lives of West African men and women.

Throughout her work, Aidoo insinuates that the transatlantic slave trade remains a lingering presence in the lives of Africans for centuries. Aidoo consistently conflates multiple, seemingly disparate historical terrors that have been inflicted upon people of African descent—in *Anowa*, she intertwines the transatlantic slave trade and the postabolition domestic trade; in *Our Sister Killjoy*, the transatlantic trade, the colonial project, Hitler's fascist Germany, missionary education, and a variety of other injustices and abuses are linked. In so doing, she reveals how the present is persistently haunted by the slave trade past. Thus, a variety of images and metaphors of the transatlantic slave trade emerge in Aidoo's work, as the trade remains a constant undercurrent that informs Aidoo's perception of both historical and contemporary life on Africa's shores.

In this chapter, I argue that through both *Anowa* and her later "novel," *Our Sister Killjoy* (which will be discussed later in the chapter), Aidoo examines the slave trade's sometimes calculated, sometimes collateral desecration of intimacy in the West African context. Throughout both works, Aidoo metaphorizes the slave trade through a variety of interruptions in intimacy—impotence, the inability to communicate, thwarted sexuality and love, separation and breakups—indicating the way the slave trade marked itself upon even the most personal and physical structures of being and feeling in Africa. As a remedy for this endemic failure, Aidoo proposes an alternative "grammar of memory," which encourages community and intimacy through a literal verbalization of a shared past, and, when communicated and recognized, can reconstruct the bonds slavery seemingly severed.

Ama Ata Aidoo opens her second play, *Anowa*, with a reflection on the transatlantic roots of the late nineteenth-century proliferation of domestic slavery in Africa that we have been discussing here. The prologue implores memory to be gentle on those African people who, during the transatlantic slave trade, were enticed to seek "protection of those that-came-from-beyond-the-horizon," those who "found a common sauce-bowl in which they play[ed] a game of dipping with the stranger,"[20] those who went "where the rumbling hunger in their bowels shall be stilled," and those who "depend for their well-being on the presence of the pale stranger in our midst" (67). This "secret" of African complicity in the slave trade, which the old man whispers to the audience of the drama, remains a significant part of the West African landscape of memory, he claims, for "those forts standing at the door of the great ocean shall remind our children and the sea bear witness" (66). The memory of ancestors who served their own needs during the era of the transatlantic slave trade serves as a backdrop for the setting of the play—the Gold Coast in 1877. Aidoo points out that this was a time when common people still suffered from desire and greed so great as to make slavery and slave trading possible, even seventy years after the British abolished the trade. Kofi, a central character of the play and the husband of the titular character, Anowa, is one of those men the Old Man describes who perpetuate the trading of slaves and the suffering that attends slavery. It is no coincidence, then, that immediately after the old man catalogs African complicities during the era of the transatlantic slave trade, Kofi is introduced for the first time.

The Old Man concludes that section with what might seem to be a non sequitur to an unsuspecting audience: "Kofi was, is, and shall always be / One of us" (67). In the Old Man's cryptic introduction, Kofi is simultaneously aligned with Africans who exploited the slave trade for their own benefit and has his membership within the community reinforced. In this way, Aidoo extends the responsibility for the slave trade and its effects across the community. Every action in the play becomes layered such that Kofi's actions take on the larger historical and communal significance with which she has endowed them here at the beginning of the play. Though the slavery *Anowa* depicts is largely domestic in nature, the prologue of the play and further images of the earlier transatlantic slave trade throughout the play indicate the intimate relationship between the transatlantic trade and the growth of the domestic trade in West Africa. Though our concern in this study is primarily the transatlantic portion of the vast trade in slaves that pervaded the West African coast for centuries, Aidoo clearly depicts the two trades as of one piece: intimately interrelated and inextricably bound.[21]

The Wayfarer's Mother

In *Anowa*, Aidoo depicts the oft-told legend of a young woman, the namesake of the play, who chooses to marry young, carefree Kofi, a man her mother decries as a "fool," "a good for nothing cassava-man," and "this-I-am-the-handsome-one-with-a-stick-between-my-teeth-in-the-market-place" (74–75). Punished by her mother for her surly independence, Anowa leaves her home with her new husband to seek her fortunes and to "walk so well" that she would "not find [her] feet back [t]here again" (79). Aidoo remarks that *Anowa* "grew directly out of a story [her mother] told . . . although as the play has come out, she can't even recognize the story she told."[22] Though the traditional folktale generally ends with Anowa's failed marriage, the altered ending that Aidoo provides leaves the idealistic young Anowa in the bind of historical reality. She does indeed find fortune with her husband, but that fortune comes at the expense of human lives—slaves that her husband buys to assist them in their labors.

Anowa is mortally distressed by the enslavement of people for her benefit and wonders if she and Kofi were meant to behave "as though other people are horses" (114). She laments that the children they have enslaved were born of mothers simply to "fan an empty chair" (112) so that Kofi may be more comfortable. She recognizes that the children whom her husband has enslaved are themselves children of some innocent woman who has purposelessly suffered the loss of her children. "Hmmm . . . woe the childless woman, they warn. Let someone go and see [the slaves'] mother, who is she? Where is she sitting while they stand here fanning an empty chair?" (112). She sympathizes with the seemingly paradoxical figure of the childless mother, who, though she birthed children, sits alone without her offspring. The pointlessness of the mother's loss strikes Anowa here as she meditates on the abuse of the children's labor. Like Samuel Crowther, Aidoo's Anowa recognizes the familial rupture that was characteristic of slavery and the slave trade. Aidoo's depiction of Anowa's failed relationships—with her parents, with her husband, and even here with the children she employs in her home—recognizes the endemic failure of intimacy that was a characteristic result of transatlantic slavery and the resultant domestic west coast trade.

Anowa explicitly articulates the perversity of relations that is characteristic of slavery—the way slavery undermines the possibility for meaningful human relationships and familial bonds. Throughout the play, Anowa repeatedly insists to her husband, Kofi Ako, that it is "wrong" and "evil" to own other humans, telling him that she would "not feel happy with slaves around," because "no man made a slave of his friend and came to much himself" (112). Fulfilling her own predictions, Anowa becomes increasingly despondent as Kofi's slave retinue grows, but she comes to a greater wisdom regarding the plight of the slave. She realizes that the slave, known as a wayfarer, is burdened not only with labor but also with the suffering resulting from a lost sense of home and familial affection, much like Crowther noted when he was torn from his mother as a child to become a slave. Anowa muses, "A wayfarer is a traveler. Therefore, to call someone a wayfarer is a painless way of saying he does not belong. That he has no home, no family, no village, no stool of his own; has no feast days, no holidays, no state, no territory" (97). Anowa forgoes discussion of the most obvious forms of suffering experienced by enslaved people, and focuses on how the men, women, and children who work to improve Kofi Ako's life suffer daily from a lack of intimacy in their lives, from a fate that denies them love, community, and familial bonds.

Though slaveholders in Anowa's community may euphemize the situation of the enslaved by calling them "wayfarers," and though the young may even refer to their slave masters as Mother and Father (112–13), Anowa insists that "an adopted child is always an adopted child and a slave child a slave" (115). She reminds us that though Kofi may encourage the children to call him Father, the status of the slave is, by virtue of its enslavement, family-less, and no amount of euphemism, no reference to tradition, and no excuse-making will resolve that rupture. Aidoo implicitly critiques the mother and father appellations—she and Kofi are markedly *not* the children's mother and father—and explicitly reminds us that these are children whose homelessness and motherlessness have been produced *through ownership*. Peter Haenger notes, "Children who were enslaved in Africa were, indeed, quite often integrated into the households of their owners, and over time, family bonds developed."[23] Nonetheless, in the purchase of their lives, Anowa suggests that she and Kofi have made the children orphans, and their calling her Mother is a perversion of the very familial bond of which she has deprived them.

Anowa's revelation regarding the status of the slave helps her to recognize that her situation as a woman, and as the wife of a slave trader, binds her to the slave and is similar to the slave's situation in many ways. She explains her virtual enslavement, saying, "I am a wayfarer with no belongings either here or there" (96). She asks Kofi Ako, "What is the difference between any of your men and me? Except that they are men and I'm a woman? None of us belongs" (97). The disintegration of familial bonds characteristic of enslavement is also experienced by Anowa, even though she ostensibly shares ownership of the slaves with Kofi. At one level, she's exiled from the intimacy of her family because she runs away to marry Kofi, but she is also silenced, forced to behave as Kofi demands, and refused the ability to make her own life decisions.

Many critics have discussed at length Anowa's comparison of herself to a slave. Unlike other literary texts that represent the slave trade in West African memory but are discussed largely for the representation of themes other than slavery, *Anowa*'s overt critique of slavery is widely analyzed. Vincent O. Odamtten claims that *Anowa* reminds us of the "complicity and active participation of African people in that degrading trafficking of human flesh"[24] and argues that Anowa's problems in her marriage stem from her decisions being "overdetermined by the ideological contradictions and the economic transformations of *that particular historical moment*."[25] The very specific historical context of Anowa's action is indeed crucial to understanding the anxieties of the text and does more to historicize domestic slavery into the transatlantic context than probably any other West African literary text of the period.

Other critics focus more specifically on *Anowa* as a feminist play. Carol Boyce Davies reads *Anowa* as depicting a continuum from slavery to colonialism to male domination, focusing on Aidoo's depiction of Kofi's acquisition of slaves and the "Big House" in which he lives with them as a mobilization of the African American trope of the "big house." Davies argues, "The 'Big House,' as acquired by the Black male, then becomes in literature by Black women a trope for Black/African National(ism) and the parallel locus of final destruction of any positive relationship between Black men and women as Black manhood aligns itself with male dominance. In the 'Big House,' a more constricting space than her village, Anowa lives as a ghost of her former self unable to come to physical terms with it as home even in a conflicted way."[26] According to Davies's formulation of Aidoo's novel in terms of African American history, Kofi believes he will be able to achieve the success he does only by fully subordinating both the men he uses as laborers and the woman he has chosen as his wife.[27]

Metaphorically enslaved in the "big house," Anowa is read as an allegory for the subordination of even the most powerful and independent of black women by the structures of male dominance inherited from the cultural importations made available to African men (and men of African descent) by the slave trade. Haiping Yan adds that Anowa is enslaved to her role in the house, "assigning her to her 'destiny' as a validation of Kofi Ako's 'lordship over the area.'"[28] Lloyd Brown affirms this reading, arguing that Anowa expresses "woman's situation as the symbol of African history—a history of slavery, colonialism, and repressive power."[29] As the symbol of all of Africa's history, then, Anowa's role is one that is made to bear a multitude of forms of oppression, enslavement, torture, and abuse, which are rooted in the historical subjugation of both people of African descent and women. Her comparison of herself to those enslaved by her husband allows for a rich allegorical reading of Africa's history, and critics have taken the unusual opportunity Aidoo has provided to discuss at length the representation of slavery and the possible parallels to the oppression of women and of the continent that such a representation might reveal.

These convincing and useful readings of the allegorical nature of Aidoo's work largely reflect the historical trajectory of women's oppression in male-dominated societies broadly construed. Anowa is read as a slave whose behavior and freedom are entirely circumscribed by her husband, who acts as if he owns her. Anowa is also interpreted as a symbol of Mother Africa: the body on which all forms of oppression are enacted. However, as C. L. Innes astutely warns us: "From her earliest work . . . Aidoo has challenged the nostalgic image of 'African mother' as symbol with a series of mothers whose characters and roles as well as their very plurality prevent them from being seen either symbolically or nostalgically."[30] The same holds true for the idea of Anowa as a slave in the big house. Thus, to dwell on a feminist allegorical reading of Anowa's disempowerment as a woman might actually sidestep some of the complexities Aidoo is depicting in the maternal, sexual, and political relationships represented in the text. Allegorical readings can fruitfully be expanded if we consider the way in which Aidoo interrogates Anowa's relationship to slavery, not only by figuring her as a slave but also by indicating the way in which the slave trade infects every aspect of her life. While allegorical readings gesture to a feminist stance that would investigate the politics of Anowa's marriage to Kofi, Aidoo's fixed attention on the rupture of familial bonds in the text requires that we explore the historical effects of slavery on intimacy more fully. Furthermore, Anowa's maternal relationship to children in the text seems to critique the long-term effects of slavery on intimacy regardless of gender or systems of male dominance.

One moment that reveals the complexities of intimacy as it is related to the slave trade is the oft-cited scene in which Anowa reflects upon her childhood interest in the slave trade. She repeatedly plies her grandmother with questions about the trade, inquiring, "Who are the pale men?" (104), "Why did they build the big houses?" (i.e., the slave castles along the coast of Ghana), and "What is a slave, Nana?" (105). As the young Anowa finally begins to understand the role played by Europeans on the coast of Africa in selling, purchasing, and kidnapping African people to become slaves in other countries, she asks the unavoidable but painful question: "Did the men of the land sell other men of the land, and women and children to pale men from beyond the horizon who looked like you or me peeled, like lobsters boiled or roasted?" (106). Unwilling to face the enormity of such a question, a question that places much of the responsibility for the trade in the hands of Africans themselves, Anowa's grandmother answers, with increasing anxiety,

> I do not know, child
> You are frightening me, child
> I was not there!
> It is too long ago!
> No one talks of these things anymore!
> All good men and women try to forget!
> They have forgotten! (106)

If Achille Mbembe diagnoses West African culture with amnesia regarding the slave trade (as discussed in chapter 1 of this study),[31] then Nana has done her best to prove him right as she attempts to forget the violent history of the trade and Africans' roles in it. In her view, there are some things that are better forgotten. "All good men and women try to forget"; and as a result, Anowa's nearly obsessive interest in slavery can only be explained, within the discourse of her own community, as the thoughts of a witch (106) or the vision of a priestess (107).

Like Baako in *Fragments* (discussed in chapter 4), Anowa's investment in uncovering the slave trade past marks her as an outsider or pariah of some kind. However, Anowa, like Baako, continues to interrogate the narrative of the past that her grandmother has outlined and that neither has been able to "forget" despite her grandmother's protests. Instead of accepting that the history of the slave trade should be forgotten, she is led to another question, a question that implies loss, but also remembrance and mourning; she asks, "What happened to those who were taken away? / Do people hear from them? / How are they?" (106). Her grandmother tells her to be quiet. And forget.

But that night, Anowa "woke up screaming hot; my body burning and sweating from a horrible dream. I dreamt I was a big, big woman. And from my insides were huge holes out of which poured men, women, and children."

Lobster men who were rushing out of the sea "rushed to where I sat and seized the men and women as they poured out of me, and they tore them apart, and dashed them to the ground and stamped upon them. And from their huge courtyards, the women ground my men and women and children on mountains of stone" (106). Here, Anowa does figure as a sort of "Mother Africa," in an allegory of the rape of Africa by Europeans who rushed onto the continent, seized its human resources, and sometimes even literally dashed them to the ground. But this dream also explores the estranged relationship between the mother and the enslaved child once again. Her fear of complicity in the production of motherless, homeless enslaved children is made literal here. Though she is "bursting" (106) with children, she is unable to protect them from the monsters on the shore who seek the complete annihilation of the newborns. It is not an abortive pregnancy that Anowa experiences, but a successful live birth, which nonetheless ends in death and destruction. It is a maternity without a bond or love, a birth of immediate mourning and loss. This nightmare of history haunts Anowa so much that she remarks, "But then, any time there is a mention of a slave, I see a woman who is me" (107). Anowa's own body becomes a site of remembrance for the violence that took place on the shores of the Atlantic, as well as a metaphor for the rupture in the bond between mothers and children all along the coast and far into the interior of West Africa.[32]

Childless Mothers and Dead Husbands

Anowa represents both the motherless slave child and the childless mother who has lost a child to the trade. Thus, when it is made clear later in the play that Anowa has been unable to have children, the news comes as no surprise. In her dream, Anowa has a vision of the futility of reproduction within an economy that values life only insofar as it can be commodified and sold. The traditional characters in Aidoo's earlier play *Dilemma of a Ghost* blame barrenness on modernization and education, when in fact the African American female lead character is more concerned with preserving her freedom.[33] In *Anowa*, traditional characters blame Anowa's barrenness (and every other problem she has) on her desire to transgress traditional African boundaries regarding a woman's role within the family structure. It is clear throughout the play that Aidoo does not subscribe to such a position. However, Aidoo does not stop at the feminist critique typical of African women writers that either implicitly or explicitly refutes the propriety of traditional African stigmatization of women who fail to birth children. Instead, she links Anowa's barrenness to a larger historical context, resisting any typical readings of the childless mother by making it explicit that her barrenness results from the violence visited on families by slaveholding and slave trading, as we shall see quite clearly as the play's action unfolds.

To understand Anowa's barrenness in the play, we cannot point to either her subordination within the community or her ostracism because of her non-participation in the reproduction of the community. We cannot even point to Anowa's physical incapacity or even her extraordinary will to resist women's subordination as a reason for her failure to reproduce. Even in the dream, Anowa herself is able to give birth to multitudes. Naana Banyiwa Horne describes Anowa's childlessness as "symptomatic of a general failure of maternal agency to engender human continuity,"[34] and in the same article claims that Anowa's "failure to have children takes on the form of female resistance to expropriation of the female womb in the perpetuation of gender oppression"[35] to defend her assertion (reminiscent of Lysistrata) that women's oppression "should be met with women withholding their ability to reproduce."[36] However, Aidoo makes it absolutely clear that it is *slavery* that estranges the mother from the child in the dream, and it is *slavery* that makes it impossible for Anowa to reproduce—what we might consider the most extreme version of the interference in the motherly bond.

The impossibility of interpreting Anowa as the source—whether by will or by circumstance—of her own barrenness is made clear at the very end of the play. Kofi mistakenly condemns Anowa for their childlessness, shouting at her, "You can't give me the only thing I want from you, a child" (116). However, though it appears without warning and though there is no medical explanation for it, we learn in the last moments of the drama that Kofi is in fact the source of the infertility. When Kofi threatens to send Anowa back to her mother, she turns the tables on him, euphemistically accusing him of being "dead," but also naming his impotence explicitly as well: "Kofi, is your manhood gone? I mean, you are like a woman" (121). Indeed, it is Kofi's infertility that causes him and Anowa to remain childless years after they have been married. Though Anowa bears the brunt of Kofi's disgust and lives with the blame for their childlessness, in the end it turns out that Kofi is the true culprit. He is infertile.

Here Aidoo divulges what I want to suggest is an open secret regarding infertility in African women's fiction and in many African women's lived experience. African women's literature is replete with examples of women who cannot conceive—female writers seemingly obsess over the state of women's fertility, dwelling as they do on women who suffer from barrenness. Aidoo, Buchi Emecheta, Flora Nwapa, and more recently Cameroonian authors Anne Tanyi-Tang and Juliana Makuchi Nfah-Abennyi, for instance, continue to explore the problem of women's infertility in more contemporary settings. Depictions of women by male authors, such as Elechi Amadi's *The Concubine* or Kola Onadipe's children's book *Koku Baboni*, also center on women who cannot have children. Aidoo's own *Dilemma of a Ghost* is centered on a female character who does not have children by choice but is understood by her African in-laws to be barren.[37] Even in *Things Fall Apart*, Okonkwo's wife, Ekwefi, mother of Ezinma, is considered inferior because before giving birth to Ezinma, she was considered barren, and in the end, she has given birth to only one living child and that, a girl. Along with *Anowa*, these fictional depictions of women could be included in something we might call a genre of infertility fiction (or at the very least, the pervasive trope of the barren woman), in which women are treated by their relatives and kin as if they need to "find out and cure what is wrong with" their wombs (93). In so many cases, when nothing can be done to cure the woman, she is abused by her family, turned out of her home, and treated as "a witch," "a devil," "everything that is evil" (100), the very way the Old Woman in the play treats Anowa.[38]

However, there is always the lurking suspicion, never spoken, in these works, that at least some of the women who remain childless are not themselves barren, but are instead married to infertile men. In Makuchi's story "The Healer," for instance, the supposedly infertile women in the town are able to get pregnant only when the traditional healer secretly sleeps with them while they are drugged, indicating clearly that it is not the woman in the marriage who is infertile.[39] Marcia C. Inhorn, a specialist in African fertility issues, notes, "Africa is a continent with a high rate of infertility, including a so-called infertility belt around its center. Although much of this infertility has been attributed to infectious scarring of female reproductive tracts, 'male factors' remain an underappreciated but a significant cause of infertility in Africa and elsewhere, contributing to more than half of all cases of infertility globally."[40] She indicates that though there are numerous reasons why men may be infertile (including a variety of problems associated with impotence, ejaculation, and intromission, but also with other problems entirely unassociated with sexual dysfunction), male reproductive problems are largely silenced in African discourse because of the persistent conflation of infertility with the loss of manhood and virility.[41] Indeed, that is how Anowa refers to Kofi's infertility, laughing at him within view of his slaves, and declaring, "So that is it. My husband is a woman now. [She giggles.] He is a corpse. He is dead wood. But less than dead wood because at least, that sometimes grows mushrooms" (122). By announcing Kofi's impotence in this way in front of Kofi's slaves, Anowa openly undermines the facade of paternalism that Kofi is hoping to engender in his slave "family." Aidoo powerfully reverses the discourse surrounding female reproduction (or the lack thereof) and stakes her claim as the one who finally makes explicit the subtext of a wide swath of African women's writing.

The moment Kofi's infertility is unveiled in the play speaks more broadly to the relationship between intimacy and the slave trade at the center of this argument and, indeed, at the center of Aidoo's work in general. Aidoo points to that rupture in familial relationships that reaches beyond the mother and child to encompass a variety of forms of bonding, including marital and sexual intimacy. Anowa suddenly comes to the realization that "for years now, I have not seen your bed" (121), which is what spurs her to conclude finally that it might be Kofi who is the cause of their childlessness. And it is not merely that Kofi is infertile, but that he was unwilling to talk to his wife about it. Anowa asks him, "Why didn't you want me to know? You could have told me" (121–22), revealing that the rupture in marital intimacy between Kofi and Anowa is more than merely sexual.

It quickly becomes clear that the cause of Kofi's impotence is not biological or the result of old age; in fact, it cannot be explained by any of the sources of infertility that Inhorn lists in her discussion of African male fertility issues. Instead, the impotence that Anowa claims Kofi suffers from is *historical*. Anowa identifies the problem immediately upon discovering the source of their childlessness and his desire to send her away. She asks him, "Is that why I must leave you? That you have exhausted your masculinity acquiring slaves and wealth?" (121). Anowa claims that his ownership of slaves meant that he had "consumed [his manhood] up" himself (122). By emasculating Kofi, Aidoo refutes the pseudoscientific claims of European social scientists of Kofi's own era who would figure the African male as virile, well-endowed, and violent. But at the same time, she reinforces the perhaps paradoxical but equally held notion that black men were impotent and powerless.[42] However, instead of seeing Kofi's condition as in any way being natural or inherent or "African," she historicizes that impotence, marking it specifically as a result of the transatlantic and domestic slave trade and their continued effects on African culture, life, and more specifically, bodies. Not in fact a slave to his passions as some scientific discourse of the time might have insisted, Kofi is quite the reverse, metaphorically enslaved himself through a lack of passion. In the consumption of human lives that Kofi indulges in by participating in the slave trade, he has also consumed his potential for procreativity. He has essentially robbed himself of the natural right to have children by any means other than through purchase, which, as Anowa points out, does not constitute a genuine parent-child relationship. He has alienated himself from his potential progeny, and he has alienated himself from Anowa.

In an article entirely focused on the uses of slavery in African women's literature titled "Slavery and Etiological Discourse in the Writings of Ama Ata Aidoo, Bessie Head, and Buchi Emecheta," Modupe Olaogun argues that *Anowa* encourages a "long view of history,"[43] which suggests that "representations of slavery are explorations of more remote or submerged causes of the problems frequently configured as neocolonial."[44] Indeed, we might understand Kofi's case as an unusual and quite fantastical rendering of a legendary figure—one that even Aidoo admits is her "pseudo-Freudian answer"[45] as to why Kofi would turn Anowa away. However, Anowa's story, as it is placed within the frame of a "long view of history" that reaches back to memories of the early slave traders on the shores of Africa, interrogates the legacy of the slave trade on successive generations of Africans. So we must extend Olaogun's preliminary claim that the slave trade is the cause of Africa's "problems" to ask ourselves: if slavery is a cause, then what are the precise *effects* on African lives?

Aidoo's answer seems to be that slavery's legacy has marked itself on the very bodies of African people, such that it does not merely sever those who might ordinarily enjoy a certain intimacy, but impedes all forms of human desire that are not consonant with the project of ever-expanding capital gain and the commodification of human life. Kofi's infertility, then, should be read as a metaphor of the slave trade that highlights the rupture the slave trade engendered in intimate relations and thus the alienation of human beings from one another and their own desires. The desire of one human being to own another has devastated the possibility for any sexual desire between man and wife. Kofi's failure to utilize his body to procreate or to be intimate with his partner reveals perhaps the most devastating of alienations. In Anowa's eyes at least, he is reduced to merely carrying a man's body around without the ability to use it. In the process of owning slaves, he has so imbibed the ideology of slavery that as he understands his slaves to be less than human, he himself is made less human. His body is diminished such that it becomes merely a shell, no longer able to function in the way it previously did. His curious lack of desire to work, which according to Anowa falls outside their tradition (114), is another sign that Kofi is alienated from the function and use of his body. For in an economy in which a person can be made an object to be utilized by another, the body is reduced to its labor alone; its more pleasurable functions and perhaps even natural desires are excised. This form of enslavement, Aidoo points out, is not limited to those whose labor has been exploited by an elite slaveholder. Indeed, within the economy of African slavery, all those who participate—at every level, even those who own slaves—are themselves enslaved.

This alienation from the body results in an inevitable repression and confinement of intimacy, desire, and affection between men and women. These human capacities function only for the purposes of expanding the project of slavery. The ideology of slavery relies on the possibility of the complete disembodiment of the person, the potential of slavery to reduce or perhaps exclude entirely the mind and the body's potential for desire, intimacy, and sexuality. Hortense Spillers elaborates on this violent economy of desire: "we could go so far as to entertain the very real possibility that 'sexuality,' as a term of implied relationship and desire, is dubiously appropriate, manageable, or accurate to *any* of the familial arrangements under a system of enslavement, from the master's family to the captive enclave."[46] As slavery undermined the possibility for sexuality as we would generally define it, through its alienation of the body from anything more than its most basic functions, the slave trade actively subverted intimacy, not only for the victims but also for the perpetrators.

The Old Man character, who serves in Aidoo's play as a sort of chorus figure along with his wife, reminds us of the dangers he foretold in the prologue, decrying Kofi's zombified slave-like existence as the result of the "unwholesome" nature of "making slaves of other men." He warns, "Money-making is like a god possessing a priest. He never will leave you, until he has occupied you, wholly changed the order of your being, and seared you through and up and down. Then only would he eventually leave you, but nothing of you except an exhausted wreck, lying prone and wondering who you are" (100). In the end, it is Kofi who is enslaved by his ownership of slaves. This possession of Kofi's body leaves him lifeless as well as literally and figuratively impotent. When the body is possessed and overcome by the desire for wealth and the subordination of others, it is made alien, becomes other than itself, enslaved by the spirits of accumulation and consumption. The Old Man ominously intones, "Those who have observed have remarked that every house is ruined where they take in slaves" (100). And indeed, Kofi's house suffers mortally from his own alienation, as both he and Anowa end up committing suicide at the end of the play, no longer able to live with their lack of intimacy or their complete alienation from the life and love they once knew.

Aidoo's depiction takes Anowa's barren condition out of the particularly divisive realm of male dominance versus female subordination. In the same moment as she explicitly reveals the open secret of male infertility and unambiguously removes the blame for childlessness from Anowa, she also exposes the way history has taken its toll on the relationship between men and women in such a way that one cannot blame either Anowa or Kofi for their lack of intimacy. It is slavery itself that comes between them, and from the beginning of the play, this domestic slavery bears the mark of a long history of West African participation in transatlantic slavery. By the end of *Anowa*, it is not clear that there is any remedy that will cure the ills of society that were born of the slave trade, not even a mythological love like Kofi and Anowa's. Aidoo's entangled slaveries—transatlantic, domestic, emotional, sexual—reveal the confluence of politics, history, and intimacy, producing in *Anowa* a tragic vision and an aborted hope for Africa's future following the slave trade.

Obstacles in the Way of Love

It may seem ironic, in light of the argument set forth here, that Ama Ata Aidoo saw *Anowa* and her other early work as entirely political and as eschewing the concerns of love and intimacy so central to other African female authors. She denied that she was interested in writing love stories, claiming in 1967 that she could not see herself "as a writer writing about lovers in Accra because, you see, there are so many other problems."[47] However, with *Our Sister Killjoy*, Ama Ata Aidoo's first "novel," she acknowledged that she was taking on the subject of love in her work. "I am beginning to say the workings of love are also political,"[48] she admitted to Adeola James in an interview. By the time she put out her next novel, *Changes: A Love Story*, she was forced to confess that "love was always more important to me than I was willing to admit twenty years or so ago in an interview of that sort."[49]

It is clear from the previous discussion that Aidoo had long been preoccupied with the intersections of love and politics and history throughout her career. Read in this light, *Our Sister Killjoy* is not an inauguration into the theme of love for Aidoo, but in fact a continuation of the interrogation of the politics of intimacy in Africa that she initiated in her early work, such as *Anowa*. As

Chimalum Nwankwo has also observed: "In [Aidoo's] works, the problems of the African woman are expressed as integral parts of the problems of colonial and post-colonial Africa. Aidoo's feminist concerns are not treated in isolation from Africa's political instability, the new master complex of the so-called elite, the atavistic problem of the rural African at the cross-roads of history, the fury and impotence of the radical African, the lure of the Western world, and so forth."[50] Regardless of Aidoo's protests, each of her novels is a kind of love story, even if she did not recognize them as such until she authored *Changes*. The politics and history that are at the center of Aidoo's writerly concerns inform the questions of intimacy and love that seem to be the motivation of her characters' personal investments. It is clear from a character like Anowa that politics, money, history, tradition, family, and memory are important to her only insofar as they determine her ability *to love*—whether that be the love of a mother toward her children or that of a wife for her husband. As a result, I would argue that the workings of love and intimacy can and should inform our understanding of Aidoo's notion of politics and history as much as any other lens.

Our Sister Killjoy, a whirlwind of a novel, similarly bears the mark of Aidoo's attention to the intersections of love and history, as they are informed by the transatlantic slave trade and other historical irruptions that have affected African lives well into the late twentieth century. It is divided into four main parts, each of which depicts a perspective on the life of the main character, Sissie, our eponymous "Sister Killjoy." The action of the novel turns on Sissie's trip to Germany, on which she is a member of a select group of international volunteers meant to work in the forests of Bavaria and participate in cultural exchange programming that might allow Germans to feel as though they had revived the spirit of internationalism that died with World War II. Though she has no idea why she's been selected, Sissie seizes her opportunity to travel, because as she puts it, at the time, "if you were an African student with the wanderlust, you travelled,"[51] despite the fact that it was "a long way from home to Europe: A cruel past, a funny present, a major desert or two, a sea, an ocean, several different languages apart" (6). As in *Anowa*, the "cruel past" is again foregrounded in the very beginning of the text, setting the stage for the historical determinants of the events to follow, which stretch beyond the 1870s setting of *Anowa* into the 1970s. During the course of her journey abroad, Sissie is involved in at least two intimate or romantic relationships, both of which are unavoidably overdetermined by the constraints of history. Both relationships are abortive in some way, and Sissie is left, after all of her international love affairs, alone, on a plane heading back to Africa, with a love letter in her hand that she is almost certain not to send.

Aidoo writes in the main section, titled "Plums": "We are the victims of our History and our Present. They place too many obstacles in the Way of Love. And we cannot enjoy even our Differences in peace" (29). This passage could serve as the thesis of the work. True to form, Aidoo's politics and concern with history are announced at the outset of the work. Here, however, Aidoo makes it clear that the history she excavates has significant effects on the structures of love and intimacy all the way into the postcolonial period. The work explicitly interrogates how the violent continuities of history—from the building of the slave castles, to the continuation of slaveholding in the 1870s, to the experiences of African women abroad in the 1970s—allow for a perpetuation of tragic consequences for African people, consequences that reach beyond the external political lives of the characters, deep into the most intimate of moments and relationships.

"Plums" is set during Sissie's volunteer vacation in Bavaria. As the section opens, Sissie stands in the shadow of a castle—a castle that is "one of the largest in all of Germany." Aidoo writes that the castle's owner had once possessed "the greatest number of serfs" (19) who "*slaved* for the Lord" (20, my emphasis). The narrator wonders in verse:

>How many
>Virgins had
>Our Sovereign Lord and Master
>Unvirgined on their nuptial nights
>For their young
>Husbands in
>Red-eyed
>Teeth-gnashing
>Agony, their
>Manhoods
>Hurting . . . (19)

The reverberation here with *Anowa* is unmistakable: the slaves working at the fort, the cost of slavery being tied to masculinity and sexuality. Though the "Master" here is not the one who has lost his manhood nor is he African, the relationship between the crime of servitude and the perversion of sexuality is evident. In "Into a Bad Dream," which acts as something of a short prologue to "Plums," Aidoo explicitly evokes the slave castles of Ghana, which are still in our minds when pages later she describes the castles of Bavaria. Like Juana in Armah's *Fragments*, she condemns all those African scholars who are unwilling to look directly into the "face of reality that is more tangible than the massive walls of the slave forts standing on our beaches" and who nonetheless do not recognize the historical specificity of Africa's present situation; instead they prefer to talk of "universal truth, universal art, universal literature and the Gross National Product" (6). The attention paid to current events and political issues ignores the context in which these concerns were born. Sissie refuses to fall prey to this desire for a blissful uninformed amnesia.

Aidoo extends the comparison between African and German architectural sites of violence when Sissie encounters German widows who mourn the loss of their young men during World War II, men whose blood was "[n]eeded to mix the concrete for / Building the walls of / The Third Reich. But / Its foundations collapsed before the walls were complete" (36). The narrative continues, "How this reminds me of the / Abome kings of Dahomey" (37). The Abome kings of Dahomey are known for operating one of the most significant slave ports in the world in the eighteenth and nineteenth centuries.[52] There, captives were brought from hundreds of miles inland to be sold in one of the most lucrative and ruthless slave markets ever known. Aidoo explicitly makes the comparison, then, that in Germany and in West Africa alike, men were considered mere pawns of avaricious governments driven by greed, and the blood that ran from the veins of the people who once inhabited those places was the figurative mortar that held up the walls of the castles of the lords of the realm in both locations. Vincent O. Odamtten confirms that "like the Bavarian castles whose walls have witnessed many crimes, 'those forts' in Ghana have been turned into police barracks, prisons and even government buildings," indicating the way in which the walls of the castles—both in Germany and in Ghana—might serve as metonymic reminders of the violence enacted within those walls over the centuries.[53] The secret histories that these walls might have witnessed are nonetheless excised from the record, "their infamous histories forgotten, or repressed."[54] Aidoo's work seems to refer repeatedly to the notion or fear that atrocities committed in sites such as slave castles might be forgotten. However, her work itself is a testimony to remembrance, to the activation of the memory of those crimes committed.

Aidoo does not spend the entire novel making explicit narrative connections between the slave trade and Africa's problems or even dramatizing explicitly the slave trade's influence on the intimate lives of the characters. Aidoo's work is nonetheless characterized by a sense of the centrality of historical continuities. The history she depicts is plagued by a varied array of violence, and that violence consistently takes a toll across generations. The slave trade repeatedly surfaces in these generally nonlinear evocations of the past, an indication of how Aidoo invests the present tense of the narrative with a lingering specter of the slave trade past. Reflecting on her work, Aidoo has commented, "I think that the whole question of how it was that so many of our people could be enslaved and sold is very important. I've always thought that it is an area that must be probed. It probably holds the keys to our future."[55] And these texts, though they situate the scenarios within a complex web of historical determinants, always return to the slave trade as a central moment that serves to illuminate the context of present iterations of violence.

Memories of Holocaust

It is in this overdetermined setting of layered oppressions that Sissie meets her new German friend, Marija. The relationship seems doomed from the start, given the histories Aidoo has set in motion, and if for no other reason than that Marija misidentifies Sissie as an Indian and thinks that Ghana might be near Canada. Sissie and Marija become fast friends nonetheless, and each evening Sissie visits Marija's house, leaving behind the ominous presence of the castle to enjoy a small meal and a bit of conversation with someone who is seemingly completely different. As their conversations wander from naming practices, to their travels, to their families, the consciousness of the narrative (whether that be Sissie's or another narrator's is not made clear) constantly moves back to historical oppressions of non-Europeans around the world. As if reiterating the early resonances between the castles of Bavaria and those of Ghana, Africa's inheritance of a history of loss that was Europe's gain haunts Sissie's relationship with Marija and creates a distance between them that no friendly banter can bridge. "Who was Marija Sommer?" the narrator asks and unhesitatingly replies,

> A daughter of mankind's
> Self-appointed most royal line,
> The House of Aryan—

> An heiress to some
> Legacy that would make you
> Bow
> Down
> Your head in
> Shame and
> Cry (48)

In Sissie's mind, Marija's German inheritance is scarred by Aryan guilt, which burdens her with the violence of Hitler's ethnic cleansing and hatred. Though the narrative makes clear that women suffered this violence as well, especially as the widows and mothers who tend the graves of the dead young soldiers, still Marija's character bears the double weight of that history—not only does she have to suffer it personally, she has to bear the responsibility for it as well.

But the weight of that inheritance also haunts Sissie. "And Our Sister?" the narrative continues:

> A Little
> Black
> Woman who
> If things were what they should have been,
> And time had not a way of
> Making nonsense of Man's
> Dreams, would
> Not
> Have been
> There
> Walking
> Where the
> Führer's feet had trod—
> A-C-H-T-U-N-G! (48)

Sissie has certainly defied what might have been her fate had the Führer had his way—as a black woman, she could very well have been forced to spend her entire life in Africa or even found herself dead as a result of her supposed racial inferiority. Despite the fact that her destiny and global politics have allowed her to be the independent young African woman that she is, her imagination is nonetheless haunted by the fact that her very existence has been determined by the success and failure of multiple interconnected international racist regimes and ideologies, which, not coincidentally, continue to make her a spectacle on the streets of Germany. This is made all too evident when the mere sight of Sissie makes an old man tremble and sweat (47). She is not able to avoid reminders that she is among a race of people who sought the extermination of another race and would have exterminated all people of African descent as well had they had the ability to extend their empire that far.

Furthermore, Sissie cannot exonerate Marija from this legacy, because, though Marija herself has no evident relationship to the Nazis, her family bears the reminder of that history—Marija's own husband is named Adolf, a not so subtle reminder of the "Lord" (as Aidoo puts it) who led Germany into World War II. Marija's son is also named Adolf, another unsubtle indication that he bears the inheritance of the violence of the Holocaust, in which Marija unwittingly participates, first in reproducing, and then in naming her son in honor of this atrocity.

Before she realizes the dangerous implications of their mingled histories, Sissie ponders for some time "what a delicious love affair she and Marija would have had if one of them had been a man" (61). Sissie quickly denies herself any desire for Marija, however, especially when she is reminded again of the impossibility of loving a white woman, as such relationships are so fraught with a history of violence. In an interview, Aidoo writes off Sissie's potential lesbian love affair as something that might happen if "you let loose an African girl in Europe," remarking that such a girl is "bound to come across all sorts of experiences, enriching, demoralizing—ah—positive, negative."[56] No matter how casual Aidoo attempts to make this relationship seem, Sissie comes across this "sort of experience" with a German woman because it allows Aidoo to explore the complex histories that would allow this experience to emerge and also prohibit its full realization.

The "delicious" possibility of a transgressive lesbian relationship with Marija emerges in Sissie's consciousness in this section, but it is immediately undermined when Sissie's memory of childhood homosocial encounters taints the fantasy. Sissie recalls a story of two girls innocently playing in bed together at boarding school, only to be interrupted and viciously reprimanded by a racist white headmistress. The woman can understand the girls' play only as "bush," a lively play on words that Aidoo reiterates repeatedly, which alternates between a meaning reflective of colonial racist overtones and another teeming with sexual implications. The schoolmarm wants to distinguish herself from what she sees as an indigenously African aberration, while the girls are all

> Giggles, giggles, giggles.
>
> Naughty African girls
> Cracking up
> To hear, and
> See
> European single woman
> Tearing up herself over
> Two girls in a bed
>
> But
> Madam,
> It is not
> Just
> Bush (67)

The response to the headmistress's shock allows the girls to shift the allegation of bad behavior onto this single woman who clearly must have the naughtier mind, as she is capable of imagining such impropriety. Regardless of the two girls' intentions, sexual or otherwise, the schoolmarm's outrage at the indiscretion of the girls figures as another form of interference in the intimate relations of African people. However, it does not stop merely at the schoolmarm's prohibition, but stretches to the internalization of that ideology within the African community. Indeed, within the African context, homosexuality has been severely curtailed by the widespread integration of evangelical Christian beliefs and practices, such that many African people will insist that African homosexuality does not exist.[57] Thus, Sissie is astutely aware that the possibilities within her relationship with Marija are severely limited by the restrictions placed on her intimacy both by the colonial gaze and by her own internalization of that gaze.

Thus confined by colonial ideology as well as the widespread African taboo against homosexuality, Sissie avoids such a restrictive designation for her relationship with Marija by dissociating herself from the feminine and imagining a way in which the affair could be played out in less transgressive terms. As she thinks she would have been the "man" in the imaginary relationship she and Marija might have pursued had things been different, "in her imagination, she was one of those black boys in one of these involvements with white girls in Europe" (61). Even this gender alteration does not allow Sissie the freedom to pursue her friend romantically because she continues to be deterred by the way the history of race relations interferes in African sexual and romantic lives. "Struck by some of the stories she had heard, she shivered, absolutely horrified" (61). She shivers when she thinks of:

Beautiful Black Bodies
Changed into elephant-gray corpses,
Littered all over the western world,
Thrown across railway tracks for
midnight expresses to mangle
just a little bit more—
Offered to cold flowing water
Buried in thickets and snow
Their penises cut. (62)

This repulsive image of the lynching of young black boys harkens to a history of enforced repressed sexuality, the policing of black men's bodies, and the continued legacy of racism, hatred, and violence that overdetermines black sexuality all around the world.

Having dissociated herself from the position of vulnerable female within the relationship, Sissie is nonetheless caught in the trap of racial hierarchies—as the imaginary man in this imaginary relationship, Sissie is still a *black* man, who would be violently punished for transgressing not the gendered but the racial barriers to love. Sissie's role as the man in the relationship gives her a momentary sense of the power she might possess in such an unbalanced relationship. She has the fantasy of male power, of colonial power even, but it is quickly shattered by her realization that race and history are still a part of the equation. Race is central to the reevaluation of her power as she remembers all the young black men who fought in Europe, had intimate relationships with white women, and despite any power they might have felt in conquering white bodily territory, they could be (not simply symbolically but literally) castrated by angry white men. Power, regardless of this newfound possibility for intimacy with white women, is still racialized such that white men have ultimate power—the power of ultimate violence. And it is no coincidence that Marija's husband, Adolf, the invisible white man who haunts Sissie and Marija's relationship, is a namesake of one of the most violent, most racist men of all time.

Marija is blissfully unaware of this inheritance and has even avoided any recognition of the distance that grows up between herself and Sissie. She slowly becomes infatuated with Sissie, substituting Sissie's friendship for her missing husband, Adolf, who appears to be at work for the duration of the novel. Marija invites Sissie upstairs for a tour of the house, but takes her into her perfectly prepared bedroom, where she slowly, timidly, and tearfully tries to kiss and fondle Sissie. However, "[a]s one does from a bad dream, impulsively, Sissie shook herself free. With too much effort, unnecessarily, so that she unintentionally hit Marija on the right cheek with the back of her hand" (64). The kiss that Marija places on Sissie's lips suddenly wakes the protagonist up from the "bad dream" that opens the novel, and it clarifies all of the tumultuous thoughts she had been having regarding slavery, colonialism, brain drain, lynching, medical experimentation, and the blood of young men. It is in this same moment, when Sissie profoundly recognizes the great gulf that separates her from Marija, that she comes to understand the collective position of those women who are made both the victims of the overwhelming oppression of such cultures and responsible for it by those from the outside like herself.

These realizations lead Sissie to be able to see that Marija's experience is defined by complete loneliness. The line of the narrative breaks into a poem, reminiscent of E. E. Cummings's poem titled "Loneliness," as it spells the word out, letter by letter, in a vertical line (65). Unlike Cummings, however, Aidoo does not set off the letters O, N, E in order to indicate the solitude of loneliness. This loneliness with which Aidoo diagnoses Marija is not solitary but *collective*. It is the shared inheritance of all those who descend from

> Bullying slavers and slave-traders.
> Solitary discoverers.
> Swamp-crossers and lion hunters.
> Missionaries who risked the cannibal's pot to bring the world to the heathen hordes.
> Speculators in gold in diamond uranium and copper
> Oil you do not even mention—
> Preachers of apartheid and zealous educators.
> Keepers of Imperial Peace and homicidal
> plantation owners.

> Monsieur Commandant and Madame the
> Commandant's wife.
> Miserable rascals and wretched whores whose only distinction in life
> was that at least they were better than the Natives . . . (65–66)

Marija's inheritance is one of loneliness that is born of centuries of historical guilt, a guilt that drives her to seek out Sissie, who she thinks might help her to heal, but who, for the very same reason, must refuse her and even strike back. But it is no coincidence that "bullying slavers and slave-traders" make this list. For Aidoo, all of these historical injustices are equivalent and ever-present.

The evocation of the slave trade at the beginning of the novel culminates in this final catalog of those who have pillaged the African continent for centuries. That Sissie cannot fulfill her budding desire to be with Marija is not simply a result of the fact that Sissie is not the man she wishes she could be or that Sissie is unable to imagine herself in a homosexual relationship. Instead, Sissie is refusing to be a victim to these histories any longer; she refuses her role as a living allegory for Africa—she will not be violated. As Sissie and Marija confront their attraction in Adolf's sterile bedroom, they also confront the detritus of historical violence that finds its way into the bedroom. This historical inheritance, which they share, makes intimacy between the two women impossible, leaving them both impotent, their love, at best, stillborn.

A Language of Love and Remembrance

In the last section of *Our Sister Killjoy*, "A Love Letter," Sissie documents her concern that her intimate thoughts and desires are hindered not only by history but by the failure of language to communicate them. She writes to her estranged African boyfriend, "My love . . . I cannot give voice to my soul and still have her heard . . . so far I have only been able to use a language that enslaved me, and therefore, the messengers of my mind always come shackled" (112). Sissie is reminded of the way Africans were enslaved by Europeans, even though they "owed them nothing. Not a cent, not a pesewa, not a kobo. . . . Yet they wanted our labor for free" (114). And since then, they have always encountered language as a problem, in that language continues to bear the mark of that early enslavement, which continues to make their thoughts captive. Though her boyfriend reprimands her for "imprison[ing] time" (113), she seeks a way she might be able to "let time move" but also "give it something to carry for us" (113), by which she seems to mean that history might indeed imprison them if they don't speak about it explicitly and recognize its impact on their present—an imprisonment of language that she clearly seeks to escape precisely by writing the letter.

Again, the past has intervened in Sissie's relationship—she and her boyfriend cannot resolve the fact that she wants to confront the power history holds in the present, and he keeps begging her to put the past behind her. As Sissie reveals through the course of her letter (which might be called an end-of-love letter as much as a love letter), Sissie is unable to maintain her relationship with her boyfriend, either physically or intellectually. The fact that her letter is never posted signifies clearly that no communication is possible. She makes it clear that history—a history inaugurated in many ways by the transatlantic slave trade and perpetuated through colonialism, as is indicated by Sissie's repeated reference to the "enslavement" of speech—has made communication even between two Ghanaians impossible because they no longer share a language that is not already tainted by history. Sissie admits that "the fact that [she] and [her boyfriend] can meet and talk at all is an advantage to the present." Nonetheless she continues, "whatever is sweet has some bitterness in it" (115). That bitterness is the fact that the language, though it connects them, still keeps them "shackled" such that even their names are not in a language they can call their own (131).

Aidoo makes it overt that it is not simply the literal ability to speak a common language that Sissie speaks of here—because of course Sissie and her boyfriend both speak English—but rather there is some hindrance to intimate language, a language of love that Sissie and her boyfriend might share, a language that could express their love and their history at the same time without conflict (116). Hortense Spillers describes the barriers to such a language that are erected as a result of the radical departures from humane ways of living that slavery engenders in this way: "Under these arrangements, the customary lexis of sexuality, including 'reproduction,' 'motherhood,' 'pleasure,' and 'desire' are thrown into unrelieved crisis."[58] The language of desire is thus undermined by the history that governs it. However, Sissie claims that "the language of love does not have to be audible. It is beyond Akan or Ewe, English or French" (113). Still, "there must be some matters which must be discussed with words. Definitely" (113). Thus, Sissie calls on her boyfriend to help her develop a "secret language. We must create this language. . . . So that we may make love with words and not fear being overheard" (116). Sissie seeks a language that not only can communicate intimate feelings and sexual desires, but one that is also able to speak the truth about the past, undeterred by events that have transpired as time blindly pressed on. Perhaps even one that might "catch up with modern versions of ancient cruelties" (116).

Sissie lists the accumulated layers of historical and contemporary cruelties:

> Burning people's farms, poisoning their rivers, and killing all their trees and plants as part of the effort to save them from a wicked philosophy.
>
> Supplying brothers with machine guns and other heavy arms because you want to stop them from slaughtering one another.
>
> Making dangerous weapons that can destroy all of the earth in one little minute in order to maintain peace.
>
> My Dear, there seem to be so many things I would like to tell you—see what I mean about language? (116)

For Sissie, love is always overdetermined by overwhelming violence; thus, successful intimacy can be created only out of a direct engagement with that violence. Nana Wilson-Tagoe argues that Sissie "is rather ambiguous about love and in fact feels that love must exist in a setting and context of politics,"[59] but it is not so much that she feels it *must* exist within that setting, but that it by necessity *does* and that lovers have to grapple with it whether they like it or not. Thus, Sissie hopes there is some way she can create a grammar of memory that can encompass both modern and ancient cruelties in a way that would liberate people in order that they might transcend this failure of intimacy.

Spillers argues that, given the collapse of language engendered by the violence of slavery, African Americans seek "1) to break apart, to rupture violently the laws of American behavior that make such a *syntax* possible; 2) to introduce a new *semantic* field/fold more appropriate to his/her own historic movement."[60] Aidoo seems to be enacting a similar invention to overcome a language that has, for centuries, described Africans as "chattel." Given the complete breakdown of gender norms, paternity and maternity, love, even language that we've seen demonstrated in her literature—a failure of all the structures of intimacy that might be taken for granted in ideal circumstances, but that she identifies as radically ruptured as a result of the slave trade and colonialism—Ama Ata Aidoo seeks to create a different grammar, a different language that might be able to describe what she experiences.

Though Sissie doesn't necessarily accomplish the creation of this language in her letter, it does seem as though Aidoo's novel has. Indeed, calling *Our Sister Killjoy* a novel minimizes what she has in fact created. By inventing a form that defies all genre boundaries, Aidoo is able to evoke all the histories that interact to create the barriers to intimacy that Sissie experiences: the slave trade, colonialism, global fascism, the postcolonial era. Aidoo does not necessarily name each one to relate a cause-and-effect or teleological narrative. However, by entangling all the iterations of violence that have intersected to create the particular historical moment in which Sissie finds herself practically impotent in all her intimate relationships, Aidoo seeks to overcome that impotence and speak in a language that averts reiterations of violence and transcends the implications of history even as its effects on the present are being witnessed.

Throughout this chapter, I have persisted in calling *Our Sister Killjoy* a novel, as do most critics and even at times Aidoo herself, though the form of *Killjoy* is not precisely what we would call a novel. Aidoo admitted that *Killjoy* makes her "unhappiest" because "it is too many words," but it is clear from the varied form of the text that Aidoo is attempting to redefine the genre she worked in, calling *Killjoy* "fiction in four episodes,"[61] and claiming she would never "describe it as a novel" herself.[62] In fact, as I have indicated within this chapter, much of *Killjoy* is written in verse. The basic novelistic narrative is written in prose style, is fairly linear in time, and presents the basic actions and dialogues of the narrative. Throughout the first three sections, however, Aidoo spontaneously breaks into verse in the midst of the narrative prose. C. L. Innes convincingly argues that Aidoo composes a mixed-genre text because it allows her to escape the constraints of traditional European genres and provides a position from which Aidoo "rewrites and reverses" colonialist representations of Africa such as that found in Conrad's *Heart of Darkness*.[63] I would add that the effect of this alternation between forms is that Aidoo performs a sort of stream-of-consciousness in which the poetry reveals the political and historical consciousness of the novel or perhaps the budding awareness of Sissie herself. It is solely through these interjections of verse that Aidoo explores the historical trajectories that lead Sissie to the moment at which she finds herself kissing Marija in Adolf's bedroom. The verse acts as a literal interruption in the narrative of the novel, and allows for an exploration of issues—both contemporary and historical—that are tangentially related to the action, expressing the implicit politics inherent in the situation explicitly explored on the page, creating a sort of political consciousness for the text.

Through this intentionally associational consciousness, Aidoo is able to highlight the silent histories that inform Sissie's experiences in the present. Kofi Owusu contends that "Aidoo mixes verse-forms with prose in her text partly because she has some very prosaic things to say about silences, but it so happens that it is verse, not prose, that is appropriately 'full of sounds and silences.'"[64] Indeed, Aidoo's poetic voice fills in those gaps with the memories of events that have been silenced and excised in official and colonial narratives of the past. If prose is the form that narrative history and official accounts of African history take, then Aidoo employs her poetry to interfere with that narrative, thereby giving a voice to those events and eras so violent that we seek to ignore and repress them though they interrupt even the most intimate of moments.

Associative but often disjunctive, lyrical but not precisely poetic, Aidoo's mixed-genre text offers an alternative to the hegemonic narrative style of the Western novel and indeed of Western and African historical discourse. She presents the historical context of the novel entirely from a position that is out of time with the narrative, as she continues to say that she recognizes the effects of the past only "from knowledge gained since" (27, 36, 51, 67, 69). This nonlinear depiction of the past reveals explicitly its presence in the present—it informs every action of the text, and is interspersed within every dialogue and every intimate moment. Aidoo avoids describing the scenes of the slave trade and colonialism as a historical narrative—even *Anowa* is simply set within the household of someone who owns slaves, but does not necessarily constitute a direct historical engagement with the past as a historical novel or epic might. Instead, she utilizes the interspersion of poetic reminiscences of past violence within the narrative of contemporary friendship and love to express the intimate relationship between the past and present, an intimacy that transcends all other intimacies. Like the other authors we have analyzed here so far, this allows Aidoo a nonnarrative, nonhegemonic means to describe how the slave trade continues to persist in contemporary life.

Aidoo is particularly committed as a writer to undoing silences, particularly those silences in West Africa regarding the slave trade and its effects on contemporary life. She herself has stated:

> I am intrigued by what processes of forgetfulness the people here used to prevent us from knowing about slaves and the slave trade because they must have done something. It is not possible that whole

populations and generations of people will be carried from one continent to another and nobody will be up and tell you about it. . . .

The oral traditions can tell you about migrations that happened about a thousand years, and yet events that happened two to three hundred years ago are completely blanketed over. Why? You know, I am interested: I am not a historian.

But definitely this is the reason why I keep coming back to this because I think it is part of what is eating us up. You can't cover up history. You know it is like a bad wound. You have to open it up and treat it.[65]

By making explicit the way the memory of past violence informs the relationship between Marija and Sissie, as well as Sissie and the rest of the world, Aidoo resists the "processes of forgetfulness" people "used" to avoid the disruptive past of the slave trade, in order to begin to think about ways she might "open up and treat" the wound of history. The wound of history is not limited to a singular injury—whether we think of that as the moment of European contact or even each iteration of a human life stolen from the continent. It is not limited even to the legacy of suffering that emanated through the West African landscape or the continued pressures on relationships between African individuals and communities. Aidoo suggests that the wound has imposed itself on the very language that African people use to describe the past, and it limits Africans' ability to speak of the horrors inflicted on the continent even to one another, thereby reducing the possibility for a restructuring of African experience, governance, economy, and intimacy. Thus, through her historical poetics, Aidoo herself creates the language that Sissie so believes must exist if we ever hope to restore intimacy and love.

As if to address the anxiety that Africans have forgotten the slave trade, Aidoo responds by suggesting that African people must find a new language if they hope to remember and to tell their own version of the story. Aidoo describes what all of the authors in this study have attempted to do with their writing; they have sought a new language—albeit metaphorical—that can express the repressed but not completely forgotten legacy of suffering that has resulted from the transatlantic slave trade. These metaphors of the slave trade—horrific as they may be—constitute a secret language of memory that communicates beyond the confines of repression, politics, history, and hegemony.

CHAPTER SIX

The Suffering of Survival

'Twas Mercy that brought me from my Pagan Land
Taught my benighted soul to understand

—Phillis Wheatley, "On Being Brought from Africa to America"

Left Behind

When African-born Phillis Wheatley was less than twenty years old, she wrote what came to be one of the most famous poems in the American literary canon, a reflection on her experience of the transatlantic slave trade. In this poem, "On Being Brought from Africa to America," she expresses her gratitude that the slave trade provided her with access to the Christian salvation and faith that she would not have had, nor indeed desired, had she remained in Africa. By utilizing the word "brought," she exposes a positive teleology for her experience of the slave trade. It simultaneously reveals her lack of agency in the process and defines as her inevitable destination the America to which she arrived, and consequently, the salvation she is guaranteed as a Christian there. Wheatley's poem provides us with an insight into the slave trade that many contemporary readers might think of as counterintuitive, as we are conditioned to understand the Middle Passage and slavery as necessarily traumatic experiences that are not to be desired and that are synonymous with devastating loss, overwhelming suffering, and often death. The nostalgia for Africa that is prevalent in African American literature from the Harlem Renaissance and onward is not obviously embraced here by Wheatley. Instead, her poem explores another view of the transatlantic slave trade, one in which the trade is understood as divine "mercy."

Though this positioning in Wheatley's poem can be understood in terms of the ideological structure of eighteenth-century American Christianity and its attendant subordination of "pagan" Africans within society, this epistemological dissonance is not completely uncommon in African thought even today. For instance, at a conference on African literatures held in Ghana in 2006, on several occasions I heard older African scholars refer to themselves as those who were "left behind" when discussing the slave trade and its effects. The poet and scholar Kwadwo Opoku-Agyemang reiterates this sentiment in the introduction to his volume of poetry titled *Cape Coast Castle* when he asks: "What of the land and the survivors [of the slave trade who were] *left behind*, the places and the people so savaged? . . . [T]ragic as the fate of all these victims is, perhaps the most horrendous experience of the victim society belonged to a group *hardly mentioned in the literature*: the damned who survived, those deprived *relatives* of the captured African."[1] A curious use of language, "left behind" might seem to imply that the Middle Passage was some longed-for journey to the Americas. In fact, the West African relationship to the slave trade can seem so conflicted that Saidiya Hartman writes, "In Ghana, they joke that if a slave ship bound for America docked off the coast today so many Ghanaians would volunteer for the passage that they would stampede one another trying to get on board."[2] Instead of indicating a desire to reach America so strong that people would be willing to endure the hardships of the slave ship, however, the use of the phrase "left behind" indicates that those who were *not* sold into servitude somehow experienced the greatest transgenerational loss; somehow they suffered to a greater extent precisely because they *survived* to see the others leave and their communities devastated by the ensuing centuries of violence and corruption.

Obviously not meant to undermine the devastating implications the slave trade held for those Africans who were actually taken away as a result of slave raids, warfare, trading, and betrayal, the linguistic turn of naming oneself as "left behind" reveals something of the ambivalent relationship that exists in West Africa regarding the transatlantic slave trade—the suffering of survival. Though seemingly paradoxical, survival necessarily meant suffering for those coastal African people whose communities and lives were often devastated by the trade. Though the violence and destruction of the slave trade is apparent, for Africans on the coast, it represented a kind of loss that engendered perhaps less predictable or less quantifiable forms of suffering for the families and neighbors of the victims, the people who were indeed "left behind." As Cathy Caruth so astutely asks, "Is the trauma the encounter with death, or the ongoing experience of surviving it?"[3] Indeed, the suffering of survival seems to haunt the rhetoric of West African discourse, as though the lost destiny is not of the salvation Wheatley described, but of the ability to escape the horror of being "left behind" to mourn.

The Suffering of Survival

What effects did the slave trade have on the populations of people who were left to suffer? How did they mourn the losses they suffered? Though there is not a significant documentary record of the forms that mourning took in the wake of slave raiding or in the shadows of the slave castles, the extraction of twelve million people from a continent and the displacement of hundreds of thousands of others surely did not go unmourned in West African cultures. In 1773, Grandy King George of Old Town begged for more reasonable men to be sent to his ports because "there is 4 of my sons gone already with Jackson and I dont want any more of them carried of by any other vausell."[4] In a letter written in Calabar to Thomas Jones in Bristol, he asks that the British slave trader look for his sons who had been pawned and then taken away in a slave ship.[5] These repeated pleas for the return of children reveal the trader's urgent concern for and inconsolable response to the departure of his family members. Even these most powerful African elites were subjected to enormous familial losses to the slave trade. For men like Grandy King George (Robin Ephraim John), an elite who participated in the trade, there was som recourse that could be taken to demand the return of their family members. However, most families were not so privileged as to have the opportunity to appeal for the retrieval of the family members they lost to the trade as these elite traders had.

Because of the nature of the loss, many of those who were "left behind" were refused the hope that they might meet their lost loved ones again in life. Ayuba Suleiman Diallo, a captive made a slave by the British, was able to return to his homeland in 1734, only to find that his family believed that "all who were sold for slaves were generally eaten or murdered, since none ever returned."[6] Given that imprisonment, torture, enslavement, murder, and cannibalism were among the terrifying fates a bereft family might imagine befell a captive, victims of the slave trade—those victims who remained in Africa—certainly mourned their losses in whatever way they could, but were likely at a loss to ritually confront the disappearance of their relatives and friends during the era of the slave trade.[7] As Stephanie E. Smallwood remarks, typically "those who disappeared into the Atlantic market . . . were never seen or heard from again," and as a result, they "were neither venerated, like the deceased, nor suspended in the balance between marginalization and integration, like local slaves, but rather consigned to an interminable purgatory."[8] Whole communities were decimated by slave raiders, children were stolen while parents were away at work, and young able-bodied people were sold, traded, and convicted into slavery. These inconceivable losses weren't necessarily thought of as permanent, nor were they in all cases understood as death. And therefore, in most communities no official outlet or ritual existed to mourn this loss.

There does not appear to be much of a record of Africans who were made captives and taken to the Americas being celebrated in elaborate funereal rituals or being lifted to the status of ancestors as the dead in most West African cultures would. This places both the victim and the bereft family members in a state of almost perpetual liminality, for as Arnold van Gennep notes in *Rites of Passage*, the funeral acts as

> a transitional period for the survivors, and they enter it through rites of separation and emerge from it through rites of integration into society (rites of the lifting of mourning). In some cases, the transitional period of the living is a counterpart of the transitional period of the deceased, and the termination of the first sometimes coincides with the termination of the second—that is, with the incorporation of the deceased into the world of the dead.[9]

But in the case of those who were lost to the slave trade, the transition to the world of the dead was not so evident, and in many cases perhaps, neither was the termination of the mourning period for those who were left behind. As J. F. Ade-Ajayi put it, "'My child is dead is infinitely more bearable than my child is missing.' When a child dies, we conduct rites, bury the child and account to the ancestors. When millions of our children were missing, and we try to avoid the subject, no rites are performed and their ghosts continue to haunt us. We need special purification rites if we are to be able to move forward."[10]

If there is little historical record of the loss people felt during the era of the slave trade, there is some evidence that people in West Africa continued to mourn the losses their ancestors suffered during the slave trade even into the twentieth century. Carolyn A. Brown studied testimonies regarding the slave trade in Igbo communities in Nigeria, where she found that "people who disappear in families leave a hole that is never filled. And this void is passed down from generation to generation."[11] Brown found that some people today openly attribute current problems in Nigeria to the effects of the transatlantic slave trade, claiming that some families have been cursed by their inappropriate participation in the trade and continue to suffer the consequences of selling their family members. In another interview, a woman reported to Brown a family story about the sale of two girls, whose disappearance caused such anguish for the girls' mother that she "was said to have cried until she went blind! She eventually died from the agony she suffered."[12] People tell that story as an explanation for the problems that family endures even today. In this particular community, people attributed great misery and suffering, both past and present, to the violence of the slave trade. These anecdotes provide some evidence as to the afterlife of the slave trade, or at the very least, its active role in the West African imagination.

What happens to people when they suffer a great loss but have no means through which to be consoled, no mechanisms by which they can ritually mourn or comprehend? And can this mourning actually continue for generations, even though the bereaved may not have experienced the loss firsthand? In regard to the continued suffering inflicted by slavery in general, the questions posed here are not new ones. Indeed, Saidiya Hartman has contemplated the same questions in the context of slavery in the Americas: "How might we understand mourning, when the event has yet to end?"[13] she wonders as she reflects upon the continued oppression of black citizens in the United States. The same question can be asked in the African context. If the economic and political changes engendered by the slave trade led to long-term demographic shifts and to a perceived devaluation of human worth, then we might argue that the mourning over the slave trade almost certainly could not have ended simply with its abolition. Just as families continue to feel a certain lack of "closure" when they are unable to bury their dead relatives, there is a sense in which the loss of at least twelve million people led generations of West Africans to seek resolution, but it seems there is no clear means of closure, and thus, the memory of the slave trade continues to haunt the imagination. When West Africans dub themselves those who were "left behind," we recognize the sense in which they suffered the immediate and incomparable loss of millions of lives, but also the way they imagine themselves to have been the perpetual survivors of that loss. Those generations who survive the trauma of the slave trade are those who are left to suffer its consequences, carry its memory, record its history, and even, as we have seen, repeat it.

Celebrating Survival?

When Saidiya Hartman traveled to Ghana to find if she could "reckon with the lives undone and obliterated in the making of human commodities"[14] during the slave trade, she found that West African people did not mourn the loss of twelve million people in the way she, as an African American, had anticipated. She concluded, as I do, that "those who stayed behind told different stories than the children of captives dragged across the sea." However, Hartman continued, "theirs wasn't a memory of loss or of captivity, but of survival and good fortune. . . . Their story of slavery was a narrative of victory, a tale of resistance and overcoming, in which the captives had been banished."[15] On hearing war chants that celebrate slave raids, Hartman unsurprisingly reels with the horror of someone who has spent years investigating the means by which people of African descent in the diaspora have managed to express their suffering in song, literature, and oral narratives. She was not prepared for the way African people distanced and protected themselves from the facts of the slave trade through taboos against discussing slave lineages, nor was she expecting the joking attitude some people took toward this gruesome history.

However, the examples of celebration she presents (as well as others that have been documented by scholars such as Adéléke Adéékó[16]) do not necessarily add up to the singularly cold, unmournful depiction of West African engagement with the slave trade that Hartman recalls encountering in *Lose Your Mother*. She is repeatedly confronted with her surprise that there were no graves she could tend and no bereaved mourners, and as a result, she argues that "theirs wasn't a memory of *loss* or of captivity, but of *survival* and good fortune."[17] Though Hartman acknowledges her personal sensitivities regarding the matter, and perhaps because of that very sensitivity, she struggles to recognize that the West African experience of the slave trade was characterized by *both survival and loss*. Hartman admits she is searching for African American forms of remembrance and ritualized mourning, but what she encounters is the fact that what we in the West call "closure" is forestalled in the African context, where the slave trade stripped people of their ability to perform final rites for people who disappeared, evidence in itself of the loss experienced by African people all along the coast.

When Hartman evokes the startling image of wanting to embrace each victim of the slave trade and whisper good-bye to them, she imagines this based, again, on the desire to memorialize those who left the coast to be taken as slaves to the Americas. She laments that "there had been no one to see them off and say I love you and we will never forget you."¹⁸ However, Hartman loses sight of all of the millions of suffering people who remained on those shores, wishing they could do just that. Even though the people she encountered did not speak of it explicitly, *loss and suffering were symptoms of survival* for many millions of people in West Africa during the period of the slave trade. Practically no one who survived lived without loss. Even the elite slave traders who profited so immensely from the trade were, as we saw with Grandy King George, sometimes plagued by the loss of their family members. The loss that Hartman experiences as an African American, then, is evidently different from that of an African, but it is not mutually exclusive of the loss that Africans experienced. Indeed, the very lack of rituals for the dead, the silence that meets her mourning, the sense of embarrassment some people feel when she mentions the slave trade, the jokes, the war songs, and the taboos—these are all signs of the long-term effects of an inexplicable encounter with a totalizing violence that has yet to be entirely worked through.

A Literature of Survival and Loss

What Hartman depicts as the callous West African celebration of survival is simply one of the ways in which West Africans have managed to incorporate the traumatic past in their narratives such that they are neither disabled by devastating loss nor unaware of its reiteration in their lives and communities. When storytellers or writers depict the slave trade, it is often through explorations of survival, but it almost always foreshadows and warns of an unfavorable reiteration of loss to come. As we have seen throughout this study, West African authors tend to mobilize the memory of the slave trade as a warning against or a reprimand for the repetition of the violence engendered by the slave trade. In Wole Soyinka's *Death and the King's Horseman*, the Praise-Singer cajoles the King's Horseman, Elesin, as he prepares himself for sacrificial suicide by saying, "In their time the great wars came and went, the little wars came and went; the white slavers came and went, they took away the heart of our race, they bore away the mind and muscle of our race. The city fell and was rebuilt; the city fell and our people trudged through mountain and forest to build a new home but—Elesin Oba do you hear me? . . . Our world was never wrenched from its true course."¹⁹ In his attempt to remind Elesin of the magnitude of his duty to follow the king into death, the Praise-Singer calls upon centuries of history as motivation. If Yoruba culture survived even the terrorizing forces of the slave trade, which deprived them of human and intellectual resources, then no threat to the power of Yoruba traditions could prevail.

The slave trade itself acts as a metaphorical reminder of the power of the Yoruba people to endure even the worst attacks upon its sovereignty, unity, and commitment to community. Though it may seem callously triumphant, the slave trade is summoned here as a means to contextualize the culture's resilience, its status as a society that has suffered its own survival. Though surviving the slave trade required much suffering—the loss of countrymen, the fall of empires, the radical displacement of people, the rebuilding of cities—Yoruba culture, and the other cultures affected by the slave trade, survived (though irrevocably altered) and would continue to survive, in spite of it, long afterward. The Praise-Singer's incantation reminds Elesin Oba and the reader that the Yoruba can face any reiteration of those crimes that may confront them precisely because of knowledge of their previous survival.

Furthermore, in contrast to the celebrations Hartman records, many of these evocations of the slave trade act as a vehicle by which African complicity can be communally discussed and denounced. In Soyinka's play, Elesin's successful completion of his suicidal duty is stalled when the British District Officer Pilkings interrupts the ceremony and imprisons the King's Horseman. He has Elesin locked inside the cellar of "the Residency," the euphemistic name given to an old slave trading post, where Pilkings remembers that "the slaves were stored before being taken down to the coast."[20] By locking Elesin inside this dungeon, Soyinka indicates the resonance between the colonial and the slave trade eras. Once again, British people are interfering with the cultural life of the Yoruba, and again they are doing so by holding Yoruba people captive. The Praise-Singer mourns Elesin's failure to resist the foreign intrusion and his own weak will, intoning, "Elesin, we placed the reins of the world in your hands yet you watched it plunge over the edge of the bitter precipice. You sat with folded arms while evil strangers tilted the world from its course and crashed it beyond the edge of emptiness. . . . Our world is tumbling in the void of strangers, Elesin."[21] The stability of the world's course is now in question, and the Praise-Singer is forced to wonder whether Elesin has single-handedly allowed the new colonizing strangers to alter the trajectory of history. There is no lack of circumspection here—even from the mouth of his very own praise-singer, Elesin's complicity in the wreckage that will result from this new incursion is magnified and censured.

Not at all a call to glorify the participation of Africans in a seeming self-betrayal, Elesin's death itself and the repetition of the praise-singer's evocation of the world tilting from its axis critiques the way British colonialism is a reiteration of slave trade violence, at the same time as he condemns African complicity in both eras. Though the Praise-Singer's very presence prohibits the possibility of amnesia regarding the brutality inflicted upon the Yoruba people during the era of the slave trade, Elesin is reprimanded for allowing that traumatic history to be replicated. Nonetheless, a celebration of survival concludes the play—the birth of a child suggests that the community will be saved from having their world completely thrown from its course. The ambivalent relationship between survival and loss is clearly revealed here.

Chinua Achebe's *Arrow of God* also depicts the triumph of African cultures over the power of the slave trade in a similarly ambivalent tone. The alliance of the six villages so central to the plot were formed, we learn at the outset of the novel, "in the very distant past," when "the hired soldiers of Abam used to strike in the dead of night, set fire to the houses and carry men, women and children into slavery."[22] A coalition was formed among the villages so that they could protect themselves from being victimized by slave raiders and traders. However, despite all warnings, it was a great challenge for the community to actively remember over time that the coalition was formed for this reason, or to mobilize it against the reenslavement of their people during the colonial period. When the colonial administration decides to build a road for their own use, they do so using unpaid labor from Umuaro, enslaving the people of the six villages even after they spent centuries in a coalition designed specifically to avoid that fate. Throughout the novel, this kind of historical repetition haunts the community, but they nonetheless persist in ignoring the desperate pleas of their highest priest, Ezeulu, who implores them to avoid entanglement with the white regime and to maintain the bonds between them that they established to protect themselves from an eerily similar adversary. Their disregard for the coalition is an allegory for the way in which repression of the memory of the slave trade has had dire consequences for African communities. Through this figuration, Achebe celebrates the mechanisms people developed to avoid their own incorporation into the slave trade, but he also reinforces the suggestion (seen time and again in West African literature) that refusal of this history makes it possible for reiterations of it to occur—and by refusing the memory, African people are complicit in that recurrence as well.

It is true indeed that, though most traces of the slave trade that we find in West African literature focus on the victims of the slave trade and those they left behind, African people are often depicted as complicit in that oppression as well. There is no question that some African people profited from the slave trade; some rare few might even be in a position, as Hartman noted, to celebrate their privilege within the system. However, representations of Africans who are the agents of oppression are not celebratory but are (perhaps at times too predictably and apologetically) critical of African participation in the recurrent violence against their own people. For the women who wage a war against unfair taxation in T. Obinkaram Echewa's *I Saw the Sky Catch Fire*, the fact that the men of their community would allow such an outrage is not surprising, as they were "mesmerized" by the white slave traders who manipulated them to leave "whatever else they were doing and begin to hunt slaves to sell to him. They kidnapped strangers and children, women and weaklings, and sold them."[23] Then, when the European traders outlawed slavery and decided to exploit the natural resources of the region, the men were ready to repeat that same behavior. And so it was again when the British concluded the women should be taxed. The exploitation of the slave trade was simply duplicated and re-duplicated, and no one was innocent. In Echewa's novel, African and British men alike participated in the replication of abuse generation after generation.

These authors are clearly not alone in their concern regarding the devastating long-term impact that the slave trade had on those West African cultures and peoples who survived the trade. In the last four chapters, we have carefully examined five major works of West African literature in terms of their engagement with the memory of the transatlantic slave trade. In every work discussed here, the slave trade is memorialized, though not necessarily in an overt or recognizable way. Individual victims are not laid to rest; ritualized ceremonies are not performed for lost children and loved ones; prayers are not said for the souls of the dead; and perpetrators are not punished. But still, this is not evidence of either the amnesia that some critics contend plagues the continent or the celebration of slave trading that Hartman encountered. Instead, the slave trade is remembered in the literature as the traces of memory embedded in the lived experiences of contemporary West African life. The authors expose the way in which any willed attempt at the refusal of remembrance or the occasional joke meant to undermine the overwhelming power of memory is not enough to impede the onslaught of its effects. And thus, the slave trade continues to reappear in the literature, in mythology and oral narratives, in metaphors and images, in whispers and gossip, to reveal the way the memory of the slave trade is not some confinable event from Africa's past, but a part of lived contemporary experience in West Africa.

The evidence collected in this study suggests that West African people have communicated and performed their grief and their suffering over generations in the shape of metaphors of the slave trade that help them to discuss, explore, and explain the traumatic memory of that era in African history. The experience that they memorialize in metaphor is even more temporally distant than what Marianne Hirsch might label "postmemory."[24] A lapse of nearly two hundred years exists between the last of the legal cargo ships holding enslaved people to leave the continent and the present day. No living survivor of the trade exists. No one is able to recall their own personal memories of suffering inflicted on them directly by callous slave traders. Still, all of the texts studied here reveal a deeply ingrained memory of the slave trade, which continues to express the suffering experienced by generations of Africans in response to the slave trade.

But this is not a literature solely born of trauma, nor does it seek to pathologize African memory, nor does it celebrate African complicity in the trade. The distinctive characteristics of trauma as we have come to describe it over the last century—the sense of amnesia or forgetting of the event itself; the latency or belatedness of the experience; the repetition, acting out, or embodiment of the traumatic event; the mourning and melancholia associated with the trauma; and the possibility for working through trauma that the psychoanalytic model suggests—are indeed all manifest in West African fictional representations of the transatlantic slave trade. However, the authors in this study clearly present a counterdiscourse to the notion that knowledge of this past and of the resultant suffering it engendered constitutes something that Africans should be ashamed of, silence, or repress. At the same time, they present no easy solutions. The authors critique slave trade violence, depict its long-term effects, and reveal contemporary reiterations of it, but do not naively contend that memory alone will heal the trauma or the failed states that indirectly resulted from it. Nonetheless, metaphors of the slave trade are activated in these texts as a vehicle, which, though painful, continues to be relevant for our understanding of the experiences of both those who were captured and those who were left behind.

EPILOGUE

The Future of the Past:

The New Historical Fiction

With the rise of African American cultural tourism, the launching of the UNESCO International Slave Routes project, the immigration of more African writers to the United States and Britain, as well as the growth of academic interest in the legacy of the slave trade, writers in the last decade (loosely the first ten years of the twenty-first century) have been even more attuned to the historical effects of the slave trade and its centrality to contemporary concerns and cultures. Wole Ogundele has correctly assessed postcolonial African literature as largely lacking a *historical novel* that explicitly depicts the era of the slave trade, writing, "Anyone interested in the historical novel cannot but be struck by the relatively small number of African novels that can be so categorized, and by the ambiguity of the contents of those few."[1] In the late twentieth century, as we have discussed, West African writers seemed to include the slave trade largely in traces and metaphors that reveal the long-term suffering exacted by the loss of twelve million people. Recently, however, that trend toward the metaphorical and away from the historical novel has changed.

In the 1990s, two novels that defied the trends described in this study were published by well-known West African authors. Ayi Kwei Armah and Syl Cheney-Coker (of Sierra Leone) wrote noteworthy novels that deal explicitly with the slave trade from the perspective of African Americans who returned to Africa to discover their ancestral homes, only to find those places unwelcoming and uncomfortable for a variety of reasons. Both novels seem to respond to the imperative espoused by the critics whose ideas launched this study—namely, the recent West African desire for an author to write historical novels that deal with the legacy of the slave trade in Africa and that respond to African American interest in and novelization of the transatlantic trade. Armah's *Osiris Rising* (1995) is a didactic take on the way the slave trade continues to haunt the relationship between African and African American people, in both their political and intimate lives, as it navigates the complicated terrain of Africa as an ancestral home for African Americans.[2] Syl Cheney-Coker's *The Last Harmattan of Alusine Dunbar* (1990) narrates the transgenerational saga of African Americans who, through a series of colonization projects, settled in what is now Sierra Leone.[3] Focused on the return of these African Americans and their invention of an Africa that was meant to serve their postslavery needs, this historical novel takes the slave trade in Africa as a foundational backdrop to the story of these colonists, but is primarily narrated as a novel of return in the postslavery era. These two texts, written by West African writers, take the African American experience of Africa as a focal point, engaging in the conversations initiated by African American neo-slave narratives and travel narratives to Africa. Still, while these texts explore the implications of the transatlantic slave trade and the "Black Atlantic" networks of knowledge that were produced by the trade and represent a transition from the metaphorized discourse studied here toward more overt engagement with the trade, these novels are not the historically grounded novels of the particularly *African experience* of the slave trade that so many critics seem to desire.

Around the same time as Armah and Cheney-Coker were writing novels of slave trade legacies, several West African poets began to take up the challenge of writing literary works that represent the African experience of the transatlantic slave trade as well. Kofi Anyidoho and Niyi Osundare both see the slave trade as part of the memory-work of their poetry. Still, as poets, their work aptly turns to oblique references and skilled metaphors that capture the image of slave trade violence on the shores of Africa. Kofi Anyidoho's poetry often depicts diaspora concerns of the Middle Passage[4] and African American anger that "your people sold ma people" and took away their "real names,"[5] but he also expresses African memories of the "Polar Bears" who "set upon our Dream and tore it into shreds."[6] Niyi Osundare's poetry echoes the "cacophony of chains"[7] and "summon[s] these scars"[8] of the "civilizing massacres of Abomey,"[9] and at last of "ankles long oblivious of the appetite of the chains."[10] Both poets recognize, as do the writers in this study, that their work "is a quest for a future alive with the energy of recovered vision, a future released from the trauma of a cyclonic past, and from the myopia of a stampeded present,"[11] but as poets, of course their language turns to metaphor and muted references, as did their fiction-writing contemporaries in the second half of the twentieth century.

Kwadwo Opoku-Agyemang, on the other hand, produced a remarkable collection of poems titled *Cape Coast Castle* in 1996, which attempts to give a voice to African people he identifies as those "left behind"[12] by the slave trade because, he claimed, "the world does not listen to silence."[13] It is no coincidence that he takes Cape Coast Castle as his focus, not only because he lives in its shadow as a resident of Cape Coast, but also because when he wrote in the mid-nineties, Cape Coast was the focal point of a surge in heritage tourism. Opoku-Agyemang's collection employs many of the same images developed by African American writers—he describes the castles and forts, the Middle Passage, the Atlantic Ocean, the sorrows of Olaudah Equiano.

Nevertheless, Opoku-Agyemang's poetry also reaches further into the interior—not simply thinking of Equiano, but of his mother as well, not only of those who embarked on slave ships but also those who were terrorized by the loss of their loved ones. In the poem "Equiano: A Mother's Song," he imagines Equiano's mother's response to the loss of her son—though she is covered in the red clay of Akan funeral mourning, she intones that she "will not be consoled."[14] In "Supplication: Equiano's Mother," she sees to the "clear bottom of torment," and wonders "Why do they not return / Those who go?"[15] His poem "Against Fear" records the long-term memory and resilient fear that remain among those African people who suffered such enormous losses to the sea. He writes:

> Thus fear the touch of water
> Simmering hot or indifferent to touch
> Fear the eddies and the storm
> The torrents and the calabash filled with tornadoes
> Fear the wave that collapses around your feet
> There is no faith in the sea
> Where my bodies were last seen
>   *   *   *
> The fashionable call to forget (O unfashionable distress!)
> Or to remember but never enough
> Fear them all, those who sing indifference
> Who live and die with the sound of nod, indifferent
> Fear lest your dawn changes its mind at night
> And take you, vein to the sea, captive again[16]

Unlike many of the authors studied in this book, Opoku-Agyemang explicitly explores the direct impact the slave trade had on its victims who remained in Africa and who suffered tremendous loss of family, love, and life nonetheless. His work is an early signal of a shift in the memorialization of the slave trade in West African fiction.

This poetic exploration of the slave trade and its implications foreshadowed the rise of a genre of historical novels that developed over the next decade. These texts deal unambiguously with the African perspective of the slave trade and its effects, and they stand in stark contrast to the metaphorical representations of the second half of the twentieth century. At least two novelists—Nigerian Obi Akwani and Ghanaian Kwakuvi Azasu—published in the first decade of the twenty-first century what literary critics would unequivocally call historical novels about the slave trade. These writers resisted the trends identified in this study, as they historically situated their characters during the period of the slave trade and took its effects on the community as the central concern of the novel. Obi Akwani's *March of Ages* (2003) is a sort of neo-slave narrative that tells the story of a village plagued by the disappearance of hundreds of people, which then focuses on the story of one who returned to tell the tale.[17] Azasu's *The Slave Raiders* (2004) vividly depicts the African communities that were eviscerated by the slave trade as well as those that resisted the trade's power.[18] In alternating sections, the novel also explores the lives of the perverse British traders whose prestige and livelihoods depended upon their deadly forays into the interior of Africa. These two novels represent what might be a sea change in the representation of the slave trade in West African literary culture.

Akwani's novel is particularly fascinating because it appears to be a deliberate heir to the traditions we have been discussing here, even as it seeks to tread the new territory of the historical novel. Akwani himself wrote that "the first challenge for literature in Africa . . . is coming to terms with the continent's heritage in slavery and colonialism,"[19] but he lamented the fact that few writers took up the challenge other than Achebe, Armah, and Ngugi. Even these writers, to Akwani's dismay, depict primarily colonialism and not slavery. Nonetheless, Akwani seems to harvest the themes that authors such as Achebe and Armah, and also Tutuola, Aidoo, and Okri employ in their depictions of the slave trade. His novel can be read as a prequel to *Things Fall Apart* or *Arrow of God* in that he sets the novel in a small Igbo village just before the era of the colonial project. The characters face some of the same concerns that Achebe's do: the timing of the harvest, the reliability of elders and religious leaders, the marriage of daughters, the childlessness of wives, the difficulties of exile, and not least, of course, the shifting economies introduced by European trade. It is here, however, that Akwani makes his mark. Insofar as he attempts to reenvision some of Achebe's work, he does so in order to infuse it with the historical context of the slave trade, which would have immediately preceded the religious and political intervention of the British that Okonkwo and his neighbors suffered. During the period described by Akwani, cowries have lost their value because of the slave trade (25), and in many ways so have the justice and faith previously associated with the Aro oracle, which has been perverted so that it serves as a tool to capture slaves (90). Akwani overtly explores the complexities of the changing economy and the complicity of Africans in it, leaving few people completely innocent and absolutely no life unaffected.

Like Tutuola's ghostly bush, Akwani's village and the trails and fields that surround it are haunted by the presence of what he calls the "dreaded menace" of the "headhunters" (45). In Akwani's historical realism, this "menace" is not a ghoulish metaphor for the horrors associated with the trade, but a terrifyingly literal group of people who threaten the village of Ozuaku and its inhabitants with kidnap, sale, and eternal exile in the Americas. He writes that "no one, not even the strongest and bravest, would want to be making their way home alone or after everyone else had left" (44). The villagers institute a sentinel system to protect the farmers from roaming raiders who might steal people as dusk settled on the fields. Families teach their children to respect the warrior class, who allow them safe passage and some modicum of security in dangerous times. People who travel to the coast tell tales of the tall ships and white people who were arriving to buy slaves from the Calabari people. "And gradually, it began to emerge that [the people who were being abducted] were being sold into an abominable kind of slavery where not only those who had offended the gods and the land, but everyone who could not defend himself, the good, the bad, the noble and the low, were sent into a fate worse than death, to a land from which it was impossible for them to find their way home. This was what chilled the hearts of all, the thought that if they were captured they would never see their beloved home again" (74). Much like the stories Obierika reports in *Things Fall Apart*, rumors spread throughout Ozuaku that it was "pale people" who took men and women to their country never to be seen again (74).

The fears that pervade much of the West African literary and storytelling tradition are present here in Akwani's novel—but this time, not in a metaphorized or muted form. Here, the fears of the slave trade are openly explored in the discussions between husbands and wives, the lessons taught to young children, the debates of the elders in the village, and the exchanges between traders stretching from the edge of the Sahara all the way to the coast. The people of Ozuaku explicitly calculate their lives in accordance with their fears, as they are terrifyingly aware of the dangerous slave raiders who lurk in their midst. Whereas Tutuola has naturalized the fear of the slave trade in the bush by revealing the way it is integrated into the oral tradition in metaphor, Akwani re-literalizes the fears, and has his characters confront the all-too-real existence of terror in the bush. He writes not of a metaphorized fear that has been passed down through the generations, but of the actual lived experience of being terrorized by kidnappers and the very practical responses the community developed to deal with them. Akwani weaves conventional stories of harvest with tales of abduction in such a way that the slave trade becomes a seamless part of the narrative—it takes shape as the absolutely conscious, relevant, and immediate context of the novel.

The slave trade becomes central even to the narrative trajectory of the novel when Ibekwe, a main character, disappears one day when he walks home alone after work despite conventional wisdom against taking such risks. Like Tutuola's and Okri's narrators, who are relegated to the status of slaves as a "body in a bag," Ibekwe, too, is "stuffed into a burlap bag, his mouth muzzled with rags and his consciousness stolen by his captors' magic" (187). His disappearance and kidnapping by slave raiders is the main conflict early in the novel and sets the stage for what is essentially a slave narrative that takes shape later in the novel when we again meet Ibekwe, whose time as a slave is elided in the narrative because of his disappearance from the community that remains central to the narrative focus.

Ibekwe's return from slavery is bittersweet, as his lover has been tormented by his disappearance and the fear that he had merely left her without a warning. Just as Samuel Crowther felt his relationship with his family had been irrevocably damaged by his enslavement, Ibekwe and Adaobi struggle to maintain their relationship after having been interrupted by the violence of the trade. For Ibekwe, his enslavement threatened the one relationship he had formed in his life on his own. For Adaobi, the slave trade took from her the opportunity to trust men and their commitment to her. She pleads with Ibekwe to understand her hesitation on his return, saying, "Do you really understand what it is like to lose someone like I lost you, to mourn him like I mourned you, even as I clung to this hope that you are still alive and will return. Do you?" (164). Adaobi was left to mourn without any real possibility for closure, and thus, even when Ibekwe returns, there still remains the scar that his disappearance and enslavement inflicted on her. Akwani unambiguously reflects on the trauma of the slave trade—the way family members of enslaved captives were left teetering in a limbo between mourning and hope, never able to complete their mourning, never able to fully believe the missing loved one was coming back. This is precisely the suffering of survival that we have been describing throughout this study.

Ibekwe was not transported to the Americas, but while he was enslaved, he did witness African captives being transported to European ships waiting at a distance from the shore at Bonny. His fellow dockworkers try to convince themselves that only those who were criminals or subversives were sold to Europeans, but Ibekwe realizes that they were all just as likely to be taken away to suffer a "slow anguished death" (171). Ibekwe's interpretation of slavery—both domestic and Atlantic—was changed on that day, and he decided that no form of slavery could be justified as punishment when the consequences were potentially so great.

More interesting than Ibekwe's transformation into an ethical thinker, however, is the response of all the men that evening as the ship departs. Akwani writes, "The feeling among the slave population that night, the lucky ones, was one of mourning. It was said that slavery in those other lands was nothing but slow anguished death and being used as human sacrifice here was better than the fate that awaited those unfortunate men and women on the boats and beyond" (171). Again, we find ourselves immersed in the complexities of West African culture that Saidiya Hartman critiques—how can people who have been so violated believe themselves to be lucky? Though this is not the celebration of the victorious slave raider, it is a mark of Akwani's willingness to explore the very complicated and ambiguous effects of the slave trade that he describes the African slaves who were left behind as both lucky and mournful. This is not necessarily a depiction of victory so much as it is a resignation to relative safety, perhaps even for just a moment.

When Ibekwe's return is later celebrated by the local griot, it is not in order to declare the community triumphant over the slave trade, but instead it serves the purpose of creating a cultural history and cultural memory that would protect them from the fate of the captives they are simultaneously mourning. Mourning and celebration, then, are not contradictions, as is evident in most West African forms of mourning in any case. While the griot sings of "the hero's struggle to escape this horrible fate," he also warns of the dangers of being brought "aboard those fearsome ships among pale men whose skins were blanched like yellow ochre, where men and women were held chained in the stinking bowels of terrible ships" (187). Indeed, this is a celebration of survival, of a refound "hero" even, but it is matched with equal mourning and pain for the loss of all those who did not return and for the fear that at any moment those who survived could also be made subject to such captivity and suffering.

Furthermore, the song ends in a mournful tone, predicting "the coming scourge of the pale people" (188). This "celebration" is undeniably mediated by the fear of the coming rise of European dominance in their region. The villagers gathered to celebrate Ibekwe's return are told to look at their own reflections in the green glass of the liquor bottles that the Europeans sold to them. As their faces become one with the weapon of their own future destruction in the mirrors of the liquor bottles, they are told to recognize in themselves "the face of a thousand sold. Innocent and guilty alike, sold into such a life of slavery and depravity that neither you nor I can describe" (188). The griot brings the community together to mourn not only for those who were lost in the past or those who had recently disappeared, but for the future that awaits them when the inevitable intrusion of European influence and subordination becomes a reality for those who were left behind.

The novel ends with an extension of that warning but in an entirely different mode. In the last scenes, Ukoha, "the high priest of Amdiaku, god of the harvest" (1), experiences a dream vision. In the dream, the only one elaborated on extensively in the novel, "a great *igbudu* (trap) had arrived and covered the whole sky over Uzuaku" (253). The trap takes him up in its tentacle-like arms, suspends him over the village, and prevents his neighbors from rescuing the high priest. From his position above the village, he could see that "their whole world seemed on the verge of change and none of them could do anything about it" (254). The evil of the trap spread like an infection in the village, pitting neighbor against neighbor, and Ukoha realized that the villages must prepare for a "descending menace" (256). What's interesting about these last few pages is that it is only here that Akwani begins to look toward the impending colonial project and its expansion into the interior that Achebe was so invested in exploring, and when Akwani depicts the colonial period, it is in abstracted and metaphorical terms. Unlike most West African authors, Akwani's main concern predates the colonial era, and is not focused on the immediacy of contemporary African problems. In fact, he reverses the usual formal gravity of the novel in such a way that it is the slave trade era to which we are directed to invest our energies and the colonial era that is metaphorized and situated in a mythical time.

Throughout the novel, Akwani makes references to the historical figures that dominated coastal trade during the period of the novel. He discusses briefly the rise and fall of Jaja, the slave who became a king; the trading empire of King Eyo Honesty II of Calabar; and the machinations of King William Koko of the Ijaw. These historical characters serve as a backdrop to this late nineteenth-century narrative and provide it the historical contextualization that many critics seek in West African fiction. The references to the changing economic climate of the late slave trade era, as Britain shifted toward securing its colonial interests, grounds Akwani's neo-slave narrative such that all that has been seen as abstracted rumors and tropes throughout the second half of the twentieth century becomes fodder for the exploration of the lives of the people who actually lived through those changes rather than those who suffered its effects generations later.

Kwakuvi Azasu similarly calls attention to his historical setting in *The Slave Raiders* by explicitly referencing historical figures and events, but instead of utilizing African history to ground his narrative in the historical world, he points to major British figures who participated in the slave trade, in particular Sir John Hawkins, a slave trader, and his cousin Sir Francis Drake, still a young boy at the time of the novel, which is set between 1565 and 1568.[20] In the novel, Bartholomé de las Casas is a central inspirational figure for the slave traders, who understood him to be the religious justification and foundation for the slave trade, in all its most brutal manifestations. The entire second book of the novel, constituting almost 150 pages, follows John Hawkins around England as he navigates the complicated social terrain of mid-sixteenth-century London politics.

If this section of the book allows England to take center stage for some time, it is not the case that England itself is allowed to be understood as the center of the world during the period. In fact, Azasu skillfully undermines the notion that England was the alpha and omega of world politics by sandwiching the British chapter between two chapters identically titled "Guinea Coast," in which the setting is explicitly the west coast of Africa and all of the action is motivated by the interests, perspectives, and agency of the Anlo people as they resist the incursion of the British "pink men." In privileging the story of the Anlo people, Azasu signals the radical epistemological upheaval he wants to enact in the text. He essentially refutes the Eurocentric notion of the triangular trade as being focalized on England, just as he undermines our historical reverence for characters such as Hawkins and Drake, valorizing instead the actions of average coastal citizens who seek to protect their homes and families and way of life. Africa is where the text begins and ends, and the African experience of the slave trade is the core concern of the novel.

The epistemological turn toward African ways of seeing the world is really what makes Azasu's novel so compelling as a historical novel. Abandoning the coded political metaphors and allegories employed by twentieth-century writers, Azasu seeks explicitly to overturn the value system that made the slave trade possible and that makes the contemporary undervaluing of African cultures and lives possible still today. Azasu doesn't merely present an image of Anlo society that upends the colonial discourse regarding African cultures; he actually reverses the polarities of primitive and civilized by pairing his valorizing portrait of the Anlo people with a scathing critique of the social conditions in England during the same period. Anlo culture before the British invaded is peaceful as a result of the good leadership of their Awomefia, who "insisted on resolving issues with neighbouring kingdoms through peaceful negotiations" (8). A well-established judicial system protects the people of the region and punishes those who disobey the law of the land.

On the other hand, England is depicted as a terrifying place without law or honor. A cruel and calculating slave trader attains knighthood despite the fact that he murders witnesses in a case against him. The church defends the man and aids him in his impunity by confirming that the impoverished (and therefore powerless) witnesses are warlocks. This conspiracy of the rich against the poor is revealed in the landscape as well—we observe London's "wretched housing conditions of the British poor," and "the most pathetic of all was the misery of the dirty urchins who scurried hungrily about the lanes, ready to snatch at the smallest crumb of mouldy bread they could sight on the rubbish heaps of the more prosperous-looking log homes" (117). The abject condition of London city life is meant to signify the larger social decay at the root of British society and is a potent reminder of the hypocrisy of British colonial discourse regarding Africa during the era of the slave trade. Azasu makes it clear that traders who deemed Africa uncivilized were themselves from a place of such misery, destitution, and class disparities that they were forced to look away, in part no doubt, as Hawkins does, because "since he had become rich, he tended to become embarrassed by the misery of the poor" (118).

Throughout the novel, Azasu cleverly reverses the valences of colonial novels, undermining as well the seemingly universal notions of beauty, knowledge, manners, law, and culture. He consistently privileges Anlo notions of beauty, overturning centuries of disparaging European judgments about the African physique. He writes of Awadada, Anlo's war leader, that "his hairy chest stood out boldly to emphasize his bravery" and that his "black lips below his huge flat nose . . . became his muscular structure splendidly. He was indeed the epitome of the perfect masculine figure among his people" (5). Azasu's appreciation of black lips and flat noses deliberately subverts the European aesthetic. On the other hand, the "pink men" are obscenely repulsive, as exemplified by the lieutenant in charge of the slave castle, Bulson, who "was as hairy as a bear and hairs grew on the back of his bear-like hands. His huge nose contrasted with his thin lips and whenever he got angry or surprised, his thin lips curled to show his rather uneven teeth which were discoloured by tobacco-smoke" (293–94). Though he is ostensibly the European equivalent to Awadada, his masculinity is figured as beastly and disgusting. Even his teeth bear the marks of his appalling habits, a habit intimately linked with the slave trade itself.

Azasu continues throughout the novel to enact these epistemological reversals, depicting British women as bloodthirsty and lascivious instead of maternal, rendering religious figures as avaricious and crude instead of inspiring, and portraying political leaders as murderers who maintain their power by any means necessary rather than unifiers who promote peace. British scientific knowledge falls short of the indigenous African knowledge, as exemplified by the fact that the British are unaware that mosquitoes can carry illness (282). Even the rotting corpses of the British soldiers smell worse than the fallen African warriors (315). Though the characters in the novel dispel the notion that Europeans were cannibals, they maintain that "they didn't eat my flesh physically, but they ate my labour," and they contend that they would rather encounter real flesh-eating cannibals (251). Azasu even utilizes the language of anthropology as a tool to mark British culture as foreign, calling the Bible "the one most sacred book in the belief system of his race" and claiming that their God is "discriminatory" because "it has a chosen people and gave birth to only one son" (254). Through this ironized voice of an anthropological observer, Azasu is able to privilege African culture and marginalize the British worldview.

The counterdiscourse that this novel produces is explicitly set amid the historical background so that the critique of British behavior, knowledge, and judgment could not possibly be ignored. Azasu's novel is an overtly political one that seeks to undermine codified Eurocentric notions of Africa and an institutionalized history of the slave trade. While his sources for Anlo history cannot provide him the abundance in terms of names and dates as the British records can, the Anlo cultural and historical perspective of the novel nonetheless allows Azasu to wage a scathing critique of some of England's most honored heroes, whose legendary glorious endeavors have to be tempered with this alternative portrait of their cruel and exploitative ventures.

What brings about such a shift in narrative structure in the early twenty-first century? Ogundele rightly wonders what historical moment would give birth to a transformation away from what he considers the suspect mythologizing of magical realism and toward a more responsible and politicized historical novel tradition in West African letters. One sign of the turning tide is the fact that in 2001, the Ghanaian Ministry of Education instituted a change in the junior secondary school curriculum that required significant lessons on the slave trade.[21] The rise in heritage tourism has no doubt highlighted the importance of the slave trade in West African history. More recently, even, African activists and leaders have begun to address the historic tragedy that took place in West Africa, but often the movement toward open public dialogue about the slave trade addresses largely African American concerns about the trade. In 1999, for instance, President Matthieu Kerekou of Benin apologized to African Americans for African complicity in the trade and lamented the continued interethnic rivalries that resulted from the trade in Africa. In 2007, President John Kufuor of Ghana made a speech suggesting that Africans should avoid ethnic and racial conflict by turning inward and considering their own complicity in the trade—a comment that was met with much rancor at home and abroad. When Kufuor used public money to build a new presidential palace and office space, he disparaged the idea that the president of a free and democratic nation should live in the shadow of the slave trade by inhabiting a former slave-trading post—this issue aroused serious debate in Ghana regarding the influence of the slave trade on contemporary politics. Despite the controversy that these comments create, the discourse regarding the slave trade is increasingly focused on the African perspective of the long-term effects of the slave trade, and engagement with the issue has begun to allow for a public debate regarding the way Africans understand, represent, and respond to the slave trade as it affected West Africans. This no doubt has an effect on the literary representation of the trade as well.

It also seems probable that the proliferation and emotional power of "Truth and Reconciliation" projects in places such as South Africa and Rwanda have had some effect on the growth of historical narration in West Africa. Some political speeches seeking to admit complicity and accept blame for the slave trade in West Africa have resulted from the drive toward mobilizing storytelling and remembrance as a political solution. It would come as no surprise, then, that literary storytelling itself would begin to reflect this form of memorialization of the past, in which the greatest criminals and the most oppressed of victims have the opportunity to either tell their own stories or have their stories told. The work to reclaim even the most painful parts of the African past has become so convincing and at the same time so pervasive that attempts to effect "healing" through literary or narrative means has nearly been mandated by the critics and authors who object to the mythologizing of Africa's past characteristic of the turn toward the magical in postcolonial fiction. Even Ben Okri, for some the exemplar of West African magical realism, has written a new novel titled *Starbook* (2007), which contends explicitly with the history of the trade and African participation in it through the depiction of imaginary confessions of those who most profited from the trade, but as is typical of Okri, the novel is still written in a mythical mode and is not a historical novel.[22] Literature that narrates the events of the past in an explicit way and that overtly confronts the complex interactions of Africans and Europeans on the coast has been embraced as a means by which a variety of contemporary problems can be wrestled with and resolved in the public sphere.

Soyinka marked the fiftieth anniversary of the independence of African nations as a moment to turn to the only commodity that "is nearly without outlay, without overheads and without any risk of sinking African nations deeper into bankruptcy, especially of the moral kind: Truth." According to Soyinka, these "unpalatable truths" can provide lessons for the future growth of the continent.[23] This new attention to the "exorcising" power of public discourse that Ogundele endorses has indeed initiated a revolution in the formal aspects of literary representation,[24] and it appears that the *future of the past* will follow a trend toward historical narratives that will explicitly interrogate the slave trade past and its centrality to the narrative of West Africa's long history.

While the turn toward historical novelization, perhaps exemplified best by Akwani's and Azasu's novels, does indeed incorporate historical figures and events into the fictional world of the text, these novels intriguingly shift attention away from the exploration of the *function* of the past in contemporary African life that was so characteristic of the earlier metaphorized depictions of the slave trade. These new historical novels localize slavery in the past, and though they point toward the way the slave trade led to the onslaught of colonialism, they anchor the trade's effects in the lived experiences of the people of the generations who directly experienced it. While this shift toward the historical novel affords Akwani the space in which to expose the effects of the slave trade—on both those who were its victims and those who were complicit in it—it loses some of the efficacy of the earlier texts to make a larger critique of the long-term effects of the trade. While it is not at all worthwhile to privilege one formal strategy over the other, what remains fascinating about the fragmented, fleeting, and metaphorical means by which Tutuola, Okri, Armah, and Aidoo (as well as the other authors discussed in this study) approach the slave trade in their writing is that it opens up possibilities for recognizing that the slave trade was not a singular experience, nor was it a confinable era. These novels indicate that the slave trade past informs the everyday lives of people long after the last human life was exchanged for guns and alcohol on the coast. For the novels discussed at length in this study do not seek to analyze the historical motivations and psyches of those ancestors past—even when set during the period of the slave trade, as Aidoo's *Anowa* is. What they seek to do is to represent the unique ways West Africans in the twentieth century have managed to survive and remember the suffering inflicted by the slave trade over the course of several centuries and well into the twenty-first century. And though that story may be told obliquely, it would be a mistake not to take heed.

NOTES

Introduction

1. Voyages: The Trans-Atlantic Slave Trade Database, http://www.slavevoyages.org.
2. Ibid.
3. For extended discussions of the significance as well as the limitations of demographic calculations of the slave trade, see David Eltis, Stephen D. Behrendt, David Richardson, and Herbert S. Klein, introduction to *The Trans-Atlantic Slave Trade: A Database on CD-Rom* (Cambridge: Cambridge University Press, 1999), 1–40; David Eltis and David Richardson, eds., *Extending the Frontiers: Essays on the New Transatlantic Slave Trade Database* (New Haven, CT: Yale University Press, 2008); Martin A. Klein, "The Impact of the Atlantic Trade on the Societies of the Western Sudan," in *The Atlantic Slave Trade: Effects on Economies, Societies, and Peoples in Africa, the Americas, and Europe*, ed. Joseph E. Inikori and Stanley L. Engerman (Durham, NC: Duke University Press, 1992), 25–48.
4. Carolyn A. Brown, "Epilogue: Memory as Resistance: Identity and the Contested History of Slavery in Southeastern Nigeria, an Oral History Project," in *Fighting the Slave Trade: West African Strategies*, ed. Sylviane A. Diouf (Athens: University of Ohio Press, 2003), 220.
5. William H. Clarke, *Travels and Explorations in Yorubaland, 1854–1858* (Ibadan, Nigeria: Ibadan University Press, 1972), 6.
6. Patrick Manning, *Slavery and African Life: Occidental, Oriental, and African Slave Trades* (Cambridge: Cambridge University Press, 1990), 2.
7. Joseph E. Inikori, "Changing Commodity Composition of Imports into West Africa, 1650–1850," in *The Transatlantic Slave Trade: Landmarks, Legacies, Expectations*, ed. James Kwesi Anquandah (Accra, Ghana: Sub-Saharan Publishers, 2007), 75.
8. See, for instance, Elisée Soumonni, "Lacustrine Villages in South Benin as Refuges from the Slave Trade," in *Fighting the Slave Trade: West African Strategies*, ed. Sylviane A. Diouf (Athens: Ohio University Press, 2003), 3–14.
9. Inikori and Engerman, *The Atlantic Slave Trade*, 3.

Chapter 1: Against Amnesia

1. Elaine Scarry, *The Body in Pain: The Making and Unmaking of the World* (New York: Oxford University Press, 1985), 16–17.
2. Rosalind Shaw, *Memories of the Slave Trade: Ritual and the Historical Imagination in Sierra Leone* (Chicago: University of Chicago Press, 2002).
3. Nicolas Argenti, *The Intestines of the State: Youth, Violence, and Belated Histories in the Cameroon Grassfields* (Chicago: University of Chicago Press, 2007).
4. Luise White, *Speaking with Vampires: Rumor and History in Colonial Africa* (Berkeley: University of California Press, 2000).
5. Kwesi J. Anquandah, *Castles and Forts of Ghana* (Atalante: Ghana Museums and Monuments Board, 1999), 24.
6. Kufuor's commissioning speech for Golden Jubilee House describes the taint of the slave trade on the president's residence. For a full recording of the speech, see "Kufuor Commissions Golden Jubilee House," ModernGhana.com, November 11, 2008, http://www.modernghana.com/news/190243/1/kufuor-commissions-golden-jubilee-house.html. See also the newspaper debates about the building of the Golden Jubilee House: Kofi Akosah-Sarpong, "The Golden Jubilee House, A Spiritual Relief," ModernGhana.com, November 26, 2008, http://www.modernghana.com/news/192256/50/the-golden-jubilee-house-a-spiritual-relief.html.
7. See Anquandah, *Castles and Forts*; and Godwin K. Agbodza and Raymond O. Agbo, *Monuments and Historical Landmarks Along the Coast* (Cape Coast: Nyakod, 2006). Recently, however, many of these buildings have been turned over to the Ghana Museums and Monuments Board and are being renovated, largely with UNESCO support. Others are ironically being privately remodeled to serve as guesthouses or restaurants.
8. For a description of the debates from a representative of the Smithsonian, see Christine Mullen Kreamer, "The Politics of Memory: Ghana's Cape Coast Castle Museum Exhibition 'Crossroads of People, Crossroads of Trade,'" *Ghana Studies* 7 (2004): 79–91; and Kreamer, "Shared Heritage, Contested Terrain: Cultural Negotiations and Ghana's Cape Coast Castle Museum Exhibition 'Crossroads of People, Crossroads of Trade,'" in *Museum Frictions: Public Cultures/Global Transformations*, ed. Ivan Karp, Corinne A. Kratz, Lynn Szwaja, and Tomás Ybarra-Frausto (Durham, NC: Duke University Press, 2006), 425. For the position of an African American expatriate who was involved in the debate, see Imakhus Vienna Robinson, "Is the Black Man's History Being Whitewashed?" *Uhuru* 9 (1994): 48–50. For anthropological and academic responses, see Edward M. Bruner, "Tourism in Ghana: The Representation of Slavery and the Return of the Black Diaspora," *American Anthropologist* 98, no. 2 (June 1996): 290–304; Brempong Osei-Tutu, "African American Reactions to the Restoration of Ghana's 'Slave Castles,'" *Public Archaeology* 3 (2004): 195–204; and Sandra Richards, "What Is to Be Remembered?: Tourism to Ghana's Slave Castle-Dungeons," *Theatre Journal* 57, no. 4 (December 2005): 617–37.
9. Pierre Nora, "Between Memory and History: Les Lieux de Mémoire," *Representations* 26 (Spring 1989): 7.

10. For a discussion that questions the veracity of the claims typically made in the tour narratives, see Brempong Osei-Tutu, "Slave Castles, African American Activism, and Ghana Memorial Entrepreneurism" (PhD diss., Syracuse University, 2009), 143, 155.

11. Bayo Holsey, *Routes of Remembrance: Refashioning the Slave Trade in Ghana* (Chicago: University of Chicago Press, 2008), 6.

12. Amissane Hackman, guided tour, May 23, 2006, Cape Coast Castle, Cape Coast, Ghana.

13. Philip Atta-Yawson, guided tour, Fort Amsterdam, Abandze, Ghana, May 27, 2006.

14. Anne C. Bailey, *African Voices of the Atlantic Slave Trade: Beyond the Silence and the Shame* (Boston: Beacon Press, 2005), 33.

15. Mahommah Gardo Baquaqua, *The Biography of Mahommah G. Baquaqua, a Native of Zoogoo, in the Interior of Africa* (Detroit: George E. Pomeroy, 1854), 34–35.

16. Philip Atta-Yawson, phone interview, January 6, 2011.

17. Guided tour, May 25, 2006, Fort Batenstein, Butre, Ghana.

18. Atta-Yawson, tour, 2006.

19. Guided tour, June 20, 2001, Fort Metal Cross, Dixcove, Ghana.

20. This study focuses entirely upon the representation of the transatlantic slave trade in West African fiction and only touches upon the issue of domestic African slavery or the trans-Saharan slave trade when it is significant to an author's depiction of transatlantic slavery. While domestic slavery is a significant concern of West African authors such as Buchi Emecheta and Amma Darko, the practice and its representation are quite different from depictions of the transatlantic slave trade and, therefore, fall outside the purview of this study. Likewise, the depiction of African American slaves returning to Africa, such as in Syl Cheney-Coker's work *The Last Harmattan of Alusine Dunbar* (New York: Heinemann, 1990), produces an entirely different set of images and themes that would be better discussed in a different study. Though some of these texts will be referenced in this study, the literature that represents the transatlantic slave trade is so diverse and vast that this study will concentrate specifically upon African experiences and representations of the transatlantic slave trade almost exclusively.

21. I will discuss a radical shift in this trend that occurs in the early twenty-first century in the epilogue of this book. One extraordinarily interesting twentieth-century exception is Beninois writer Paul Hazoumé's 1938 French-language novel *Doguicimi* (Washington, DC: Three Continents Press, 1990), in which a young heroine uncovers the fact that the hidden depths of corruption in her hometown are fueled by the European trade on the coast. This study concentrates on Anglophone writing in part because of the enormous difference in traditions that grew out of the various colonial experiences. However, as Robin Law notes, even Hazoumé's remarkable historical novel gives only a nod to the fact that slaves are being traded on the coast. As Law argues, what was more interesting was what the king of Dahomey was receiving in the trade—guns. Robin Law, "The Atlantic Slave Trade in Local History Writing in Ouidah," in *Africa and Trans-Atlantic Memories: Literary and Aesthetic Manifestations of Diaspora and History*, ed.

Naana Opoku-Agyemang, Paul E. Lovejoy, and David V. Trotman (Trenton, NJ: Africa World Press, 2008), 260–61.

22. For a discussion of Francophone representations of the slave trade, see Christopher L. Miller, *The French Atlantic Triangle: Literature and Culture of the Slave Trade* (Durham, NC: Duke University Press, 2008).

23. George Lakoff and Mark Johnson, *Metaphors We Live By* (Chicago: University of Chicago Press, 1980), 193.

24. Ato Quayson, *Calibrations: Reading for the Social* (Minneapolis: University of Minnesota Press, 2003), 87.

25. Nicolas Argenti and Katharina Schramm, eds., *Remembering Violence: Anthropological Perspectives on Intergenerational Transmission* (New York: Berghahn Books, 2010), 19.

26. Shaw, *Memories of the Slave Trade*, 22.

27. See, for instance (on Emecheta), Ikem Stanley Okoye, "The Representation of Slavery at Bonny and Asaba: The Traditional Visual Arts Interrogate Modern Literature," in Opoku-Agyemang, Lovejoy, and Trotman, *Africa and Trans-Atlantic Memories*, 65–66; and (on Armah) Benaouda Lebdai, "Armah's Obsessions with the 'Middle Passage': Reality and Symbols," in Opoku-Agyemang, Lovejoy, and Trotman, *Africa and Trans-Atlantic Memories*, 405–16.

28. Chinua Achebe, *Things Fall Apart* (New York: Anchor Books, 1994), 141.

29. Buchi Emecheta, *The Slave Girl* (New York: George Braziller, 1977), 26.

30. Ayi Kwei Armah, *Two Thousand Seasons* (Oxford: Heinemann, 1973), 204.

31. Ibid., 15.

32. Ibid., 2.

33. Ibid., 171.

34. Ibid., 204.

35. Quayson, *Calibrations*, xv.

36. Jennifer Wenzel, *Bulletproof: Afterlives of Anticolonial Prophecy in South Africa and Beyond* (Chicago: University of Chicago Press, 2009), 6, my emphasis.

37. Marcus Wood, *Blind Memory: Visual Representations of Slavery in England and America, 1780–1865* (New York: Routledge, 2000), 11.

38. Femi Osofisan, *The Oriki of a Grasshopper and Other Plays* (Washington, DC: Howard University Press, 1995), 13.

39. F. Odun Balogun, *Adjusted Lives: Stories of Structural Adjustments* (Trenton, NJ: Africa World Press, 1995), 13–15.

40. Ibid., 97.

41. Lakoff and Johnson, *Metaphors We Live By*, 163.

42. Paul Ricoeur, *The Rule of Metaphor: Multi-Disciplinary Studies of the Creation of Meaning in Language* (Toronto: University of Toronto Press, 1975), 197.

43. See, for instance, Emmanuel Akyeampong, "History, Memory, Slave-Trade and Slavery in Anlo (Ghana)," *Slavery and Abolition* 22 (2001): 1–24; Bailey, *African Voices of the Atlantic Slave Trade*; Shaw, *Memories of the Slave Trade*; and Argenti, *Intestines of the State*.

44. Achille Mbembe, "African Modes of Self-Writing," *Public Culture* 14, no. 1 (2002): 259.

45. Ibid., 260.

46. Bogumil Jewsiewicki and Valetin Y. Mudimbe, "Africans' Memories and Contemporary History of Africa," *History and Theory* 32 (1993): 1.

47. Ibid., 9.

48. Ibid., 10.

49. Kwadwo Opoku-Agyemang, "A Crisis of Balance: The (Mis)Representation of Colonial History and the Slave Experience as Themes in Modern African Literature," in *Nationalism vs. Internationalism: (Inter)National Dimensions of Literatures in English*, ed. Wolfgang Zach and Ken L. Goodwin (Tübingen, Germany: Stauffenburg Verlag, 1996), 219.

50. Mbembe, "African Modes," 260.

51. Akyeampong. "History, Memory, Slave-Trade and Slavery," 1.

52. Martin A. Klein, "Studying the History of Those Who Would Rather Forget: Oral History and the Experience of Slavery," *History in Africa* 16 (1989): 211.

53. See Stephen D. Behrendt, A. J. H. Latham, and David Northrup, eds., *The Diary of Antera Duke, an Eighteenth-Century African Slave Trader* (New York: Oxford University Press, 2010).

54. Law, "The Atlantic Slave Trade," 269.

55. Klein, "Studying the History," 209.

56. Holsey, *Routes of Remembrance*, 56–57.

57. Ibid., 143–44.

58. Ibid., 122–48.

59. Theodor W. Adorno, "What Does Coming to Terms with the Past Mean?" in *Bitburg in Moral and Political Perspective*, ed. Geoffrey H. Hartman (Bloomington: Indiana University Press, 1986), 115.

60. Ibid.

61. Mbembe, "African Modes," 260.

62. Wole Ogundele, "Devices of Evasion: The Mythic Versus the Historical Imagination in the Postcolonial African Novel," *Research in African Literatures* 33, no. 3 (Fall 2002): 137.

63. Rosalind Shaw, "Afterword: Violence and the Generation of Memory," in *Remembering Violence: Anthropological Perspectives on Intergenerational Transmission*, ed. Nicolas Argenti and Katharina Schramm (New York: Berghahn Books, 2010), 259.

64. Ibid., 253.

65. Argenti and Schramm, *Remembering Violence*, 12.

66. Argenti, *Intestines of the State*, 22.

67. Hayden White, *The Content of the Form: Narrative Discourse and Historical Representation* (Baltimore: Johns Hopkins University Press, 1987), 5–6.

68. Toni Morrison, "The Site of Memory," *Inventing the Truth: The Art and Craft of Memoir*, ed. William Zinsser (Boston: Houghton Mifflin, 1987), 124.

69. For discussion of the notion of a "usable past" in the literature of the Americas, see Lois Parkinson Zamora, *The Usable Past: The Imagination of History in Recent Fiction of the Americas* (Cambridge: Cambridge University Press, 1997).

70. See Bernard W. Bell, *The Afro-American Novel and Its Tradition* (Amherst: University of Massachusetts Press, 1987); Ashraf H. A. Rushdy, *Neo-Slave Narratives: Studies in the Social Logic of a Literary Form* (New York: Oxford University Press, 1999); George B. Handley, *Post-Slavery Literatures in the Americas: Family Portraits in Black and White* (Charlottesville: University Press of Virginia, 2000); and Timothy J. Cox, *Postmodern Tales of Slavery in the Americas: From Alejo Carpentier to Charles Johnson* (New York: Garland, 2001).

71. See, for instance, Aimé Césaire, *Notebook of a Return to the Native Land*, trans. and ed. Clayton Eshleman and Annette Smith (1949; Middletown, CT: Wesleyan University Press, 2001); Edward Kamau Brathwaite, *The Arrivants: A New World Trilogy* (Oxford: Oxford University Press, 1973); and Brathwaite, *Middle Passages* (New York: New Directions, 1992); Alejo Carpentier, *Explosion in a Cathedral* (New York: Farrar, Straus and Giroux, 1962); Miguel Barnet, *Biography of a Runaway Slave*, trans. W. Nick Hill (New York: Pantheon, 1994); Derek Walcott, *Omeros* (New York: Farrar, Straus and Giroux, 1990); and Maryse Condé, *I, Tituba, Black Witch of Salem* (New York: Ballantine, 1992).

72. Eduoard Glissant, *Caribbean Discourse: Selected Essays*, trans. J. Michael Dash (Charlottesville: University of Virginia Press, 1989), 133, 144.

73. Handley, *Post-Slavery Literatures*, 5.

74. Paul Gilroy, *The Black Atlantic: Modernity and Double Consciousness* (Cambridge, MA: Harvard University Press, 1993), 4.

75. Ibid., 4, my emphasis.

76. Paul Tiyambe Zeleza, "Rewriting the African Diaspora: Beyond the Black Atlantic," *African Affairs* 104, no. 414 (2005): 37. For critiques of Gilroy's omission of Africa in his formulation of the black Atlantic, see also Joan Dyan, "Paul Gilroy's Slaves, Ships, and Routes: The Middle Passage as Metaphor," *Research in African Literatures* 27, no. 4 (Winter 1996): 7–14; Michael J. C. Echeruo, "An African Diaspora: The Ontological Project," in *The African Diaspora: African Origins and New World Identities*, ed. Isidore Okpewho, Carole Boyce Davies, and Ali A. Mazrui (Bloomington: Indiana University Press, 1999), 3–18; Laura Chrisman, "Rethinking Black Atlanticism," *Black Scholar* 30, nos. 3–4 (2000): 12–17; and Charles Piot, "Atlantic Aporias: Africa and Gilroy's Black Atlantic," *South Atlantic Quarterly* 100, no. 1 (2001): 155–70.

77. Orlando Patterson, *Slavery and Social Death: A Comparative Study* (Cambridge, MA: Harvard University Press, 1982), 38.

78. In Toni Morrison's *Beloved* (New York: Penguin, 1987), for instance, the ghostly character of Beloved seemingly dies and is born again in the figurative space of the slave ship.

79. F. Abiola Irele, *The African Imagination: Literature in Africa and the Black Diaspora* (Oxford: Oxford University Press, 2001), 54–56.

80. Holsey, *Routes of Remembrance*, 59.

81. Ogundele, "Devices of Evasion," 131.

82. Chinua Achebe, *Morning Yet on Creation Day: Essays* (New York: Anchor Press, 1975), 71–72.

83. Stephanie Newell, *West African Literatures: Ways of Reading* (Oxford: Oxford University Press, 2006), 28 (on Negritude's influence); 88 (on Achebe's cultural nationalism); 125 (on second-generation adoption of oral forms).

84. Tim Woods, *African Pasts: Memory and History in African Literatures* (Manchester, UK: Manchester University Press, 2007), 6.

85. Ibid., 5.

86. Ayi Kwei Armah, "Don't Mention Slavery," *New African* (July 2006), http://goliath.ecnext.com/coms2/gi_0199-5788357/Don-t-mention-slavery-Special.html.

87. See, for instance, Derek Wright, "Ayi Kwei Armah and the Significance of His Novels and Histories," *International Fiction Review* 17, no. 1 (Winter 1990): 36; and Hugh Webb, "The African Historical Novel and the Way Forward," *African Literature Today* 11 (1980): 34–35.

88. Maureen N. Eke, "Diasporic Ruptures and (Re)membering History: Africa as Home and Exile in *Anowa* and *The Dilemma of a Ghost*," in *Emerging Perspectives on Ama Ata Aidoo*, ed. Ada Uzoamaka Azodo and Gay Wilentz (Trenton, NJ: Africa World Press, 1999), 64–66.

89. See Mildred A. Hill-Lubin, "Ama Ata Aidoo and the African Diaspora: Things 'All Good Men and Women Try to Forget,' But I Will Not Let Them," in Azodo and Wilentz, *Emerging Perspectives*, 45–60; and Angeletta KM Gourdine, "Slavery in the Diaspora Consciousness: Ama Ata Aidoo's Conversations," in Azodo and Wilentz, *Emerging Perspectives*, 27–44.

90. Adéléké Adéèkó, *The Slave's Rebellion: Literature, History, Orature* (Bloomington: Indiana University Press, 2005).

91. Julia Sun-Joo Lee, *The American Slave Narrative and the Victorian Novel* (New York: Oxford University Press, 2010), 19.

92. Ogundele, "Devices of Evasion," 137n10.

93. Ricoeur, *The Rule of Metaphor*, 185.

94. Holsey, *Routes of Remembrance*, 16.

Chapter 2: Magical Capture in a Landscape of Terror

1. Olaudah Equiano, *The Interesting Narrative of the Life of Olaudah Equiano, or Gustavus Vassa, the African, Written by Himself*, ed. Werner Sollors (New York: Norton, 2001), 32. Future references to this work will be indicated parenthetically and will cite this particular edition.

Some scholars argue that at such a temporal and geographical distance as Equiano was when he wrote his narrative, he could not have remembered in such detail the nature of commerce and warfare in the region. For claims that the African portions of Equiano's narrative may have some falsified or misremembered details, see Vincent Carretta, *Equiano, the African: Biography of a Self-Made Man* (Athens: University of Georgia Press, 2005). Regardless of Carretta's scrutiny of Equiano's naval records and naming strategies,

Equiano's description of the raids on the coast are quite accurate representations of the way the trade operated and are supported by Africanist scholars of the trade. For the most convincing and thorough critique of Carretta's stance, see Paul E. Lovejoy, "Autobiography and Memory: Gustavus Vassa, alias Olaudah Equiano, the African," *Slavery and Abolition* 27, no. 3 (December 2006): 317–47. See also Angelo Costanza, *Surprizing Narrative:Olaudah Equiano and the Beginnings of Black Autobiography* (Westport, CT: Greenwood Press, 1987), in which Costanza argues that though Equiano does utilize Anthony Benezet's work for his opening chapter and cites him, the second chapter in which he describes his capture is certainly a memory of his own experiences. See also Sylviane A. Diouf, ed., *Fighting the Slave Trade: West African Strategies* (Athens: Ohio University Press, 2003), for evidence regarding children and others resisting the trade. Furthermore, it can be argued that such a traumatic experience would no doubt leave a permanent impression on Equiano's memory and could, therefore, be remembered quite vividly.

2. G. I. Jones, "Olaudah Equiano: Introduction," in *Africa Remembered: Narratives by West Africans from the Era of the Slave Trade*, ed. Philip D. Curtin (Madison: University of Wisconsin Press, 1968), 67.

3. Joseph C. Miller, *Way of Death: Merchant Capitalism and the Angolan Slave Trade, 1730–1830* (Madison: University of Wisconsin Press, 1988), 380.

4. Amos Tutuola, *The Palm-Wine Drinkard and My Life in the Bush of Ghosts* (New York: Grove, 1994), 70. Future references to this work will be indicated parenthetically and will cite this particular edition.

5. See Bernth Lindfors, *Critical Perspectives on Amos Tutuola* (Washington, DC: Three Continents Press, 1975), for an extensive collection of reviews of *My Life*.

6. For example, David Byrne, the lead singer of the 1970s and '80s post–punk rock band Talking Heads, and Brian Eno made a collaborative concept album titled *My Life in the Bush of Ghosts* (Warner Brothers, 1981). The contemporary artist Neil Roberts created a series of paintings and drawings thematically conceived as a reflection on *My Life* and utilizing the distinctive chapter titles of Tutuola's novel, such as "On the Queer Way to Homeward" and "Invisible Magnetic Missive Sent to Me from Home." A gallery of these works can be found at his website: http://www.neilroberts.com.au/checklist.asp?fID=253.

7. Harold R. Collins, "Founding a New National Literature: The Ghost Novels of Amos Tutuola," in Lindfors, *Critical Perspectives on Amos Tutuola*, 64.

8. David Whittaker, "Realms of Liminality: The Mythic Topography of Amos Tutuola's *Bush of Ghosts*," *SOAS Literary Review* 3 (Spring 2001): 16.

9. Oyekan Owomoyela, *Amos Tutuola Revisited* (New York: Twayne Publishers, 1999), 25.

10. Ato Quayson, *Strategic Transformations in Nigerian Writing: Orality and History in the Work of Rev. Samuel Johnson, Amos Tutuola, Wole Soyinka, and Ben Okri* (Bloomington: Indiana University Press, 1997), 55.

11. Olatunji Ojo, "The Organization of the Atlantic Slave Trade in Yorubaland, ca. 1777 to ca. 1856," *International Journal of African Historical Studies* 41, no. 1 (2008): 77–78;

and Kristin Mann, *Slavery and the Birth of an African City: Lagos, 1760–1900* (Bloomington: University of Indiana Press, 2007), 39.

12. Mann, *Slavery*, 40.

13. Ibid., 40–44.

14. Ibid., 35.

15. Ojo, "The Organization of the Atlantic Slave Trade," 80.

16. Mann, *Slavery*, 51.

17. Samuel Johnson, *The History of the Yorubas: From the Earliest Times to the Beginning of the British Protectorate* (London: Routledge, 1966), 225–26; and Toyin Falola and Ann Genova, eds., *Historical Dictionary of Nigeria* (Lanham, MD: Scarecrow Press, 2009), s.v. "Abeokuta."

18. Patrick Manning, *Slavery and African Life: Occidental, Oriental, and African Slave Trades* (Cambridge: Cambridge University Press, 1990), 68–69.

19. While there is certainly an undeniable fear of the forest in literature, oral narratives, and mythologies all over the world, the analysis presented here is invested in the way Tutuola's particular manifestation of that fear is informed by the specific history, experience, and memory of slave raids in West Africa.

20. Rev. Geoffrey Parrinder, foreword to Tutuola, *The Palm-Wine Drinkard*, 10.

21. Brenda Cooper, *Magical Realism in West African Fiction: Seeing with a Third Eye* (London: Routledge, 1998), 41.

22. Isidore Okpewho, *African Oral Literature: Backgrounds, Character, and Continuity* (Bloomington: Indiana University Press, 1992), 110.

23. For an extended debate of Tutuola's demerits, see the chapter titled "The Controversy in West Africa" in Lindfors, *Critical Perspectives on Amos Tutuola*, 27–44.

24. Quayson, *Strategic Transformations*, 62.

25. F. Abiola Irele, *The African Experience in Literature and Ideology* (Bloomington: Indiana University Press, 1981), 178.

26. Jonathan A. Peters, "English-Language Fiction from West Africa," in *A History of Twentieth-Century African Literatures*, ed. Oyekan Owomoyela (Lincoln: University of Nebraska Press, 1993), 23.

27. Afolabi Afolayan, "Languages and Sources of Amos Tutuola," in Lindfors, *Critical Perspectives on Amos Tutuola*, , 206.

28. Walter J. Ong, *Orality and Literacy: The Technologizing of the Word* (London: Routledge, 1982), 148.

29. Quayson, *Strategic Transformations*, 46.

30. Rosalind Shaw, *Memories of the Slave Trade: Ritual and the Historical Imagination in Sierra Leone* (Chicago: University of Chicago Press, 2002), 11.

31. It is no coincidence that none of these are the white or "skinless," cannibalistic ghosts Equiano (and other slave narrators) describes when he meets European traders on the coast. The slave raiders who attacked the young narrator and his brother in the bush are African, thus the living dead of the bush are sometimes unidentifiable ghosts but are also sometimes people who look just like the narrator and his family; sometimes they are even

his family members. This reflects the memory of those African raiders who invaded small towns in the interior in search of wealth in the form of human chattel.

32. Diana Mafe, "'A Wilderness of the Mind': Representations of the Bush in Yoruba Fiction" (paper presented at Eco-Imagination: African Diasporan Literatures and Sustainability, Annual African Literature Association Conference, Tucson, Arizona, March 10–14, 2010).

33. Gilles Deleuze and Felix Guattari, *A Thousand Plateaus: Capitalism and Schizophrenia* (Minneapolis: University of Minnesota Press, 1987), 446.

34. Roger D. Abrahams, "The Disobedient Sisters," in *African Folktales: Traditional Stories of the Black World* (New York: Pantheon, 1983), 143–44.

35. Christian G. A. Oldendorp, *Historie der caribischen Inseln Sanct Thomas, Sanct Crux und Sanct Jan, inbesondere der dasigen Neger und der Mission der evangelischen Brüder under denselben*, ed. Gudrun Meier, Stephan Palmié, Peter Stein, and Horst Ulbricht, vol. 1 (Berlin: Verlag für Wissenschaft und Bildung, 2000–2002), 483. Translated for the author by Silke Brodersen. I thank John Thornton for pointing out this passage to me.

36. Naana Jane Opoku-Agyemang, "The Living Experience of the Slave Trade in Sankana and Gwollu: Implications for Tourism," in *The Transatlantic Slave Trade: Landmarks, Legacies, Expectations*, ed. James Kwesi Anquandah (Accra, Ghana: Sub-Saharan Publishers, 2007), 219.

37. D. O. Fagunwa, *The Forest of a Thousand Daemons: A Hunter's Saga*, trans. Wole Soyinka (London: Nelson, 1982), 61.

38. Amos Tutuola, *Simbi and the Satyr of the Dark Jungle* (San Francisco: City Lights Books, 1955), 13(kidnapped); 15 (made slaves); 127–34 (carried in sacks).

39. Ben Okri, *The Famished Road* (New York: Anchor Books, 1991), 110–11.

40. Emmanuel N. Obiechina, *Language and Theme: Essays on African Literature* (Washington, DC: Howard University Press, 1990), 36.

41. Ibid., 37.

42. Achille Mbembe, "Life, Sovereignty, and Terror in the Fiction of Amos Tutuola," *Research in African Literatures* 34, no. 4 (Winter 2003): 1.

43. Sigmund Freud, "Mourning and Melancholia," in *The Standard Edition of the Complete Psychological Works of Sigmund Freud*, ed. James Strachey, vol. 14 (London: Hogarth, 1953–1973), 243.

44. Sigmund Freud, "Analysis of a Phobia in a Five-year-old Boy," in *Standard Edition*, vol. 10, 122.

45. Alessia Ricciardi, *The Ends of Mourning: Psychoanalysis, Literature, Film* (Stanford, CA: Stanford University Press, 2003), 21.

46. Robert Elliot Fox, "Tutuola and the Commitment to Tradition," *Research in African Literatures* 29 (1998): 207.

47. Ong, *Orality and Literacy*, 97.

48. Marianne Hirsch, *Family Frames: Photography, Narrative, and Postmemory* (Cambridge, MA: Harvard University Press, 1997), 243.

49. Fox, "Tutuola and the Commitment," 207.

Chapter 3: Geographies of Memory

1. In his narrative, Baquaqua's hometown is spelled Zoogoo, but according to scholars Robin Law and Paul E. Lovejoy, his hometown is most probably the present-day town of Djougou. Robin Law and Paul E. Lovejoy, eds., *The Biography of Mahommah Gardo Baquaqua: His Passage from Slavery to Freedom in Africa and America* (Princeton, NJ: Marcus Weiner, 2001), 17.

2. Mahommah Gardo Baquaqua, *The Biography of Mahommah G. Baquaqua, a Native of Zoogoo, in the Interior of Africa* (Detroit: George E. Pomeroy, 1854), 32. Future references to this work will be indicated parenthetically and will cite this particular edition.

3. Anne C. Bailey, *African Voices of the Atlantic Slave Trade: Beyond the Silence and the Shame* (Boston: Beacon Press, 2005), 33.

4. Allan D. Austin, *African Muslims in Antebellum America: Transatlantic Stories and Spiritual Struggles* (London: Routledge, 1997), 159.

5. For a thorough explication of the route by which Baquaqua's coffle is moved toward the shore and thus into slavery, see Law and Lovejoy, *The Biography of Mahommah Gardo Baquaqua*, 35–39. The translations of the town names that follow all come from Law and Lovejoy's remapping of Baquaqua's journey.

6. Ben Okri, *The Famished Road* (New York: Anchor Books, 1991). Future references to this work will be indicated parenthetically and will cite this particular edition.

7. See for instance, Brenda Cooper, *Magical Realism in West African Fiction: Seeing with a Third Eye* (London: Routledge, 1998); Renata Oliva, "Re-Dreaming the World: Ben Okri's Shamanic Realism," in *Coterminous Worlds: Magical Realism and Contemporary Post-Colonial Literature in English*, ed. Elsa Linguanti, Francesco Casotti, and Carmen Concilio (Amsterdam: Rodopi, 1999), 171–96; Derek Wright, "Postmodernism as Realism: Magic History in Recent West African Fiction," in *Contemporary African Fiction* (Bayreuth: Bayreuth African Studies, 1997), 181–207; and Anjali Roy, "Post-Modern or Post-Colonial? Magic Realism in Okri's *The Famished Road*," in *The Post-Colonial Condition of African Literature*, ed. Daniel Gover, John Conteh-Morgan, and Jane Bryce (Trenton, NJ: Africa World Press, 2000), 23–39. For a debate regarding the postcolonial, postmodern, cosmopolitan, and allegorical implications of the novel, see Douglas McCabe, "'Higher Realities': New Age Spirituality in Ben Okri's *The Famished Road*," *Research in African Literatures* 36, no. 4 (Winter 2005): 1–21; Esther de Bruijn, "Coming to Terms with New Ageist Contamination: Cosmopolitanism in Ben Okri's *The Famished Road*," *Research in African Literatures* 38, no. 4 (Winter 2007): 170–86; and Douglas McCabe, "Doug McCabe's Response to Esther de Bruijn's Essay," *Research in African Literatures* 38, no. 4 (Winter 2007): 227–33.

8. This reading is inspired by Rosalind Shaw's brief discussion of the "magical capacities" of the river in *The Famished Road* in *Memories of the Slave Trade: Ritual and the Historical Imagination in Sierra Leone* (Chicago: University of Chicago Press, 2002), 3.

9. Paul Gilroy, *The Black Atlantic: Modernity and Double Consciousness* (Cambridge, MA: Harvard University Press, 1993), 197.

10. See for instance, Margaret Cezair-Thompson, "Beyond the Postcolonial Novel: Ben Okri's *The Famished Road* and Its '*Àbíkú*' Traveler," *Journal of Commonwealth Literature* 31, no. 2 (1996): 33–45; Arlene A. Elder, "Narrative Journeys: From Orature to Postmodernism in Soyinka's *The Road* and Okri's *The Famished Road*," in *Multiculturalism and Hybridity in African Literatures*, ed. Hal Wylie and Bernth Lindfors (Trenton, NJ: Africa World Press, 2000), 409–516; Bode Sowande, "The Metaphysics of *Àbíkú*: A Literary Heritage in Ben Okri's *The Famished Road*," *Matatu: Journal for African Culture and Society* 23–24 (2001): 73–82; and David C. L. Lim, *The Infinite Longing for Home: Desire and the Nation in Selected Writings of Ben Okri and K. S. Maniam* (Amsterdam: Rodopi, 2004), 62–66.

11. Toyin Falola, *The History of Nigeria* (Westport, CT: Greenwood Press, 1999), 32.

12. Patrick Manning, *Slavery and African Life: Occidental, Oriental, and African Slave Trades* (Cambridge: Cambridge University Press, 1990), 24.

13. Ibid.

14. For extensive discussion of the *àbíkú* and *ògbánje* phenomena, see Douglas McCabe, "Histories of Errancy: Oral Yoruba *Àbíkú* Texts and Soyinka's 'Àbíkú,'" *Research in African Literatures* 33, no. 1 (Spring 2002): 46–74; and Chinwe Achebe, *The World of the Ogbanje* (Enugu, Nigeria: Fourth Dimension, 1986), respectively.

15. Ibid.

16. Modupe Oduyoye, *Yoruba Names: Their Structure and Their Meanings* (Ibadan, Nigeria: Daystar Press, 1972), 78–79.

17. Wilhelmina J. Donkoh, "Legacies of the Transatlantic Slave Trade in Ghana: Definitions, Understanding and Perceptions," in *The Transatlantic Slave Trade: Landmarks, Legacies, Expectations*, ed. James Kwesi Anquandah (Accra, Ghana: Sub-Saharan Publishers, 2007), 308.

18. Wole Soyinka, "Àbíkú," in *Early Poems* (Oxford: Oxford University Press, 1998), 24–26.

19. John Pepper Clark-Bekederemo, "Àbíkú," in *Collected Poems, 1958–1988* (Washington, DC: Howard University Press, 1991), 3–4.

20. For a thorough description of the liminal and ambivalent status of the *àbíkú*, see McCabe, "Histories of Errancy."

21. Chikwenye Okonjo Ogunyemi, "An Àbíkú-Ogbanje Atlas: A Pre-Text for Rereading Soyinka's *Aké* and Morrison's *Beloved*," *African American Review* 36, no. 4 (Winter 2002): 666, my emphasis.

22. Christopher N. Okonkwo, *A Spirit of Dialogue: Incarnations of Ogbanje, the Born-to-Die, in African American Literature* (Knoxville: University of Tennessee Press, 2008), 40.

23. Buchi Emecheta, *The Slave Girl* (New York: George Braziller, 1977). Emecheta's novel makes a compelling connection between the transatlantic slave trade and domestic African child slavery. For more on Emecheta's novel, see chapter 1 in this study; for more on domestic slavery's connection to the transatlantic trade, see chapter 5 on Ama Ata Aidoo.

24. Clark-Bekederemo, "Àbíkú," 4.

25. Misty Bastian, "Irregular Visitors: Narratives about *Ogbaanje* (Spirit Children) in Southern Nigerian Popular Writing," in *Readings in African Popular Fiction*, ed. Stephanie Newell (Bloomington: Indiana University Press, 2002), 62, my emphasis.

26. McCabe, "Histories of Errancy," 49.

27. Ibid., 46.

28. In this discussion of metonymy, I depart from Roman Jakobson's more rigid differentiation and polarization of metaphor and metonymy. See Roman Jakobson, "Two Aspects of Language and Two Types of Aphasic Disturbances," in *Selected Writings*, vol. 2 (The Hague, Netherlands: Mouton, 1971), 239–59.

29. Rosalind Shaw, "Afterword: Violence and the Generation of Memory," in *Remembering Violence: Anthropological Perspectives on Intergenerational Transmission*, ed. Nicolas Argenti and Katharina Schramm (New York: Berghahn Books, 2010), 253.

30. Carl Jung, "Mysterium Coniunctionis," in *Collected Works of C. G. Jung*, ed. Sir Herbert Read (New York: Pantheon, 1966), 365.

31. Thanks to Suzanne Blier for pointing this out to me.

32. Achille Mbembe, "Life, Sovereignty, and Terror in the Fiction of Amos Tutuola," *Research in African Literatures* 34, no. 4 (Winter 2003): 7.

33. Benedict Anderson, *Imagined Communities* (London: Verso, 1983), 184.

34. James Clifford, "Notes on Travel and Theory," *Inscriptions* 5 (1989): 88.

35. Rosi Braidotti, "Difference, Diversity, and Nomadic Subjectivity," *Labrys: Etudes feministes* 1–2 (July/December 2002), www.unb.br/ih/his/gefem/labrys1_2/rosi2.html.

36. Jacques Derrida, *Archive Fever: A Freudian Impression* (Chicago: University of Chicago Press, 1996), 4n10.

37. Pierre Nora, "Between Memory and History: Les Lieux de Mémoire," *Representations* 26 (Spring 1989): 8.

38. Ibid., 7.

39. Ibid., 13.

40. Ibid., 7.

41. Ibid., 8.

42. Ibid., 8.

43. Elisée Soumonni, "Lacustrine Villages in South Benin as Refuges from the Slave Trade," in *Fighting the Slave Trade: West African Strategies*, ed. Sylviane A. Diouf (Athens: Ohio University Press, 2003), 6–11.

44. Adama Guèye, "The Impact of the Slave Trade on Cayor and Baol: Mutations in Habitat and Land Occupancy," in Diouf, *Fighting the Slave Trade*, 55.

45. John N. Oriji, "Igboland, Slavery, and the Drums of War and Heroism," in Diouf, *Fighting the Slave Trade*, 127.

46. Walter Hawthorne, "Strategies of the Decentralized: Defending Communities from Slave Raiders in Coastal Guinea-Bissau, 1450–1815," in Diouf, *Fighting the Slave Trade*, 159.

47. Wole Ogundele, "Devices of Evasion: The Mythic Versus the Historical Imagination in the Postcolonial African Novel," *Research in African Literatures* 33, no. 3 (Fall 2002): 137.

48. Nora, "Between Memory and History," 15.
49. Valetin Y. Mudimbe, *The Idea of Africa* (Bloomington: Indiana University Press, 1994), 134.

Chapter 4: The Curse of Constant Remembrance

1. Stephen D. Behrendt, A. J. H. Latham, and David Northrup, eds., *The Diary of Antera Duke, an Eighteenth-Century African Slave Trader* (New York: Oxford University Press, 2010), 184.
2. Ibid., 192.
3. Ibid., 149. This reflects the translation provided by Behrendt, Latham, and Northrup for "Did Drishst whit men" (148).
4. From Paul E. Lovejoy and David Richardson, "Letters of the Old Calabar Slave Trade, 1760–89," in *Genius in Bondage: Literature of the Early Black Atlantic*, ed. Vincent Carretta and Philip Gould (Louisville: University of Kentucky Press, 2000), 106–7.
5. Jane Guyer, "Wealth-in-People, Wealth-in-Things: Introduction," *Journal of African History* 36 (1995): 84.
6. J. D. Fage, *Ghana: A Historical Interpretation* (Madison: University of Wisconsin Press, 1959), 48.
7. Ibid.
8. Behrendt, Latham, and Northrup, *The Diary of Antera Duke*, 46.
9. Jane Parish, "The Dynamics of Witchcraft and Indigenous Shrines Among the Akan," *Africa* 69 (1999): 426.
10. William Lawson, *The Western Scar: The Theme of the Been-to in West African Fiction* (Athens: Ohio University Press, 1982), 10.
11. Ayi Kwei Armah, *Fragments* (Oxford: Heinemann, 1970). Future references to this work will be indicated parenthetically and will cite this particular edition.
12. G. Ojong Ayuk, "The Lust for Material Well-Being in *The Beautyful Ones Are Not Yet Born* and *Fragments* by Ayi Kwei Armah," *Présence Africaine* 132 (1984): 33.
13. Lawson, *The Western Scar*, 73.
14. Ayuk, "The Lust for Material Well-Being," 39.
15. Even in *The Beautyful Ones Are Not Yet Born*, which is almost exclusively concerned with Nkrumah's Ghana, Armah's interest in this historical relationship is prefigured, as "The Man" makes reference to the connection between the current state of affairs and the legacy of the slave trade: "He could have asked if anything was supposed to have changed after all, from the days of chiefs selling their people for the trinkets of Europe. But he thought again of the power of the new trinkets and of their usefulness, and of the irresistible desire they brought" (149). Armah clearly links what he considers the continued misrule of Ghana to the mentality of consumerism that allowed for the historical dislocation of so many West African people as a result of the slave trade. Ayi Kwei Armah, *The Beautyful Ones Are Not Yet Born* (Oxford: Heinemann, 1968).

16. Pierre Nora, "Between Memory and History: Les Lieux de Mémoire," *Representations* 26 (Spring 1989): 13.

17. Translation: "Every man creates unconsciously / Like breathing / But the artists feels creation / His act engages his whole self / His beloved pain strengthens him." My gratitude to Samuel Ray for the translation.

18. Translation: "It depends on the passerby / Whether I am a tomb or a treasure / Whether I speak or fall silent / It's only due to you / Friend, don't enter without desire." My gratitude to Samuel Ray for the translation.

19. Jean Paul Sartre, *Nausea* (New York: New Directions, 1969), 91.

20. Ayi Kwei Armah, "Teaching Creative Writing," *West Africa* 20 (May 1985): 994.

21. Jonathan A. Peters, "English-Language Fiction from West Africa," in *A History of Twentieth-Century African Literatures*, ed. Oyekan Owomoyela (Lincoln: University of Nebraska Press, 1993), 29.

22. Geneviève Fabre, "The Slave Ship Dance," in *Black Imagination and the Middle Passage*, ed. Maria Diedrich, Henry Louis Gates Jr., and Carl Pedersen (New York: Oxford University Press, 1999), 39.

23. Julia Kristeva, *Powers of Horror: An Essay on Abjection* (New York: Columbia University Press, 1982), 1.

24. Ibid., 2.

25. Ibid., 9.

26. Ibid., 4.

27. Ibid., 9.

28. Ibid., 4.

29. For foundational texts regarding the Melanesian Cargo Cults, see Francis E. Williams's *The Vailala Madness and the Destruction of Native Ceremonies in the Gulf Division* (Port Moresby: E. G. Baker, 1923); Peter Worsley's *The Trumpet Shall Sound: A Study of "Cargo" Cults in Melanesia* (London: MacGibbon and Kee, 1957); Peter Lawrence's *Road Belong Cargo: A Study of the Cargo Movement in the Southern Madang District, New Guinea* (Manchester, UK: Manchester University Press, 1964); G. W. Trompf, ed., *Cargo Cults and Millenarian Movements* (Berlin: Mouton de Gruyter, 1990); and Lamont Lindstrom's *Cargo Cult: Strange Stories of Desire from Melanesia and Beyond* (Honolulu: University of Hawaii Press, 1993).

30. Robert Fraser, *The Novels of Ayi Kwei Armah: A Study in Polemical Fiction* (London: Heinemann, 1980), 38.

31. Derek Wright, "Fragments: The Cargo Connection," *Kunapipi* 7, no. 1 (1985): 46.

32. Wole Soyinka, "Between Truths and Indulgences," The Root, July 21, 2010, http://www.theroot.com/views/between-truths-and-indulgences.

33. Fraser, *The Novels of Ayi Kwei Armah*, 36.

34. Elaine Scarry, *The Body in Pain: The Making and Unmaking of the World* (New York: Oxford University Press, 1985), 4.

35. William Wells Brown, "Lecture," *The Narrative of William W. Brown, a Fugitive slave. And a Lecture Delivered before the Female Anti-Slavery Society of Salem, 1847* (Reading, MA: Addison-Wesley, 1969), 82.

36. Tim Woods, *African Pasts: Memory and History in African Literatures* (Manchester, UK: Manchester University Press, 2007), 33.
37. Shoshana Felman and Dori Laub, *Testimony: Crises of Witnessing in Literature, Psychoanalysis, and History* (New York: Routledge, 1992), 74.
38. Ayo Mamadu, "Making Despair Bearable: Armah's *The Beautyful Ones Are Not Yet Born* and *Fragments*," *Neohelicon* 10, no. 2 (1983): 242.
39. Lawson, *The Western Scar*, 79.
40. D. S. Izevbaye, "Ayi Kwei Armah and the 'I' of the Beholder," in *Critical Perspectives on Ayi Kwei Armah*, ed. Derek Wright (Washington, DC: Three Continents Press, 1992), 23.
41. Derek Wright, *Ayi Kwei Armah's Africa: The Sources of His Fiction* (London: Hans Zell, 1989), 139.
42. Ibid., 148.
43. Fraser, *The Novels of Ayi Kwei Armah*, 36.
44. Lawson, *The Western Scar*, 73.
45. Kofi Owusu, "Armah's F-R-A-G-M-E-N-T-S: Madness as Artistic Paradigm," *Callaloo* 11, no. 2 (Spring 1988): 361.
46. Ibid., 361.
47. Luce Irigiray, *This Sex Which Is Not One* (Ithaca, NY: Cornell University Press, 1977), 136.
48. Ibid., 29.
49. Diedrich, Gates, and Pedersen, introduction to *Black Imagination and the Middle Passage*, 8.
50. Paul Gilroy, *The Black Atlantic: Modernity and Double Consciousness* (Cambridge, MA: Harvard University Press, 1993), 16.
51. Cathy Caruth, *Unclaimed Experience: Trauma, Narrative, and History* (Baltimore: Johns Hopkins University Press, 1996), 4–5.
52. Sigmund Freud, *Moses and Monotheism*, trans. Katherine Jones (New York: Knopf, 1937), 157.
53. Kristeva, *Powers of Horror*, 208.

Chapter 5: Childless Mothers and Dead Husbands

1. Mary McCarthy, *Social Change and the Growth of British Power in the Gold Coast: The Fante States, 1807–1874* (Lanham, MD: University Press of America, 1983), 76.
2. Paul E. Lovejoy and David Richardson, "British Abolition and Its Impact on Slave Prices Along the Atlantic Coast of Africa, 1783–1850," *Journal of Economic History* 55, no. 1 (March 1995): 99–100, 114–15.
3. Ivor Wilks, *Asante in the Nineteenth Century: The Structure and Evolution of a Political Order* (Cambridge: Cambridge University Press, 1975), 178.
4. Ibid., 179–89.

5. Ibid., 675. Wilks notes that Cruickshank claimed, "Ashantee wars are never undertaken expressly to supply this demand," and in 1820, Osei Bonsu confirmed that he "cannot make war to catch slaves in the bush, like a thief."

6. Ibid., 177–78.

7. McCarthy, *Social Change*, 81.

8. Robin Law, *Ouidah: The Social History of a West African Slaving "Port," 1727–1892* (Athens: Ohio University Press, 2004), 160.

9. J. F. Ade Ajayi and Robert S. Smith, *Yoruba Warfare in the Nineteenth Century* (Ibadan, Nigeria: Ibadan University Press, 1971), 9.

10. Samuel Crowther, Letter from Fourah Bay College, February 22, 1837, Church Missionary Society Archive (Marlborough, Wiltshire, England: Adam Matthew Publications, 1996).

11. For a compelling discussion of this conflicted return, see Adéléke Adéèkó, "Writing Africa Under the Shadow of Slavery," *Research in African Literatures* 40, no. 4 (Winter 2009): 20–22.

12. Christian G. A. Oldendorp, *History of the Mission of the Evangelical Brethren on the Caribbean Islands of St. Thomas, St. Croix, and St. John*, ed. Johann Jakob Bossart, trans. Arnold R. Highfield (Ann Arbor, MI: Karoma, 1987), 214.

13. Samuel Crowther, "Journal of Samuel Crowther for the Quarter Ending Sep. 25, 1846," Church Missionary Society Archive (Marlborough, Wiltshire, England: Adam Matthew Publications, 1996).

14. Ibid.

15. Ibid.

16. Frederick Douglass, *Narrative of the Life of Frederick Douglass, an American Slave* (New York: Penguin, 1983), 48.

17. Samuel Crowther, quoted in Sarah Tucker, *Abbeokuta, or Sunrise Within the Tropics: An Outline of the Origin and Progress of the Yoruba Mission* (New York: Robert Carter, 1854), 277.

18. Kwabena O. Akurang-Parry, "'A Smattering of Education' and Petitions as Sources: A Study of African Slaveholders' Responses to Abolition in the Gold Coast Colony, 1874–1875," *History in Africa* 27 (2000): 41.

19. Peter Haenger, *Slave and Slaveholders on the Gold Coast*, ed. J. J. Shaffer and Paul E. Lovejoy, trans. Christina Handford (Basel, Switzerland: P. Schlettwein, 2000), 155.

20. Ama Ata Aidoo, *The Dilemma of a Ghost and Anowa* (New York: Longman, 1965), 66. Future references to this work will be indicated parenthetically and will cite this particular edition.

21. In this chapter, unlike in the other chapters in this study, domestic slavery and the transatlantic slave trade are often referred to simultaneously, a reflection of Aidoo's self-conscious conflation, indicative of the inextricable relationship of the two.

22. Adeola James, *In Their Own Voices: African Women Writers Talk* (London: James Currey, 1990), 19.

23. Haenger, *Slave and Slaveholders*, 161.

24. Vincent O. Odamtten, *The Art of Ama Ata Aidoo: Polylectics and Reading Against Neocolonialism* (Gainesville: University Press of Florida, 1994), 52.

25. Ibid., 58.

26. Carol Boyce Davies, *Black Women, Writing and Identity* (New York: Routledge, 1994), 66.

27. Ibid., 71.

28. Haiping Yan, "Staging Modern Vagrancy: Female Figures of Border Crossings in Ama Ata Aidoo and Caryl Churchill," *Theatre Journal* 54, no. 2 (2002): 248.

29. Lloyd Brown, *Women Writers in Black Africa* (Westport, CT: Greenwood Press, 1981), 98.

30. C. L. Innes, "Mothers or Sisters? Identity, Discourse, and Audience in the Writing of Ama Ata Aidoo and Mariama Ba," in *Motherlands: Black Women's Writing from Africa, the Caribbean and South Asia*, ed. Susheila Nasta (London: Women's Group, 1991), 133.

31. Achille Mbembe, "African Modes of Self-Writing," *Public Culture* 14, no. 1 (2002): 259.

32. African American critics often read this dream as a representation of Aidoo's commitment to those people of African descent who were the victims of the slave trade. Mildred A. Hill-Lubin claims that Aidoo is "equally troubled about what has happened to the men, women, and children who have been taken beyond the horizon" (46); and Angeletta KM Gourdine argues that the play is centered on "why Africans sold their brothers to the whites" (61) and on the "diaspora orphanage created by slavery" (63). Though it is true that Anowa wonders what happened to those who were sold away from the shore, and Aidoo's work in general does concern itself with the African American descendants of the African victims of the trade (particularly in *Dilemma of a Ghost*), Aidoo's main commitment is to understanding the effects of the trade on the lives and cultures of Africans. The diaspora, Europe, and the Americas are not central to her interest, as they are for most African American writers. Instead, as I argue in the introduction, it is critical that we read Aidoo's writing (as well as other African writers who depict the slave trade or its effects) as an investigation into African memory and African responses to the trade. In particular we must analyze how those representations differ from African American representations, depart from African American desires for reunion and reparations, and reveal a particularity of African experience that need not be mediated by African American discourses regarding the trade. See Mildred A. Hill-Lubin, "Ama Ata Aidoo and the African Diaspora: Things 'All Good Men and Women Try to Forget,' But I Will Not Let Them," in *Emerging Perspectives on Ama Ata Aidoo*, ed. Ada Uzoamaka Azodo and Gay Wilentz (Trenton, NJ: Africa World Press, 1999), 45–60; and Angeletta KM Gourdine, "Slavery in the Diaspora Consciousness: Ama Ata Aidoo's Conversations," in Azodo and Wilentz, *Emerging Perspectives*, 27–44.

33. See, for instance, Karen Chapman, "'Introduction' to Ama Ata Aidoo's 'Dilemma of a Ghost,'" *Sturdy Black Bridges: Visions of Black Women in Literature*, ed. Roseann Bell, Bettye J. Parker, and Beverly Guy-Sheftall (New York: Anchor Books, 1979), 33.

34. Naana Banyiwa Horne, "The Politics of Mothering: Multiple Subjectivity and Gendered Discourse in Aidoo's Plays," in Azodo and Wilentz, *Emerging Perspectives*, 321.

35. Ibid., 322.

36. Ibid.

37. See Buchi Emecheta, *The Joys of Motherhood* (New York: George Braziller, 1979); Flora Nwapa, *Efuru* (Oxford: Heinemann, 1966); Anne Tanyi-Tang, "My Bundle of Joy," in *Ewa and Other Plays* (Yaoundé, Cameroon: Editions CLE, 2000); Juliana Makuchi Nfah-Abennyi, "The Healer," in *Your Madness Not Mine: Stories of Cameroon* (Athens: Ohio University Press, 1999); Elechi Amadi, *The Concubine* (Oxford: Heinemann, 1975); Kola Onadipe, *Koku Baboni* (Ibadan, Nigeria: African Universities Press, 1965); Ama Ata Aidoo, *The Dilemma of a Ghost and Anowa* (New York: Longman,1965).

38. For critical reflection on the barren mother figure in African literature, see Jane Bryce-Okunlola, "Motherhood as a Metaphor for Creativity in Three African Women's Novels: Flora Nwapa, Rebeka Njau, and Bessie Head," in Nasta, *Motherlands*, 200–218.

39. Makuchi Nfah-Abennyi, "The Healer," 1–11.

40. Marcia C. Inhorn, "Sexuality, Masculinity, and Infertility in Egypt: Potent Troubles in Marital and Medical Encounters," *African Masculinities: Men in Africa from the Late Nineteenth Century to the Present*, ed. Lahoucine Ouzgane and Robert Morrell (New York: Palgrave Macmillan, 2005), 289.

41. Ibid.

42. For a brief history of European and American scientific (and proto-scientific) discussion of black male virility, see Arthur F. Saint-Aubin, "A Grammar of Black Masculinity: A Body of Science," in Ouzgane and Morrell, *African Masculinities*; and John S. Haller Jr., *Outcasts from Evolution: Scientific Attitudes of Racial Inferiority, 1859–1900* (Urbana: University of Illinois Press, 1971). Both these texts have extensive bibliographies of eighteenth- and nineteenth-century scientific discourses regarding black male sexuality.

43. Modupe Olaogun, "Slavery and Etiological Discourse in the Writings of Ama Ata Aidoo, Bessie Head, and Buchi Emecheta," *Research in African Literatures* 33, no. 2 (Summer 2002): 171.

44. Ibid., 172.

45. Maxine MacGregor, "Interview with Ama Ata Aidoo," in *African Writers Talking*, ed. Cosmo Pieterse and Dennis Duerden (London: Heinemann, 1970), 23.

46. Hortense Spillers, "Mama's Baby, Papa's Maybe: An American Grammar Book," *Diacritics* 17, no. 2 (Summer 1987): 76.

47. James, *In Their Own Voices*, 14.

48. Ibid.

49. Rosemary Marangoly George and Helen Scott, "'A New Tail to an Old Tale": An Interview with Ama Ata Aidoo," *NOVEL: A Forum on Fiction* 26, no. 3 (Spring 1993): 305.

50. Chimalum Nwankwo, "The Feminist Impulse and Social Realism in Ama Ata Aidoo's *No Sweetness Here* and *Our Sister Killjoy*," in *Ngambika: Studies of Women in African Literature*, ed. Carol Boyce Davies and Anne Adams Graves (Trenton, NJ: Africa World Press, 1986), 152.

51. Ama Ata Aidoo, *Our Sister Killjoy: Or Reflections from a Black-Eyed Squint* (New York: Longman, 1977), 59. Future references to this work will be indicated parenthetically and will cite this particular edition.

52. Law, *Ouidah*, 1.
53. Odamtten, *The Art of Ama Ata Aidoo*, 123.
54. Ibid.
55. James, *In Their Own Voices*, 20.
56. Ibid., 16.
57. Nii Ajen, "West African Homoeroticism: West African Men Who Have Sex with Men," *Boy-Wives and Female Husbands: Studies of African Homosexualities*, ed. Stephen O. Murray and Will Roscoe (New York: St. Martin's Press, 1998), 130.
58. Spillers, "Mama's Baby," 76.
59. Nana Wilson-Tagoe, "Ama Ata Aidoo with Nana Wilson-Tagoe," in *Writing Across Worlds: Contemporary Writers Talk*, ed. Susheila Nasta (New York: Routledge, 2004), 296.
60. Spillers, "Mama's Baby," 79.
61. James, *In Their Own Voices*, 20.
62. Ibid., 15.
63. Innes, "Mothers or Sisters?" 140.
64. Kofi Owusu, "Canons Under Siege: Blackness, Femaleness and Ama Ata Aidoo's *Our Sister Killjoy*," *Callaloo* 13, no. 2 (Spring 1990): 354.
65. Theo Vincent, *Seventeen Black and African Writers on Literature and Life* (Lagos: Centre for Black and African Arts and Civilization, 1981), 6–7.

Chapter 6: The Suffering of Survival

1. Kwadwo Opoku-Agyemang, *Cape Coast Castle: A Collection of Poems* (Accra, Ghana: Afram Publications, 1996), 5, my emphasis.
2. Saidiya Hartman, *Lose Your Mother: A Journey Along the Atlantic Slave Route* (New York: Farrar, Straus and Giroux, 2007), 170. Bayo Holsey notes that she often heard this same comment in Ghana in her book *Routes of Remembrance: Refashioning the Slave Trade in Ghana* (Chicago: University of Chicago Press, 2008), 214–15.
3. Cathy Caruth, *Unclaimed Experience: Trauma, Narrative, and History* (Baltimore: Johns Hopkins University Press, 1996), 7.
4. Paul E. Lovejoy and David Richardson, "Letters of the Old Calabar Slave Trade: 1760–1789," *Genius in Bondage: Literature of the Early Black Atlantic*, ed. Vincent Carretta and Philip Gould (Louisville: University of Kentucky Press, 2000), 103.
5 Ibid., 105.
6. Ayuba Suleiman Diallo, "Some Memoirs of the Life of Job, the Son of Solomon the High Priest of Boonda in Africa; Who Was a Slave about Two Years in Maryland; and afterwards Being Brought to England, Was Set Free, and Sent to His Native Land in the Year 1734," in *Africa Remembered: Narratives by West Africans from the Era of the Slave Trade*, ed. Philip D. Curtin (Madison: University of Wisconsin Press, 1968), 57.
7. In fact, in some cases, family members would have been prohibited from mourning the victims of the trade. Among the Yoruba, the death of a young person was considered

"horrifying, an unnatural calamity, and always due to ill will," and could not be memorialized publicly. Similarly, for some among the Temne of present-day Sierra Leone, the disappearance of large numbers of people indicated the haunting of vicious bush spirits and even possibly witchcraft. See Peter Morton-Williams, "Yoruba Responses to the Fear of Death," *Africa: Journal of the International African Institute* 39, no. 1 (January 1960): 34; and Rosalind Shaw, *Memories of the Slave Trade: Ritual and the Historical Imagination in Sierra Leone* (Chicago: University of Chicago Press, 2002), 49, 222; Shaw notes that marking a person as a witch might itself have been a means of supplying people to the slave trade.

8. Stephanie E. Smallwood, *Saltwater Slavery: A Middle Passage from Africa to American Diaspora* (Cambridge, MA: Harvard University Press, 2007), 61.

9. Arnold van Gennep, *The Rites of Passage* (London: Routledge, 1965), 47.

10. J. F. Ade-Ajayi, "Remembering the Slave Trade," in *The Transatlantic Slave Trade: Landmarks, Legacies, Expectations*, ed. James Kwesi Anquandah (Accra, Ghana: Sub-Saharan Publishers, 2007), 367.

11. Carolyn A. Brown, "Epilogue: Memory as Resistance: Identity and the Contested History of Slavery in Southeastern Nigeria, an Oral History Project," in *Fighting the Slave Trade: West African Strategies*, ed. Sylviane A. Diouf (Athens: University of Ohio Press, 2003), 224.

12. Ibid., 222.

13. Saidiya Hartman, "The Time of Slavery," *South Atlantic Quarterly* 101, no. 4 (Fall 2002): 758.

14. Hartman, *Lose Your Mother*, 6.

15. Ibid., 233.

16. Adélékè Adéèkó, "Oral Poetry and Hegemony: Yorùbá *Oríkì*," in *African Literatures at the Millennium*, ed. Arthur Drayton, Omofolabo Ajayi-Soyinka, and I. Peter Ukpokodu (Trenton, NJ: Africa World Press, 2007), 12–15.

17. Hartman, *Lose Your Mother*, 232.

18. Ibid., 54.

19. Wole Soyinka, *Death and the King's Horseman*, ed. Simon Gikandi (New York: Norton, 2003), 6.

20. Ibid., 47.

21. Ibid., 62.

22. Chinua Achebe, *Arrow of God* (New York: Anchor Books, 1969), 14–15.

23. T. Obinkaram Echewa, *I Saw the Sky Catch Fire* (New York: Penguin, 1992), 32.

24. Marianne Hirsch, *Family Frames: Photography, Narrative, and Postmemory* (Cambridge, MA: Harvard University Press, 1997), 243.

Epilogue: The Future of the Past

1. Wole Ogundele, "Devices of Evasion: The Mythic versus the Historical Imagination in the Postcolonial African Novel," *Research in African Literatures* 33, no. 3 (Fall 2002): 126.

2. Ayi Kwei Armah, *Osiris Rising: A Novel of Africa Past, Present and Future* (Senegal: Per Ankh, 1995).

3. Syl Cheney-Coker, *The Last Harmattan of Alusine Dunbar: A Novel of Magical Vision* (New York: Heinemann, 1990).

4. Kofi Anyidoho, "HavanaSoul," in *Ancestrallogic and Caribbeanblues* (Trenton, NJ: Africa World Press, 1993), 16–17.

5. Kofi Anyidoho, "Lolita Jones," in *Ancestrallogic and Caribbeanblues*, 27.

6. Kofi Anyidoho, "Children of the Land," in *Ancestrallogic and Caribbeanblues*, 44.

7. Niyi Osundare, "For Eldred Durosimi Jones at 71," in *Pages from the Book of the Sun: New and Selected Poems* (Trenton, NJ: Africa World Press, 2002), 34.

8. Niyi Osundare, "Scars of Unremembrance," in *Horses of Memory* (Ibadan, Nigeria: Heinemann, 1999), 33.

9. Niyi Osundare, "Feathered Heels," in *Pages from the Book of the Sun*, 37.

10. Osundare, "Scars of Unremembrance," 35.

11. Anyidoho, *Ancestrallogic*, xii.

12. Opoku-Agyemang, *Cape Coast Castle*, 4.

13. Ibid., 7.

14. Kwadwo Opoku-Agyemang, "Equiano: A Mother's Song," in *Cape Coast Castle*, 66.

15. Kwadwo Opoku-Agyemang, "Supplication: Equiano's Mother," in *Cape Coast Castle*, 25–26.

16. Kwadwo Opoku-Agyemang, "Against Fear," in *Cape Coast Castle*, 75–76.

17. Obi Akwani, *March of Ages* (Enugu, Nigeria: Fourth Dimension, 2003). Future references to this work will be indicated parenthetically and will cite this particular edition.

18. Kwakuvi Azasu, *The Slave Raiders* (Accra, Ghana: Yamens Press, 2004). Future references to this work will be indicated parenthetically and will cite this particular edition.

19. Obi Akwani, "Book Review: Moaning Pessimists: A Review of the Novel, *Fragments* by Ayi Kwei Armah," http://www.imdiversity.com/villages/global/arts_culture_media/Fragments.asp.

20. In the novel, Francis Drake is a young son of a poor neighbor instead of Hawkins's second cousin. Azasu's novel is filled with these kinds of inaccuracies. Another example is the fact that Las Cassas appears at an event in the novel after the time of his own actual death. Azasu's cover page notes, "This is not a work of history. It is fictitious in every detail. The characters in it are, therefore, only fabrications of a fertile mind and bear no resemblance to any person, living or dead." Of course his characters do very much resemble major figures in British history both in name and in action, but the author has indeed taken significant poetic license with them. Though his historical research is sometimes not on par with other comparable historical novels (and though typos make some of the chronological events impossible—the books ends in "1508," though the chronological action of the novel otherwise takes place entirely between 1565 and 1568, for instance), this novel is no doubt explicitly meant to evoke a very specific set of major players in sixteenth-century England and to critique their involvement in the transatlantic slave trade. It is thus clear that this is a historical novel, even if it is at times historically inaccurate.

21. Ella Keren, "The Atlantic Slave Trade in West African History Text Books," in *Africa and Trans-Atlantic Memories: Literary and Aesthetic Manifestations of Diaspora and History*, ed. Naana Opoku-Agyemang, Paul E. Lovejoy, and David V. Trotman (Trenton, NJ: Africa World Press, 2008), 242.

22. Ben Okri, *Starbook* (London: Rider, 2007).

23. Wole Soyinka, "Between Truths and Indulgences, Part Two," The Root, July 21, 2010, http://www.theroot.com/views/between-truths-and-indulgences-part-two.

24. Ogundele, "Devices of Evasion," 137.

BIBLIOGRAPHY

Literary:

Achebe, Chinua. *Arrow of God.* New York: Anchor Books, 1969.
———. *Things Fall Apart.* New York: Anchor Books, 1994. First published 1959.
Aidoo, Ama Ata. *The Dilemma of a Ghost and Anowa.* New York: Longman, 1965.
———. *Our Sister Killjoy.* New York: Longman, 1977.
Akwani, Obi. *March of Ages.* Enugu, Nigeria: Fourth Dimension, 2003.
Amadi, Elechi. *The Concubine.* London: Heinemann, 1975.
Anyidoho, Kofi. *Ancestrallogic and Caribbeanblues.* Trenton, NJ: Africa World Press, 1993.
Armah, Ayi Kwei. *The Beautyful Ones Are Not Yet Born.* Oxford: Heinemann, 1968.
———. *Fragments.* Oxford: Heinemann, 1969.
———. *The Healers: A Novel.* Oxford: Heinemann, 1978.
———. *Osiris Rising: A Novel of Africa Past, Present and Future.* Popenguine, Senegal: Per Ankh, 1995.
———. *Two Thousand Seasons: A Novel.* Oxford: Heinemann, 1973.
Azasu, Kwakuvi. *The Slave Raiders.* Accra, Ghana: Yamens Press, 2004.
Balogun, F. Odun. *Adjusted Lives: Stories of Structural Adjustments.* Trenton, NJ: Africa World Press, 1995.
Barnet, Miguel. *Biography of a Runaway Slave.* Translated by W. Nick Hill. New York: Pantheon, 1994. First published 1968.
Brathwaite, Edward Kamau. *The Arrivants: A New World Trilogy.* Oxford: Oxford University Press, 1973.
———. *Middle Passages.* New York: New Directions, 1992.
Carpentier, Alejo. *Explosion in a Cathedral.* New York: Farrar, Straus and Giroux, 1962.
Césaire, Aimé. *Notebook of a Return to the Native Land.* Translated and edited by Clayton Eshleman and Annette Smith. Middletown, CT: Wesleyan University Press, 2001. First published 1949.
Cheney-Coker, Syl. *The Last Harmattan of Alusine Dunbar: A Novel of Magical Vision.* Oxford: Heinemann, 1990.
Clark-Bekederemo, John Pepper. *Collected Poems, 1958–1988.* Washington, DC: Howard University Press, 1991.

Condé, Maryse. *I, Tituba, Black Witch of Salem.* New York: Ballantine, 1992.
Echewa, T. Obinkaram. *I Saw the Sky Catch Fire.* New York: Penguin, 1992.
Emecheta, Buchi. *The Joys of Motherhood.* New York: George Braziller, 1979.
———. *The Slave Girl.* Oxford: Heinemann, 1995.
Fagunwa, Daniel O. *Forest of a Thousand Daemons: A Hunter's Saga.* Translated by Wole Soyinka. London: Nelson, 1982.
Hazoumé, Paul. *Doguicimi.* Translated by Richard Bjornson. Washington, DC: Three Continents Press, 1990. First published 1938.
Morrison, Toni. *Beloved.* New York: Penguin, 1987.
Nfah-Abennyi, Juliana Makuchi. *Your Madness Not Mine: Stories of Cameroon.* Athens: Ohio University Press, 1999.
Nwapa, Flora. *Efuru.* London: Heinemann, 1966.
Okri, Ben. *The Famished Road.* New York: Anchor Books, 1991.
———. *Starbook: A Magical Tale of Love and Regeneration.* London: Rider, 2007.
Onadipe, Kola. *Koku Baboni.* Ibadan, Nigeria: African Universities Press, 1965.
Opoku-Agyemang, Kwadwo. *Cape Coast Castle: A Collection of Poems.* Accra, Ghana: Afram, 1996.
Osofisan, Femi. *The Oriki of a Grasshopper and Other Plays.* Washington, DC: Howard University Press, 1995.
Osundare, Niyi. *Horses of Memory.* Ibadan, Nigeria: Heinemann, 1999.
———. *Pages from the Book of the Sun: New and Selected Poems.* Trenton, NJ: Africa World Press, 2002.
Saro-Wiwa, Ken. "Africa Kills Her Sun." In *Anchor Book of Modern African Stories.* Edited by Nadezda Obradovic, 210–21. New York: Anchor Books, 1994.
Sartre, Jean Paul. *Nausea.* New York: New Directions, 1969.
Soyinka, Wole. *Death and the King's Horseman.* New York: Hill and Wang, 1975.
———. *Early Poems.* Oxford: Oxford University Press, 1998.
Tanyi-Tang, Anne. *Ewa and Other Plays.* Yaounde, Cameroon: Editions CLE, 2000.
Tutuola, Amos. *The Palm-Wine Drinkard and My Life in the Bush of Ghosts.* New York: Grove, 1954.
———. *Simbi and the Satyr of the Dark Jungle.* San Francisco: City Lights Books, 1955.
Walcott, Derek. *Omeros.* New York: Farrar, Straus and Giroux, 1900.

Scholarly:

Abrahams, Roger D. "The Disobedient Sisters." In *African Folktales: Traditional Stories of the Black World*, 143–44. New York: Pantheon, 1983.
Achebe, Chinua. *Morning Yet on Creation Day: Essays.* New York: Anchor Press, 1975.
Achebe, Chinwe. *The World of the Ogbanje.* Enugu, Nigeria: Fourth Dimension, 1986.
Ade-Ajayi, J. F. "Remembering the Slave Trade." In *The Transatlantic Slave Trade: Landmarks, Legacies, Expectations*, edited by James Kwesi Anquandah, 365–70. Accra, Ghana: Sub-Saharan Publishers, 2007.

Adéèkó, Adélékè. "Oral Poetry and Hegemony: Yorùbá Oríkì." In *African Literatures at the Millennium*, edited by Arthur Drayton, Omofolabo Ajayi-Soyinka, and I. Peter Ukpokodu, 6–19. Trenton, NJ: Africa World Press, 2007.

———. *The Slave's Rebellion: Literature, History, Orature*. Bloomington: Indiana University Press, 2005.

———. "Writing Africa Under the Shadow of Slavery." *Research in African Literatures* 40, no. 4 (Winter 2009): 1–22.

Adorno, Theodor W. "What Does Coming to Terms with the Past Mean?" In *Bitburg in Moral and Political Perspective*, edited by Geoffrey H. Hartman, 114–15. Bloomington,: Indiana University Press, 1986.

Agbodza, Godwin K., and Raymond O. Agbo. *Monuments and Historical Landmarks Along the Coast*. Cape Coast: Nyakod, 2006.

Ajayi, J. F. Ade, and Robert S. Smith. *Yoruba Warfare in the Nineteenth Century*. Ibadan, Nigeria: Ibadan University Press, 1971.

Ajen, Nii. "West African Homoeroticism: West African Men Who Have Sex with Men." In *Boy-Wives and Female Husbands: Studies of African Homosexualities*, edited by Stephen O. Murray and Will Roscoe, 129–40. New York: St. Martin's Press, 1998.

Akurang-Parry, Kwabena O. "'A Smattering of Education' and Petitions as Sources: A Study of African Slaveholders' Responses to Abolition in the Gold Coast Colony, 1874–1875." *History in Africa* 27 (2000): 39–60.

Akwani, Obi. "Book Review: Moaning Pessimists: A Review of the Novel, *Fragments* by Ayi Kwei Armah." http://www.imdiversity.com/villages/global/arts_culture_media/Fragments.asp.

Akyeampong, Emmanuel. "History, Memory, Slave-Trade and Slavery in Anlo (Ghana)." *Slavery and Abolition* 22 (December 2001): 1–24.

Anderson, Benedict. *Imagined Communities*. London: Verso, 1983.

Anquandah, Kwesi. *Castles and Forts of Ghana*. Atalante: Ghana Museums and Monuments Board, 1999.

Antze, Paul, and Michael Lambek. *Tense Past: Cultural Essays in Trauma and Memory*. London: Routledge, 1996.

Argenti, Nicolas. *The Intestines of the State: Youth, Violence, and Belated Histories in the Cameroon Grassfields*. Chicago: University of Chicago Press, 2007.

Argenti, Nicolas, and Katharina Schramm, eds. *Remembering Violence: Anthropological Perspectives on Intergenerational Transmission*. New York: Berghahn Books, 2010.

Armah, Ayi Kwei. "Don't Mention Slavery." *New African* (July 2006). http://goliath.ecnext.com/coms2/gi_0199-5788357/Don-t-mention-slavery-Special.html.

———. "Teaching Creative Writing." *West Africa* 20 (May 1985): 994–95.

Atta-Yawson, Philip. Interview by the author. Fort Amsterdam, Abandze, Ghana. May 27, 2006.

———. Phone interview by the author. January 6, 2011.

Austen, Ralph. *African Economic History: Internal Development and External Dependency*. London: James Curry Press, 1987.

———. "The Slave Trade as History and Memory: Confrontations of Slaving Voyage Documents and Communal Traditions." *William and Mary Quarterly* 58 (2001): 229–44.

Austin, Allan D. *African Muslims in Antebellum America: Transatlantic Stories and Spiritual Struggles*. London: Routledge, 1997.

Ayuk, G. Ojong. "The Lust for Material Well-Being in *The Beautyful Ones Are Not Yet Born* and *Fragments* by Ayi Kwei Armah." *Présence Africaine* 132 (1984): 33–43.

Azodo, Ada Uzoamaka, and Gay Wilentz, eds. *Emerging Perspectives on Ama Ata Aidoo*. Trenton, NJ: Africa World Press, 1999.

Bailey, Anne C. *African Voices of the Atlantic Slave Trade: Beyond the Silence and the Shame*. Boston: Beacon Press, 2005.

———. "Breaking Silence and a Break with the Past: African Oral Histories and the Transformations of the Atlantic Slave Trade in Southern Ghana." In *Relocating Postcolonialism*, edited by David Theo Goldberg and Ato Quayson, 122–42. Oxford: Blackwell, 2002.

Bal, Mieke. *Acts of Memory: Cultural Recall in the Present*. Hanover, NH: Dartmouth College, University Press of New England, 1998.

Bartlett, Richard. "Taking Centre Stage in History." In *African Review of Books*. http://www.africanreviewofbooks.com/Review.asp?offset=45&book_id=93.

Baquaqua, Mahommah Gardo. *The Biography of Mahommah G. Baquaqua*. Detroit: George E. Pomeroy, 1854.

Bastian, Misty. "Irregular Visitors: Narratives about *Ogbaanje* (Spirit Children) in Southern Nigerian Popular Writing." In *Readings in African Popular Fiction*, edited by Stephanie Newell, 59–67. Bloomington: Indiana University Press, 2002.

Baum, Robert M. *Shrines of the Slave Trade: Diola Religion and Society in Precolonial Senegambia*. Oxford: Oxford University Press, 1999.

Behrendt, Stephen D., A. J. H. Latham, and David Northrup, eds. *The Diary of Antera Duke, an Eighteenth-Century African Slave Trader*. New York: Oxford University Press, 2010.

Bell, Bernard W. *The Afro-American Novel and Its Tradition*. Amherst: University of Massachusetts Press, 1987.

Braidotti, Rosi. "Difference, Diversity, and Nomadic Subjectivity." *Labrys: Études féministes* 1–2 (July/December 2002). www.unb.br/ih/his/gefem/labrys1_2/rosi2.html.

Brown, Carolyn A. "Epilogue: Memory as Resistance: Identity and the Contested History of Slavery in Southeastern Nigeria, an Oral History Project." In *Fighting the Slave Trade: West African Strategies*, edited by Sylviane A. Diouf, 219–26. Athens: University of Ohio Press, 2003.

Brown, Lloyd. *Women Writers in Black Africa*. Westport, CT: Greenwood Press, 1981.

Brown, William Wells. "Lecture." *The Narrative of William W. Brown, a Fugitive Slave. And a Lecture Delivered before the Female Anti-Slavery Society of Salem, 1847*. Reading, MA: Addison-Wesley, 1969.

Bruijn, Esther de. "Coming to Terms with New Ageist Contamination: Cosmopolitanism in Ben Okri's *The Famished Road*." *Research in African Literatures* 38, no. 4 (Winter 2007): 170–86.

Bruner, Edward. "Tourism in Ghana: The Representation of Slavery and the Return of the Black Diaspora." *American Anthropologist* 98, no. 2 (1996): 290–304.

Bryce-Okunlola, Jane. "Motherhood as a Metaphor for Creativity in Three African Women's Novels: Flora Nwapa, Rebeka Njau, and Bessie Head." In *Motherlands: Black Women's Writing from Africa, the Caribbean and South Asia*, edited by Susheila Nasta, 200–218. London: Women's Group, 1991.

Byrne, David, and Brian Eno. "My Life in the Bush of Ghosts." Audio CD. Warner Brothers, 1981.

Carretta, Vincent. "Olaudah Equiano or Gustavus Vassa? New Light on an Eighteenth-Century Question of Identity." *Slavery and Abolition* 20, no. 3 (1999): 96–105.

Caruth, Cathy, ed. *Trauma: Explorations in Memory*. Baltimore: Johns Hopkins University Press, 1995.

———. *Unclaimed Experience: Trauma, Narrative, and History*. Baltimore: Johns Hopkins University Press, 1996.

Cezair-Thompson, Margaret. "Beyond the Postcolonial Novel: Ben Okri's *The Famished Road* and Its 'Abiku' Traveler." *Journal of Commonwealth Literature* 31, no. 2 (1996): 33–45.

Chapman, Karen. "'Introduction' to Ama Ata Aidoo's 'Dilemma of a Ghost.'" In *Sturdy Black Bridges: Visions of Black Women in Literature*, edited by Roseann Bell, Bettye J. Parker, and Beverly Guy-Sheftall, 25–39. New York: Anchor Books, 1979.

Chrisman, Laura. "Rethinking Black Atlanticism." *Black Scholar* 30, nos. 3–4 (2000): 12–17.

Clarke, William H. *Travels and Explorations in Yorubaland, 1854–1858*. Ibadan, Nigeria: Ibadan University Press, 1972.

Clifford, James. "Notes on Travel and Theory." *Inscription* 5 (1989): 177–88.

Collins, Harold R. "Founding a New National Literature: The Ghost Novels of Amos Tutuola." In *Critical Perspectives on Amos Tutuola*, edited by Bernth Lindfors, 43–54. Washington, DC: Three Continents Press, 1975.

Connerton, Paul. *How Societies Remember*. Cambridge: Cambridge University Press, 1989.

Conservation and Tourism Development Plan for Cape Coast, Central Region, Ghana. http://hitchcock.itc.virginia.edu/CapeCoastArchive/.

Cooper, Brenda. *Magical Realism in West African Fiction: Seeing with a Third Eye*. London: Routledge, 1998.

Cooper, Frederick. *Africa Since 1940: The Past of the Present*. Cambridge: Cambridge University Press, 2002.

Costanzo, Angelo. *Surprizing Narrative: Olaudah Equiano and the Beginnings of Black Autobiography*. New York: Greenwood Press, 1987.

Cox, Timothy J. *Postmodern Tales of Slavery in the Americas: From Alejo Carpentier to Charles Johnson*. New York: Garland, 2001.

Crowther, Samuel. "Journal of Samuel Crowther for the Quarter Ending Sep. 25, 1846." Church Missionary Society Archive. Marlborough, Wiltshire, England: Adam Matthew Publications, 1996.

———. Letter from Fourah Bay College. February 22, 1837. Church Missionary Society Archive. Marlborough, Wiltshire, England: Adam Matthew Publications, 1996.

Curtin, Philip D., ed. *Africa Remembered: Narratives by West Africans from the Era of the Slave Trade*. Madison: University of Wisconsin Press, 1968.

Davidson, Basil. *The African Slave Trade*. Boston: Little, Brown, 1961.

Davies, Carol Boyce. *Black Women, Writing and Identity*. NewYork: Routledge, 1994.

Deleuze, Gilles, and Felix Guattari. *A Thousand Plateaus: Capitalism and Schizophrenia*. Minneapolis: University of Minnesota Press, 1987.

Derrida, Jacques. *Archive Fever: A Freudian Impression*. Chicago: University of Chicago Press, 1996.

Diallo, Ayuba Suleiman. "Some Memoirs of the Life of Job, the Son of Solomon the High Priest of Boonda in Africa; Who Was a Slave about two Years in Maryland; and afterwards Being Brought to England, Was Set Free, and Sent to His Native Land in the Year 1734." In *Africa Remembered: Narratives by West Africans from the Era of the Slave Trade*, edited by Philip D. Curtin, 17–59. Madison: University of Wisconsin Press, 1968.

Diedrich, Maria, Henry Louis Gates Jr., and Carl Pedersen. "The Middle Passage between History and Fiction: Introductory Remarks." In *Black Imagination and the Middle Passage*, 5–20. New York: Oxford University Press, 1999.

Diouf, Sylviane A., ed. *Fighting the Slave Trade: West African Strategies*. Athens: Ohio University Press, 2003.

Donkoh, Wilhelmina J. "Legacies of the Transatlantic Slave Trade in Ghana: Definitions, Understanding, and Perceptions." In *The Transatlantic Slave Trade: Landmarks, Legacies, Expectations*, edited by James Kwesi Anquandah, 305–25. Accra, Ghana: Sub-Saharan Publishers, 2007.

Douglass, Frederick. *Narrative of the Life of Frederick Douglass, an American Slave*. New York: Penguin, 1983.

Dyan, Joan. "Paul Gilroy's Slaves, Ships, and Routes: The Middle Passage as Metaphor." *Research in African Literatures* 27, no. 4 (Winter 1996): 7–14.

Echeruo, Michael J. C. "An African Diaspora: The Ontological Project." In *The African Diaspora: African Origins and New World Identities*, edited by Isidore Okpewho, Carole Boyce Davies, and Ali A. Mazrui, 3–18. Bloomington: Indiana University Press, 1999.

Egejuru, Phanuel Akubueze. *Black Writers, White Audience: A Critical Approach to African Literature*. Hicksville, NY: Exposition Press, 1978.

Eke, Maureen N. "Diasporic Ruptures and (Re)membering History: Africa as Home and Exile in *Anowa* and *The Dilemma of a Ghost*." In *Emerging Perspectives on Ama Ata Aidoo*, edited by Ada Uzoamaka Azodo and Gay Wilentz, 61–78. Trenton, NJ: Africa World Press, 1999.

Elder, Arlene A. "Narrative Journeys: From Orature to Postmodernism in Soyinka's *The Road* and Okri's *The Famished Road*." In *Multiculturalism and Hybridity in African Literatures*, edited by Hal Wylie and Bernth Lindfors, 409–16. Trenton, NJ: Africa World Press, 2000.

Eltis, David, Stephen D. Behrendt, David Richardson, and Herbert S. Klein. Introduction to *The Trans-Atlantic Slave Trade: A Database on CD-ROM*. Cambridge: Cambridge University Press, 1999.
Eltis, David, and David Richardson, eds. *Extending the Frontiers: Essays on the New Transatlantic Slave Trade Database*. New Haven, CT: Yale University Press, 2008.
Equiano, Olaudah. *The Interesting Narrative of the Life of Olaudah Equiano, or Gustavus Vassa, the African, Written by Himself*. Edited by Werner Sollors. New York: Norton, 2001.
Fabre, Geneviève. "The Slave Ship Dance." In *Black Imagination and the Middle Passage*, edited by Maria Diedrich, Henry Louis Gates Jr., and Carl Pedersen, 33–46. New York: Oxford University Press, 1999.
Fage, J. D. *Ghana: A Historical Interpretation*. Madison: University of Wisconsin Press, 1959.
———. "Slavery and the Slave Trade in the Context of West African History." *Journal of African History* 10, no. 3 (1969): 393–404.
Falola, Toyin. *The History of Nigeria*. Westport, CT: Greenwood Press, 1999.
Falola, Toyin, and Ann Genova, eds. *Historical Dictionary of Nigeria*. Lanham, MD: Scarecrow Press, 2009.
Fanon, Frantz. *Black Skins, White Masks*. New York: Grove, 1967.
———. *The Wretched of the Earth*. New York: Grove, 1963.
Felman, Shoshana, and Dori Laub. *Testimony: Crises of Witnessing in Literature, Psychoanalysis, and History*. New York: Routledge, 1992.
Foucault, Michel. *Language, Counter-Memory, Practice*. Ithaca, NY: Cornell University Press, 1980.
Fox, Robert Elliot. "Tutuola and the Commitment to Tradition." *Research in African Literatures* 29 (1998): 203–8.
Fraser, Robert. *The Novels of Ayi Kwei Armah: A Study in Polemical Fiction*. London: Heinemann, 1980.
Freud, Sigmund. "Analysis of a Phobia in a Five-Year Old Boy." In vol. 10 of *The Standard Edition of the Complete Psychological Works of Sigmund Freud* (3–149). London: Hogarth, 1953–1973.
———. "Analysis Terminable and Interminable." In vol. 23 of *The Standard Edition of the Complete Psychological Works of Sigmund Freud* (211–53). London: Hogarth, 1953–1973.
———. *Beyond the Pleasure Principle*. New York: Penguin, 2003.
———. *Moses and Monotheism*. Translated by Katherine Jones. New York: Knopf, 1937.
———. "Mourning and Melancholia." In vol. 14 of *The Standard Edition of the Complete Psychological Works of Sigmund Freud* (237–58). London: Hogarth, 1953–1973
———. "Remembering, Repeating, and Working Through." In vol. 12 of *The Standard Edition of the Complete Psychological Works of Sigmund Freud* (145–56). London: Hogarth, 1953–1973.
George, Rosemary Marangoly, and Helen Scott. "'A New Tail to an Old Tale': An Interview with Ama Ata Aidoo." *NOVEL: A Forum on Fiction* 26, no. 3 (Spring 1993): 297–308.

Gilroy, Paul. *The Black Atlantic: Modernity and Double Consciousness*. Cambridge, MA: Harvard University Press, 1993.

Glissant, Eduoard. *Caribbean Discourse: Selected Essays*. Translated by J. Michael Dash. Charlottesville: University of Virginia Press, 1989. First published 1981.

Goldberg, David Theo, and Ato Quayson, eds. *Relocating Postcolonialism*. Oxford: Blackwell, 2002.

"Golden Jubilee House: A Spiritual Relief, The." ModernGhana.com. Accessed November 26, 2008. http://www.modernghana.com/news/192256/50/the-golden-jubilee-house-a-spiritual-relief.html.

Gourdine, Angeletta KM. "Slavery in the Diaspora Consciousness: Ama Ata Aidoo's Conversations." In *Emerging Perspectives on Ama Ata Aidoo*, edited by Ada Uzoamaka Azodo and Gay Wilentz, 27–44. Trenton, NJ: Africa World Press, 1999.

Guèye, Adama. "The Impact of the Slave Trade on Cayor and Baol: Mutations in Habitat and Land Occupancy." In *Fighting the Slave Trade: West African Strategies*, edited by Sylviane A. Diouf, 50–61. Athens: Ohio University Press, 2003.

Guyer, Jane. "Wealth-in-People, Wealth-in-Things—Introduction." *Journal of African History* 36 (1995): 83–90.

Hackman, Amissane. Interview by the author. Cape Coast Castle, Cape Coast, Ghana. May 23, 2006.

Haenger, Peter. *Slaves and Slaveholders on the Gold Coast*. Edited by J. J. Shaffer and Paul E. Lovejoy. Translated by Christina Handford. Basel, Switzerland: P. Schlettwein, 2000.

Halbwachs, Maurice. *On Collective Memory*. Chicago: University of Chicago Press, 1992.

Haller, John S., Jr. *Outcasts from Evolution: Scientific Attitudes of Racial Inferiority, 1859–1900*. Urbana: University of Illinois Press, 1971.

Handler, Jerome. "Survivors of the Middle Passage: Life Histories of Enslaved Africans in British America." *Slavery and Abolition* 23, no. 1 (April 2002): 25–56.

Handley, George B. *Post-Slavery Literatures in the Americas: Family Portraits in Black and White*. Charlottesville: University Press of Virginia, 2000.

Hartman, Saidiya. *Lose Your Mother: A Journey Along the Atlantic Slave Route*. New York: Farrar, Straus and Giroux, 2007.

———. "The Time of Slavery." *South Atlantic Quarterly* 101, no. 4 (Fall 2002): 757–77.

Hawthorne, Walter. "Strategies of the Decentralized: Defending Communities from Slave Raids in Coastal Guinea-Bissau, 1450–1815." In *Fighting the Slave Trade: West African Strategies*, edited by Sylviane A. Diouf, 152–69. Athens: Ohio University Press, 2003.

Hill-Lubin, Mildred A. "Ama Ata Aidoo and the African Diaspora: Things 'All Good Men and Women Try to Forget,' But I Will Not Let Them." In *Emerging Perspectives on Ama Ata Aidoo*, edited by Ada Uzoamaka Azodo and Gay Wilentz, 45–60. Trenton, NJ: Africa World Press, 1999.

Hirsch, Marianne. *Family Frames: Photography, Narrative, and Postmemory*. Cambridge, MA: Harvard University Press, 1997.

Holsey, Bayo. *Routes of Remembrance: Refashioning the Slave Trade in Ghana*. Chicago: University of Chicago Press, 2008.

Horne, Naana Banyiwa. "The Politics of Mothering: Multiple Subjectivity and Gendered Discourse in Aidoo's Plays." In *Emerging Perspectives on Ama Ata Aidoo*, edited by Ada Uzoamaka Azodo and Gay Wilentz, 303–32. Trenton, NJ: Africa World Press, 1999.

Inhorn, Marcia C. "Sexuality, Masculinity, and Infertility in Egypt: Potent Troubles in Marital and Medical Encounters." In *African Masculinities: Men in Africa from the Late Nineteenth Century to the Present*, edited by Lahoucine Ouzgane and Robert Morrell, 289–304. New York: Palgrave Macmillan, 2005.

Inikori, Joseph E. "Changing Commodity Composition of Imports into West Africa, 1650–1850." In *The Transatlantic Slave Trade: Landmarks, Legacies, Expectations*, edited by James Kwesi Anquandah, 57–80. Accra, Ghana: Sub-Saharan Publishers, 2007.

———, ed. *Forced Migrations: The Impact of the Export Slave Trade on African Societies*. New York: Africana Publishing, 1982.

———. *Slavery and the Rise of Capitalism*. Kingston, Jamaica: University of West Indies Press, 1993.

Inikori, Joseph E., and Stanley L. Engerman, eds. *The Atlantic Slave Trade: Effects on Economies, Societies, and Peoples in Africa, the Americas, and Europe*. Durham, NC: Duke University Press, 1992.

Innes, C. L. "Mothers or Sisters? Identity, Discourse, and Audience in the Writing of Ama Ata Aidoo and Mariama Ba." In *Motherlands: Black Women's Writing from Africa, the Caribbean and South Asia*, edited by Susheila Nasta, 129–51. London: Women's Group, 1991.

Irele, F. Abiola. *The African Experience in Literature and Ideology*. London: Heinemann, 1981.

———. *The African Imagination: Literature in Africa and the Black Diaspora*. Oxford: Oxford University Press, 2001.

———. "Tradition and the African Writer: D. O. Fagunwa, Amos Tutuola, and Wole Soyinka." In *Perspectives on Wole Soyinka: Freedom and Perspective*, edited by Biodun Jeyifo, 3–26. Jackson: University of Mississippi Press, 2001.

Irigiray, Luce. *This Sex Which Is Not One*. Ithaca, NY: Cornell University Press, 1977.

Izevbaye, D. S. "Ayi Kwei Armah and the 'I' of the Beholder." In *Critical Perspectives on Ayi Kwei Armah*, edited by Derek Wright, 22–33. Washington, DC: Three Continents Press, 1992.

Jakobson, Roman. "Two Aspects of Language and Two Types of Aphasic Disturbances." In vol. 2 of *Selected Writings* (239–59). The Hague, Netherlands: Mouto, 1971.

James, Adeola. *In Their Own Voices: African Women Writers Talk*. London: James Currey, 1990.

Jewsiewicki, Bogumil, and Valetin Y. Mudimbe. "Africans' Memories and Contemporary History of Africa." *History and Theory* 32 (1993): 1–11.

Johnson, Samuel. *The History of the Yorubas: From the Earliest Times to the Beginning of the British Protectorate*. London: Routledge, 1966.

Jones, G. I. "Olaudah Equiano: Introduction." In *Africa Remembered: Narratives by West Africans from the Era of the Slave Trade*, edited by Philip D. Curtin, 60–69. Madison: University of Wisconsin Press, 1968.

Jung, Carl. *Mysterium Coniunctionis: Collected Works of C. G. Jung*. Edited by Sir Herbert Read. Princeton: Pantheon, 1966.

Keren, Ella. "The Atlantic Slave Trade in West African History Text Books." In *Africa and Trans-Atlantic Memories: Literary and Aesthetic Manifestations of Diaspora and History*, edited by Naana Opoku-Agyemang, Paul E. Lovejoy, and David V. Trotman, 235–55. Trenton, NJ: Africa World Press, 2008.

Klein, Martin A. "The Impact of the Atlantic Trade on the Societies of the Western Sudan." In *The Atlantic Slave Trade: Effects on Economies, Societies, and Peoples in Africa, the Americas, and Europe*, edited by Joseph E. Inikori and Stanley L. Engerman, 25–48. Durham, NC: Duke University Press, 1992.

———. "Studying the History of Those Who Would Rather Forget: Oral History and the Experience of Slavery." *History in Africa* 16 (1989): 209–17.

Kreamer, Christine Mullen. "The Politics of Memory: Ghana's Cape Coast Castle Museum Exhibition 'Crossroads of People, Crossroads of Trade.'" *Ghana Studies* 7 (2004): 79–91.

———. "Shared Heritage, Contested Terrain: Cultural Negotiations and Ghana's Cape Coast Castle Museum Exhibition 'Crossroads of People, Crossroads of Trade.'" In *Museum Frictions: Public Cultures/Global Transformations*, edited by Ivan Karp, Corinne A. Kratz, Lynn Szwaja, and Tomás Ybarra-Frausto, 425–68. Durham, NC: Duke University Press, 2006.

Kristeva, Julia. *Powers of Horror: An Essay on Abjection*. New York: Columbia University Press, 1982.

"Kufuor commissions Golden Jubilee House." ModernGhana.com. Accessed November 11, 2008. http://www.modernghana.com/news/190243/1/kufuor-commissions-golden-jubilee-house.html.

LaCapra, Dominick. *Writing History, Writing Trauma*. Baltimore: Johns Hopkins University Press, 2001.

Lakoff, George, and Mark Johnson. *Metaphors We Live By*. Chicago: University of Chicago Press, 1980.

Law, Robin. "The Atlantic Slave Trade in Local History Writing in Ouidah." In *Africa and Trans-Atlantic Memories: Literary and Aesthetic Manifestations of Diaspora and History*, edited by Naana Opoku-Agyemang, Paul E. Lovejoy, and David V. Trotman, 257–74. Trenton, NJ: Africa World Press, 2008.

———. *Ouidah: The Social History of a West African Slaving "Port," 1727–1892*. Athens: Ohio University Press, 2004.

Law, Robin, and Paul E. Lovejoy. *The Biography of Baquaqua: His Passage from Slavery to Freedom in Africa and America*. Princeton, NJ: Markus Wiener, 2001.

Lawrence, Peter. *Road Belongs Cargo: A Study of the Cargo Movement in the Southern Madang District, New Guinea*. Manchester, UK: Manchester University Press, 1964.

Lawson, William. *The Western Scar: The Theme of the Been-To in West African Fiction*. Athens: Ohio University Press, 1982.

Lebdai, Benaouda. "Armah's Obsessions with the 'Middle Passage:' Reality and Symbols." In *Africa and Trans-Atlantic Memories: Literary and Aesthetic Manifestations of Diaspora and History*, edited by Naana Opoku-Agyemang, Paul E. Lovejoy, and David V. Trotman, 405–16. Trenton, NJ: Africa World Press, 2008.

Lee, Julia Sun-Joo. *The American Slave Narrative and the Victorian Novel.* New York: Oxford University Press, 2010.

LeGoff, Jacques. *History and Memory.* New York: Columbia University Press, 1977.

Lim, David C. L. *The Infinite Longing for Home: Desire and the Nation in Selected Writings of Ben Okri and K. S. Maniam.* Amsterdam: Rodopi, 2004.

Lindfors, Bernth. "Amos Tutuola: Literary Syncretism and the Yoruba Folk Tradition." In *European Language Writing in Sub-Saharan Africa*, edited by Albert S Gerard, 632–49. Budapest: Akad Kiado, 1986.

———. *Critical Perspectives on Amos Tutuola.* Washington, DC: Three Continents Press, 1975.

Lindstrom, Lamont. *Cargo Cult: Strange Stories of Desire from Melanesia and Beyond.* Honolulu: University of Hawaii Press, 1993.

Lovejoy, Paul E. "Autobiography and Memory: Gustavus Vassa, alias Olaudah Equiano, the African." *Slavery and Abolition* 27, no. 3 (December 2006): 317–47.

———. *Transformations in Slavery: A History of Slavery in Africa.* Cambridge: Cambridge University Press, 2000.

Lovejoy, Paul E., and David Richardson. "British Abolition and Its Impact on Slave Prices Along the Atlantic Coast of Africa, 1783–1850." *Journal of Economic History* 55, no. 1 (March 1995): 98–119.

———. "Letters of the Old Calabar Slave Trade: 1760–1789." In *Genius in Bondage: Literature of the Early Black Atlantic*, edited by Vincent Carretta and Philip Gould, 89–115. Louisville: University of Kentucky Press, 2000.

Lukacs, Georg. *The Historical Novel.* Lincoln: University of Nebraska Press, 1983.MacGregor, Maxine. "Interview with Ama Ata Aidoo." In *African Writers Talking*, edited by Cosmo Pieterse and Dennis Duerden, 19–27. London: Heinemann, 1970.

Mafe, Diana. "A Wilderness of the Mind Representations of the Bush in Yoruba Fiction." Paper presented at Eco-Imagination: African Diasporan Literatures and Sustainability, Annual African Literature Association Conference. Tucson, Arizona, March 10–14, 2010.

Mamadu, Ayo. "Making Despair Bearable: Armah's *The Beautyful Ones Are Not Yet Born* and *Fragments*." *Neohelican* 10, no. 2 (1983): 231–49.

Mann, Kristin. *Slavery and the Birth of an African City: Lagos, 1760–1900.* Bloomington: University of Indiana Press, 2007.

Manning, Patrick. *Slavery and African Life: Occidental, Oriental, and African Slave Trades.* Cambridge: Cambridge University Press, 1990.

Mbembe, Achille. "African Modes of Self-Writing." *Public Culture* 14, no. 1 (Fall 2002): 239–73.

———. "Life Sovereignty, and Terror in the Fiction of Amos Tutuola." *Research in African Literatures* 34, no. 4 (Winter 2003): 1–26.

———. *On the Postcolony*. Berkeley: University of California Press, 2001.
McCabe, Douglas. "'Higher Realities': New Age Spirituality in Ben Okri's The Famished Road." *Research in African Literatures* 36, no. 4 (Winter 2005): 1–21.
———. "Histories of Errancy: Oral Yoruba *Abiku* Tales and Soyinka's 'Abiku.'" *Research in African Literatures* 33, no. 1 (Spring 2002): 45–74.
———. "Doug McCabe's Response to Esther de Bruijn's Essay." *Research in African Literatures* 38, no. 4 (Winter 2007): 227–33.
McCarthy, Mary. *Social Change and the Growth of British Power in the Gold Coast: The Fante States, 1807–1874*. Lanham, MD: University Press of America, 1983.
Miller, Christopher L. *The French Atlantic Triangle: Literature and Culture of the Slave Trade*. Durham, NC: Duke University Press, 2008.
Miller, Joseph C. "Presidential Address: History and Africa/Africa and History." *American Historical Review* 104, no. 1 (February 1999): 1–32.
———. *Way of Death: Merchant Capitalism and the Angolan Slave Trade, 1730–1830*. Madison: University of Wisconsin Press, 1988.
Morrison, Toni. "Memory, Creation, and Writing." *Thought* 59 (December 1984): 385–90.
———. "The Site of Memory." In *Inventing the Truth: The Art and Craft of Memoir*, edited by William Zinsser, 103–24. Boston: Houghton Mifflin, 1987.
———. "Unspeakable Things Unspoken." *Michigan Quarterly Review* 18, no. 1 (Winter 1989): 9–34.
Morton-Williams, Peter. "Yoruba Responses to the Fear of Death." *Africa: Journal of the International African Institute* 39, no. 1 (January 1960): 34–40.
Mudimbe, V. Y. *The Idea of Africa*. Bloomington: Indiana University Press, 1994.
Newell, Stephanie, ed. *Readings in African Popular Fiction*. Bloomington: Indiana University Press, 2002.
———. *West African Literatures: Ways of Reading*. Oxford: Oxford University Press, 2006.
———. *Writing African Women: Gender, Popular Culture and Literature in West Africa*. London: Zed Books, 1997.
Nora, Pierre. "Between Memory and History: Les Lieux de Mémoire." *Representations* 26 (Spring 1989): 7–24.
Nunn, Nathan. "Slavery, Institutional Development, and Long-Run Growth in Africa, 1400–2000." August 2005 (1–46). http://ipc.umich.edu/edts/pdfs/empirical_slavery.pdf.
Nwankwo, Chimalum. "The Feminist Impulse and Social Realism in Ama Ata Aidoo's *No Sweetness Here* and *Our Sister Killjoy*." In *Ngambika: Studies of Women in African Literature*, edited by Carol Boyce Davies and Anne Adams Graves, 151–59. Trenton, NJ: Africa World Press, 1986.
Obiechina, Emmanuel N. *Language and Theme: Essays on African Literature*. Washington, DC: Howard University Press, 1990.
Odamtten, Vincent O. *The Art of Ama Ata Aidoo: Polylectics and Reading Against Neocolonialism*. Gainesville: University Press of Florida, 1994.

Oduyoye, Modupe. *Yoruba Names: Their Structure and Their Meanings*. Ibadan, Nigeria: Daystar Press,1972.
Ogundele, Wole. "Devices of Evasion: The Mythic versus the Historical Imagination in the Postcolonial African Novel." *Research in African Literatures* 33, no. 3 (Fall 2002): 125–39.
Ogunyemi, Chikwenye Okonjo. "An Abiku/Ogbanje Atlas: A Pre-text for Rereading Soyinka's *Ake* and Morrison's *Beloved*." *African American Review* 36, no. 4 (Winter 2002): 663–79.
Ojo, Olatunji. "The Organization of the Atlantic Slave Trade in Yorubaland, ca. 1777 to ca. 1856." *International Journal of African Historical Studies* 41, no. 1 (2008): 77–78.
Okonkwo, Christopher N. *A Spirit of Dialogue: Incarnations of Ogbanje, the Born-to-Die, in African American Literature*. Knoxville: University of Tennessee Press, 2008.
Okoye, Ikem Stanley. "The Representation of Slavery at Bonny and Asaba: The Traditional Visual Arts Interrogate Modern Literature." In *Africa and Trans-Atlantic Memories: Literary and Aesthetic Manifestations of Diaspora and History*, edited by Naana Opoku-Agyemang, Paul E. Lovejoy, and David V. Trotman, 63–90. Trenton, NJ: Africa World Press, 2008.
Okpewho, Isadore. "African Mythology and Africa's Political Impasse." *Research in African Literatures* 29 (1998): 1–15.
———. *African Oral Literature: Backgrounds, Character, and Continuity*. Bloomington: Indiana University Press, 1992.
Olaogun, Modupe. "Slavery and Etiological Discourse in the Writings of Ama Ata Aidoo, Bessie Head, and Buchi Emecheta." *Research in African Literatures* 33, no. 2 (Summer 2002): 171–93.
Oldendorp, Christian G. A. *Historie der caribischen Inseln Sanct Thomas, Sanct Crux und Sanct Jan, inbesondere der dasigen Neger und der Mission der evangelischen Brüder under denselben*. Edited by Gudrun Meier, Stephan Palmié, Peter Stein, and Horst Ulbricht. 4 vols. Berlin: Verlag für Wissenschaft und Bildung, 2002.
———. *History of the Mission of the Evangelical Brethren on the Caribbean Islands of St. Thomas, St. Croix, and St. John*. Edited by Johann Jakob Bossart. Translated by Arnold R. Highfield. Ann Arbor, MI: Karoma, 1987.
Oliva, Renata. "Re-Dreaming the World: Ben Okri's Shamanic Realism." In *Coterminous Worlds: Magical Realism and Contemporary Post-Colonial Literature in English*, edited by Elsa Linguanti, Francesco Casotti, and Carmen Concilio, 171–96. Amsterdam: Rodopi, 1999.
Ong, Walter J. *Orality and Literacy: The Technologizing of the Word*. London: Routledge, 1982.
Opoku-Agyemang, Kwadwo. "A Crisis of Balance: The (Mis)Representation of Colonial History and the Slave Experience as Themes in Modern African Literature." In *Nationalism vs. Internationalism: (Inter)National Dimensions of Literatures in English*, edited by Wolfgang Zach and Ken L. Goodwin, 219–28. Tübingen, Germany: Stauffenburg Verlag, 1996.

Opoku-Agyemang, Naana J. "The Living Experience of the Slave Trade in Sankana and Gwollu: Implications for Tourism." In *The Transatlantic Slave Trade: Landmarks, Legacies, Expectations*, edited by James Kwesi Anquandah, 210–24. Accra, Ghana: Sub-Saharan Publishers, 2007.

Oriji, John N. "Igboland, Slavery, and the Drums of War and Heroism." In *Fighting the Slave Trade: West African Strategies*, edited by Sylviane A. Diouf, 121–31. Athens: Ohio University Press, 2003.

Osei-Tutu, Brempong. "African American Reactions to the Restoration of Ghana: Slave Castles." *Public Archaeology* 3 (2004): 195–204.

———. "Slave Castles, African American Activism, and Ghana Memorial Entrepreneurism." PhD diss., Syracuse University, 2009.

Owomoyela, Oyekan. *Amos Tutuola Revisited*. New York: Twayne Publishers, 1999.

Owusu, Kofi. "Armah's F-R-A-G-M-E-N-T-S: Madness as Artistic Paradigm." *Callaloo* 11, no. 2 (Spring 1988): 361–70.

———. "Canons Under Siege: Blackness, Femaleness and Ama Ata Aidoo's *Our Sister Killjoy*." *Callaloo* 13, no. 2 (Spring 1990): 341–63.

Parish, Jane. "The Dynamics of Witchcraft and Indigenous Shrines Among the Akan." *Africa* 69, no. 3 (1999): 426–47.

Parrinder, Geoffrey. Forward to *The Palm-Wine Drinkard and My Life in the Bush of Ghosts*. New York: Grove, 1994.

Patterson, Orlando. *Slavery and Social Death: A Comparative Study*. Cambridge, MA: Harvard University Press, 1982.

Pedersen, Carl. "Sea Change: The Middle Passage and the Trans-Atlantic Imagination." In *Black Columbiad*, edited by Werner Sollors and Maria Diedrich, 42–51. Cambridge, MA: Harvard University Press, 1994.

Peters, Jonathan A. "English-Language Fiction from West Africa." In *A History of Twentieth-Century African Literatures*, edited by Oyekan Owomoyela, 9–48. Lincoln: University of Nebraska Press, 1993.

Piot, Charles. "Atlantic Aporias: Africa and Gilroy's Black Atlantic." *South Atlantic Quarterly* 100, no. 1 (2001): 155–70.

Quayson, Ato. *Calibrations: Reading for the Social*. Minneapolis: University of Minnesota Press, 2003.

———. *Strategic Transformations in Nigerian Writing: Orality and History in the Work of Rev. Samuel Johnson, Amos Tutuola, Wole Soyinka, and Ben Okri*. Bloomington: Indiana University Press, 1997.

Report of the Proceedings of the Conference on Preservation of Elmina and Cape Coast. May 11–12, 1994.

Ricciardi, Alessia. *The Ends of Mourning: Psychoanalysis, Literature, Film*. Stanford, CA: Stanford University Press, 2003.

Richards, Sandra. "What Is to Be Remembered?: Tourism to Ghana's Slave Castle-Dungeons." *Theatre Journal* 57, no. 4 (December 2005): 617–37.

Ricoeur, Paul. *Memory, History, Forgetting*. Chicago: University of Chicago Press, 2006.

———. *The Rule of Metaphor: Multi-disciplinary Studies of the Creation of Meaning in Language*. Toronto: University of Toronto Press, 1975.
Robinson, Imakhus Vienna. "Is the Black Man's History Being Whitewashed?" *Uhuru* 9 (1994): 48–50.
Rodney, Walter. *How Europe Underdeveloped Africa*. Washington, DC: Howard University Press, 1972.
Roy, Anjali. "Post-Modern or Post-Colonial? Magic Realism in Okri's *The Famished Road*." In *The Post-Colonial Condition of African Literature*, edited by Daniel Gover, John Conteh-Morgan, and Jane Bryce, 23–39. Trenton, NJ: Africa World Press, 2000.
Rushdy, Ashraf H. A. *Neo-Slave Narratives: Studies in the Social Logic of a Literary Form*. New York: Oxford University Press, 1999.
Saint-Aubin, Arthur F. "A Grammar of Black Masculinity: A Body of Science." In *African Masculinities*, edited by Lahoucine Ouzgane and Robert Morrell, 23–42. New York: Palgrave Macmillan, 2005.
Scarry, Elaine. *The Body in Pain: The Making and Unmaking of the World*. New York: Oxford University Press, 1985.
Shaw, Rosalind. "Afterword: Violence and the Generation of Memory." In *Remembering Violence: Anthropological Perspectives on Intergenerational Transmission*, edited by Nicolas Argenti and Katharina Schramm, 251–59. New York: Berghahn Books, 2010.
———. *Memories of the Slave Trade: Ritual and the Historical Imagination in Sierra Leone*. Chicago: University of Chicago Press, 2002.
Slaughter, Joseph. "One Track Minds: Markets, Madness, Metaphors, and Modernism in Postcolonial Nigerian Fiction." In *African Writers and Their Readers: Essays in Honor of Bernth Lindfors*, edited by Toyin Falola, 55–89. Trenton, NJ: Africa World Press, 2002.
Smallwood, Stephanie E. *Saltwater Slavery: A Middle Passage from Africa to American Diaspora*. Cambridge, MA: Harvard University Press, 2007.
Soumonni, Elisée. "Lacustrine Villages in South Benin as Refuges from the Slave Trade." In *Fighting the Slave Trade: West African Strategies*, edited by Sylviane A. Diouf, 3–14. Athens: Ohio University Press, 2003.
Sowande, Bode. "The Metaphysics of Abiku: A Literary Heritage in Ben Okri's *The Famished Road*." *Matatu: Journal for African Culture and Society* 23–24 (2001): 73–82.
Soyinka, Wole. "Between Truths and Indulgences." *Root* (July 21, 2010).http://www.theroot.com/views/between-truths-and-indulgences.
———. "Between Truths and Indulgences, Part Two." The Root, July 21, 2010. http://www.theroot.com/views/between-truths-and-indulgences-part-two.
———. *The Burden of Memory, The Muse of Forgiveness*. New York: Oxford University Press, 1999.
Sparks, Randy J. *The Two Princes of Calabar: An Eighteenth Century Atlantic Odyssey*. Cambridge, MA: Harvard University Press, 2004.
Spillers, Hortense. "Mama's Baby, Papa's Maybe: An American Grammar Book." *Diacritics* 17 (Summer 1987): 64–81.

———. "The Politics of Intimacy: A Discussion." In *Sturdy Black Bridges: Visions of Black Women in Literature*, edited by Roseanne Bell, 87–106. New York: Anchor Press/Doubleday, 1979.

Thornton, John. *Africa and Africans in the Making of the Atlantic World, 1400–1800*. Cambridge: Cambridge University Press, 1992.

Trompf, G. W., ed. *Cargo Cults and Millenarian Movements*. Berlin: Mouton de Gruyter, 1990.

Tucker, Sarah. *Abbeokuta, or Sunrise Within the Tropics: An Outline of the Origin and Progress of the Yoruba Mission*. New York: Robert Carter, 1854.

Turner, Victor. *The Ritual Process: Structure and Anti-Structure*. New York: Aldine DeGruyter, 1995.

van Gennep, Arnold. *The Rites of Passage*. London: Routledge, 1965.

Vincent, Theo. *Seventeen Black and African Writers on Literature and Life*. Lagos: Centre for Black and African Arts and Civilization, 1981.

Voyages: The Trans-Atlantic Slave Trade Database. http://www.slavevoyages.org.

Webb, Hugh. "The African Historical Novel and the Way Forward." *African Literature Today* 11 (1980): 24–38.

Wenzel, Jennifer. *Bulletproof: Afterlives of Anticolonial Prophecy in South Africa and Beyond*. Chicago: University of Chicago Press, 2009.

White, Hayden. *The Content of the Form: Narrative Discourse and Historical Representation*. Baltimore: Johns Hopkins University Press, 1987.

———. *Figural Realism: Studies in the Mimesis Effect*. Baltimore: Johns Hopkins University Press, 1999.

White, Luise. *Speaking with Vampires: Rumor and History in Colonial Africa*. Berkeley: University of California Press, 2000.

Whittaker, David. "Realms of Liminality: The Mythic Topography of Amos Tutuola's *Bush of Ghosts*." *SOAS Literary Review* 3 (Spring 2001): 1–18.

Wilks, Ivor. *Asante in the Nineteenth Century: The Structure and Evolution of a Political Order*. Cambridge: Cambridge University Press, 1975.

Williams, Francis E. *The Vailala Madness and the Destruction of Native Ceremonies in the Gulf Division*. Port Moresby: E. G. Baker, 1923.

Wilson-Tagoe, Nana. "Ama Ata Aidoo with Nana Wilson-Tagoe." In *Writing Across Worlds: Contemporary Writers Talk*, edited by Susheila Nasta, 292–300. New York: Routledge, 2004.

Wood, Marcus. *Blind Memory: Visual Representations of Slavery in England and America, 1780–1865*. New York: Routledge, 2000.

Woods, Tim. *African Pasts: Memory and History in African Literatures*. Manchester, UK: Manchester University Press, 2007.

Worsley, Peter. *The Trumpet Shall Sound: A Study of "Cargo" Cults in Melanesia*. London: MacGibbon and Kee, 1957.

Wright, Derek. "Ayi Kwei Armah and the Significance of His Novels and Histories." *International Fiction Review* 17, no. 1 (Winter 1990): 29–40.

———. *Ayi Kwei Armah's Africa: The Sources of His Fiction*. London: Hans Zell, 1989.

———. "Fragments: The Cargo Connection." *Kunapipi* 7, no. 1 (1985): 45–58.
———. "Postmodernism as Realism: Magic History in Recent West African Fiction." In *Contemporary African Fiction*. Bayreuth: Bayreuth African Studies, 1997. Yan, Haiping. "Staging Modern Vagrancy: Female Figures of Border Crossings in Ama Ata Aidoo and Caryl Churchill." *Theatre Journal* 54, no. 2 (2002): 245–62.
Zamora, Lois Parkinson. *The Usable Past: The Imagination of History in Recent Fiction of the Americas*. Cambridge: Cambridge University Press, 1997.
Zeleza, Paul Tiyambe. "Rewriting the African Diaspora: Beyond the Black Atlantic." *African Affairs* 104, no. 414 (2005): 35–68.

INDEX

àbíkú: as metaphor for Nigeria, 80, 88–89; as metaphor for slave trade loss, 84–87, 94; as metonym, 87–88; in Okri, 80–89; in Tutuola, 67. See also *ògbánje*

abolition (of the slave trade): failures related to, 13, 51, 52, 133–34; traumatic legacy after, 73, 104, 140, 173

Achebe, Chinua: anticolonial writing and, 42–43; *Arrow of God*, 177, 183–84; concern with slave trade, 183; *Things Fall Apart*, 23–24, 84, 149, 183–84

Adéèkó, Adélékè, 44, 174

Adjusted Lives (Balogun), 32

Adorno, Theodor W., 37

Afolayan, Afolabi, 55

"African Modes of Self-Writing" (Mbembe), 33–34, 37–38

Afrocentrism, 34–35, 42

Aidoo, Ama Ata, 1, 5–6, 44; *Anowa* (see *Anowa* [Aidoo]); *Changes*, 153; desecration of intimacy and, 140; *Dilemma of a Ghost*, 147, 149, 212n32; grammar of memory and, 5–6, 140, 165–66; love stories and, 153–55, 164; on slave trade, 167–68; *Our Sister Killjoy* (see *Our Sister Killjoy* [Aidoo])

Akwani, Obi, 6, 183–84; historical novel and, 183, 188; *March of Ages* (see *March of Ages* [Akwani]); slave trade amnesia and, 183

Akyeampong, Emmanuel, 35

alternative history, 22, 39, 98–100, 103

Amadi, Elechi: *The Concubine*, 149

amnesia, 33–46; African American literature and, 39–42; African involvement in the slave trade and, 36; British colonial powers and, 36–37; mapping as response to, 103; Mbembe and, 37–38, 146; Opoku-Agyemang and, 34–35; slave ship image and, 40–41; trauma and, 179; Tutuola and, 73; West African literature and, 3–4, 33–46

Anderson, Benedict, 94

Anlo, 17, 75, 188–90

Anowa (Aidoo), 5, 139–53; African American slavery and, 144, 212n32; Anowa as wayfarer, 143–44; Anowa's dream in, 212n32; barrenness in, 147–48; familial rupture of slavery in, 142–43, 145, 150–51; as feminist play, 144–45; Kofi's infertility in, 148–52; Kofi, the slave trade and, 141, 150

Anyidoho, Kofi, 181

Argenti, Nicolas, 10, 21, 39

Armah, Ayi Kwei, 1, 25, 43–44, 139; *The Beautyful Ones Are Not Yet Born*, 110, 208n15; on creative writing, 117–18; historical novel and, 26–28, 43, 180–81, 183; Ghanaian independence and, 110–11; *Fragments* (see *Fragments* [Armah]); metaphor and, 28–29, 116, 117, 120, 121, 124, 193; *Osiris Rising*, 181; *Two Thousand Seasons* (see *Two Thousand Seasons* [Armah])

Arrow of God (Achebe), 177, 183

Asante people, 134

Atta-Yawson, Philip, 17, 18

Austin, Allan D., 75

Ayuk, Ojong, 111
Azasu, Kwakuvi, 6, 183, 192; anticolonial worldview and, 188–91; historical novel and, 183, 188–91; *Slave Raiders* (see *Slave Raiders* [Azasu])

Bailey, Anne C., 17, 75
Balogun, F. Odun: *Adjusted Lives*, 32
Baquaqua, Mahommah Gardo, 75–79
Barnet, Miguel, 40
Bastian, Misty, 87
Beautyful Ones Are Not Yet Born, The (Armah), 110, 208n15
"been-to" characters, 109–10, 123
Behrendt, Stephen D., 109
Beloved (Morrison), 42
Black Atlantic, 41, 46, 48, 130, 181
body in the bag, trope of the, 5, 6, 32, 33, 54, 61–68, 72–73, 87–88, 89, 185
Braidotti, Rosi, 96
Brathwaite, Kamau, 40
Brown, Carolyn A., 2, 172–73
Brown, Lloyd, 144–45
Brown, William Wells, 125
Byrne, David, 202n6

Cape Coast Castle, 13–17, 23, 134, 182; hidden tunnel and, 16–17; memorial plaque on, *15*
Cape Coast Castle (Opoku-Agyemang), 170, 182
Carpentier, Alejo, 40
Caruth, Cathy, 131, 170–71
Casas, Bartholomé de las, 188
castles, slave-trading, 11–20; cultural discourse of fear and, 18–19; door of no return and, 13, 16–17; institutionalized memory and, 16; "lies" and, 16–19; as metaphors, 13, 14; as reverberations of slave trade violence, 18–20. *See also specific castles and forts*
Césaire, Aimé, 40
Changes (Aidoo), 153
Cheney-Coker, Syl: *The Last Harmattan of Alusine Dunbar*, 181, 197n20
Christiansborg Castle (Osu), 11–12, 112

civil rights movement (US), 40
Clark-Bekederemo, John Pepper, 84, 86
Clarke, William H., 2
Clifford, James, 95
Collins, Harold R., 49
Columbus, Christopher, 17
Concubine, The (Amadi), 149
Condé, Maryse, 40
Conrad, Joseph: *Heart of Darkness*, 166
consumer culture in West Africa, 108–9, 110, 111, 208n15
Crowther, Samuel Ajayi, 135–38, 139, 143, 185
Cummings, E. E., 162
Curtin, Philip D., 48

Dahomey, 51, 76, 78, 197n21; Abome kings of, 156; Oyo and, 135
Darko, Amma, 197n20
Davies, Carol Boyce, 144
Death and the King's Horseman (Soyinka): African complicity in the slave trade in, 176–77; Elesin in, 175–77; Praise Singer in, 175–77; metaphor and, 176
Deleuze, Gilles, 59
Derrida, Jacques, 96
Diallo, Ayuba Suleiman, 171
Diedrich, Maria, 129
Dilemma of a Ghost (Aidoo), 147, 149, 212n32
Douglass, Frederick, 79, 138
Drake, Sir Francis, 188
Duke, Antera, 36, 106–7, 109, 111

Echewa, T. Obinkaram: *I Saw the Sky Catch Fire*, 178
Eke, Maureen N., 44
Elmina Castle, 14
Emecheta, Buchi, 23, 149, 197n20; *The Slave Girl*, 24–25, 86, 206n23
England: abolition of the slave trade and, 133; mid-sixteenth century and, 188–89, 191, 216n20; Tutuola and, 50
Eno, Bryan, 202n6
Equiano, Olaudah, 5–6, 47–49, 53, 63–64, 182, 201–2n11, 203n31
"Equiano: A Mother's Song" (Opoku-Agyemang), 182

INDEX

Fabre, Geneviève, 121
Fage, J. D., 108
Fagunwa, D. O.: *Forest of a Thousand Daemons*, 63
Falola, Toyin, 82–83
Famished Road, The (Okri), 5, 63; *àbíkú* and, 80, 84–89; as allegory for Nigeria, 5, 32, 79, 80–81, 87, 90, 92; aquamarine beginnings and, 93, 94, 100; Azaro as traveler/cartographer, 91–97, 100–101; Azaro's father, 83, 102; Azaro's mother and historical amnesia, 81–83; historical novel and, 104; Madame Koto in, 89–90, 92–94; as magical realism, 79, 104; memory and, 93–97; metaphor in, 79, 81, 84–85, 87, 88, 100; *milieux de mémoire*, 99–100, 101; modernity in, 79–81, 87, 90, 99–101, 104; as novel of hope, 102; the photographer in, 97–99; the river/road, 79–80, 87, 89, 90–91
Fante people, 134
Felman, Shoshana, 126
Flagstaff House (Golden Jubilee House), 11–12
forest (bush), fear of, 4, 54, 56–58, 82, 93, 203n19, 215n7
Forest of a Thousand Daemons (Fagunwa), 63
forts, slave trading. *See* castles, slave-trading; *specific castles and forts*
Fort Amsterdam, 17
Fort Batenstein, 17
Fort Metal Cross, 18
Fragments (Armah), 5; abjection in, 122, 124–27, 128, 132; Baako as "been-to" character, 110, 123; Baako as writer, 111, 114–15, 116–20, 122, 125, 126–29; Baako in Paris, 113–14; Baako's body as memory in, 121–22; Baako's illness in, 110–12, 120–21, 125; Baako's madness, 127–29; Baako's screenplays and, 116–18; cargo cults of Melanesia and, 122–24; Christiansborg Castle (Osu) and, 112–13, 116–17; the "curse" of constant remembrance, 112–13, 122, 129, 131; Efua (Baako's mother), 112–13; Ghanaian history and, 114–15, 116–20, 123, 131; Juana, 112–13, 116, 123, 128; materialism and, 109–11; Naana, 129–30; trauma and, 111, 113, 116–18, 125–27, 131; rejection of Baako's work in, 188–189; Sartre's Roquentin and, 115; slave trade consumerism in, 109–10; unassimilated past and, 131
Fraser, Robert, 125
Freud, Sigmund, 69–71, 131

Gates, Henry Louis, Jr., 129
Gennep, Arnold van: *Rites of Passage*, 172
Ghana, 42, 43; consumerism and corruption in, 109–10; historical education in, 36–37, 191; seat of government of, 11–12. *See also Anowa* (Aidoo); castles, slave trading; *Fragments* (Armah); *Our Sister Killjoy* (Aidoo)
Ghezo, King, 135
Gilroy, Paul, 40–41, 79, 130
Glissant, Edouard, 40
Grandy King George (Ephraim Robin John), 107–9, 111, 171
guns, 23–24, 82, 116, 165, 193, 197n21

Hackman, Amissane, 16
Haenger, Peter, 139, 143
Handley, George B., 40
Hartman, Saidiya, 170, 173, 174–76, 178, 186
Hawkins, John, 188, 189
Hayden, Robert, 40
Hazoumé, Paul: *Doguicimi*, 197n21
"Healer, The" (Makuchi), 149
Heart of Darkness (Conrad), 166
Hirsch, Marianne, 3, 73, 179

historical novel, 6, 20, 26, 38–39, 45, 103–5, 180–83, 191–93, 197n21. *See also individual writers and works*
Hitler, Adolf, 17, 140, 158–59
Holocaust, 37, 159
Holsey, Bayo, 16, 37, 45

infertility, 148–53
Inhorn, Marcia C., 149–50
Inikori, Joseph E., 2

Innes, C. L., 145, 166
Irele, F. Abiola, 55
I Saw the Sky Catch Fire (Echewa), 6, 178
Izevbaye, D. S., 127

Jakobson, Roman, 207n28
James, Adeola, 153
Jewsiewicki, Bogumil, 34, 35
John, Ephraim Robin. *See* Grandy King George
Johnson, Charles, 40
Johnson, Mark, 21

Kerekou, Matthieu, 191
Klein, Martin A., 35, 36
Koku Baboni (Onadipe), 149
Komenda Castle, 12
Kristeva, Julia, 121, 131–32
Kufuor, John, 11, 191
Kuti, Ransome, 136

Lagos, 51, 135
Lakoff, George, 21
Last Harmattan of Alusine Dunbar, The (Cheney), 181, 197n20
Laub, Dori, 126
Law, Robin, 36, 76
Lawson, William, 111, 127
Lee, Julia Sun-Joo, 44
left behind, 6, 42, 52, 169–73, 177–78, 182, 186–87
Lose Your Mother (Hartman), 174–75
Lovejoy, Paul E., 76, 134

Mafe, Diana, 58
magical realism, 79, 104, 191
Mamadu, Ayo, 127
Manning, Patrick, 2, 52
March of Ages (Akwani), 183–88; body in the bag in, 185; historical figures in, 188; as historical novel, 183, 188; Ibekwe's return from slavery, 185–87; as slave narrative, 183, 185
Mbembe, Achille, 3, 47, 68, 92, 93, 146; "African Modes of Self-Writing," 33–34, 37–38
McCabe, Douglas, 87

McCarthy, Mary, 134
memory, alternative, 3, 4, 45, 140; collective, 3, 21, 45; countermemory, 10, 30, 40, 42; institutionalized, 16, 19; of loss, 3; and metaphor, 21, 30, 35, 39; Nora and, 14; repression of, 177; and rumor, 24; transgenerational, 6, 10, 18, 21, 22, 30, 38–39, 87, 88, 131; trauma and, 5. *See also* amnesia; *individual writers and works*
metaphor: *àbíkú* as, 84–87; alternative memory and, 3–4, 22; amnesia and, 3, 7, 33, 35, 38, 45, 73; body in the bag and, 5, 6, 61–65, 87–88, 89, 185; of captivity and enslavement, 4, 58–59; castles and, 11–13; definitions of, 9–10, 21; of estranged mothers, 34, 137–38; flexibility of, 7, 21, 31–33; of globalization, 79; as grammar of memory, 168; guns as, 23–24; historical novels and, 38; importance of, 30–31, 33; impotent body/infertility as, 5–6, 140, 151–52; invention of, 7; as language of slave trade memory, 23; legacy of violence and, 38; lies and, 16–19; memory and, 7, 30, 33, 39, 45; metonyms and, 87–88; as mnemonic devices, 17, 19–20; politics and, 4, 21–22, 29–30, 32, 43–44; politics of, 39–46; reading for, 20–33; slave ship as, 31–32, 40–42, 44, 170; of slave trade, defined, 1, 4, 7, 10–11, 21–23, 31, 33; of suffering, 179; "the way" as, 28–29; as transgenerational communication, 6, 10, 18, 21, 30–31, 38–39, 87–88; trauma and, 5, 10, 21, 22, 31, 61, 69, 179; twenty-first-century departure from, 6, 180–81, 183–84, 191–93, 197n21; witchcraft and, 34–35. *See also individual writers and works*
metonymy, 21, 87–88, 207n28
Middle Passage, 3, 4, 41, 79, 80, 98, 111, 114, 121, 129, 169, 170, 181, 182
Miller, Joseph C., 48
Mills, John Atta, 11–12
Moore, Samuel, 77
Morrison, Toni, 39, 40; *Beloved*, 42, 200n78
Mudimbe, Valetin Y., 34, 35, 105

INDEX

My Life in the Bush of Ghosts (Tutuola), 5; as allegory for Nigeria, 49–50, 51, 71, 72; body in the bag and, 48, 61–65, 67; cautionary tale and, 54–56; cultural memory and, 74; cycle of enslavement and, 65–68; Equiano and, 47; framing narrative of, 49–50, 73; Freud and, 69–70; ghostly enslavement in, 89; layered temporalities in, 73; magical capture in, 56–59; memories of unlaid ghosts in, 68–71; metallic ghosts in, 60–61; narrative and form in, 55–56; oral narratives and, 49–50, 54; physical and emotional dislocation and, 53–54; psychic power of slavery and, 59; slave-raiding conflicts and, 52; the Smelling-Ghost and, 61, 64–65; time setting and, 49–54; traumatic repetition and, 56, 69–71; violence and terror, enduring effects of, 68–69; Yoruba folklore and, 49, 51, 58

Negritude, 42
Nfah-Abennyi, Julianna Makuchi: "The Healer," 149
Nigeria: failures of independence in, 43; historical education in, 42; twentieth-century politics in, 90–91, 92, 173. See also *Famished Road* (Okri); and *My Life in the Bush of Ghosts* (Tutuola)
Nkrumah, Kwame, 11, 42, 110, 208n15
Nora, Pierre, 14, 99–100, 104, 113
Nwankwo, Chimalum, 154
Nwapa, Flora, 149

Obiechina, Emmanuel N., 66
Odamtten, Vincent O., 144, 156
ògbánje, 84, 86, 87. See also *àbíkú*
Ogundele, Wole, 38, 42, 44–45, 103–4, 180, 191, 192
Ogunyemi, Chikwenye, 85
Okonkwo, Christopher N., 85
Okpewho, Isidore, 55
Okri, Ben, 1, 4–5, 105; body in the bag and, 32; *The Famished Road* (see *Famished Road, The* [Okri]); *Starbook*, 192
Oldendorp, Christian G. A., 62–63, 136

Onadipe, Kola: *Koku Baboni*, 149
"On Being Brought from Africa to America" (Wheatley), 169–70
Ong, Walter J., 55, 72
Opoku-Agyemang, Kwadwo: "Against Fear," 182; *Cape Coast Castle*, 170, 182–83; "Equiano: A Mother's Song," 182; on historical amnesia, 34–35; "Supplication: Equiano's Mother," 182
Opoku-Agyemang, Naana Jane, 63
oríkì, 44
Oriki of a Grasshopper (Osofisan), 31–32
Oshunmare, 91
Osiris Rising (Armah), 181
Osofisan, Ferni: *Oriki of a Grasshopper*, 31–32
Osundare, Niyi, 181–82
Our Sister Killjoy (Aidoo), 5, 139–40; "A Love Letter," 163; *Anowa* and, 155–56; black sexuality and, 161–62; genre and, 153–54, 166–67; grammar of memory in, 165–66; historical continuities and, 157; homosexual relationship in, 159–62; language, love and, 164–65; language, past violence and, 168; loneliness in, 162–63; Nazis, Aryan guilt and, 157–59; Sissie and Marija, 157–61; Sissie's trip to Germany, 154; sites of violence in, 156; verse in, 166–67
Owomoyela, Oyekan, 50
Owusu, Kofi, 128, 167
Oyo Empire, 51, 83, 135

Parish, Jane, 109
Parrinder, Geoffrey, 68
Patterson, Orlando, 41–42
Pedersen, Carl, 129
Peters, Jonathan A., 119
postmemory, 73, 179

Quayson, Ato, 3, 21, 29, 50, 55, 56

Ricciardi, Alessia, 70
Richardson, David, 134
Ricoeur, Paul, 33, 45
Rites of Passage (Gennep), 172
Roberts, Neil, 202n6

Sango, 93
Saro-Wiwa, Ken, 106
Scarry, Elaine, 9, 125
Schramm, Katharina, 21, 39
Senegambia region, 103
Shaw, Rosalind, 3, 10, 22, 35, 38–39, 88
Simbi and the Satyr of the Dark Jungle (Tutuola), 63
Slave Girl, The (Emecheta), 23, 24–25, 86
Slave Raiders, The (Azasu), 183, 188–91, 216n20; England in, 188–90; epistemological reversals in, 189–90; Eurocentric notions of Africa and, 190–91; historical figures in, 188; historical novel and, 189, 216n20
slave ships, 4; in Armah, 26; as chronotopes, 40–42, 44; Duke on the welcoming of, 106–7; Ghanaian joke about, 170; Morrison on, 200n78; in Osofisan, 31–32; Samuel Crowther and, 136; West African fiction and, 42–43; as wonder, 78
slave trade: abolition, effects of, 133–35, 139; African Americans and, 4, 197n20, 211n21; African complicity in, 5, 19, 26, 34, 35–37, 102, 141, 144, 147, 176–79, 184, 191; amnesia and, 33–39; British colonial powers and, 36–37; characteristics of trauma and, 179; as cultural and economic exchange, 107–9; as "divine mercy," 169–70; familial separation and, 136–39; Ghanaian schools and, 191; increased demand for slaves and, 2; kidnapping raids and, 48; the left behind and, 170; literature of survival and loss and, 175–79; memorialization of in literature, 178; modernity and, 109; mourning period and, 172–73; personal and social costs of, 2; reading for metaphor and, 20–33; suffering of survival and, 170, 171–73; transatlantic versus domestic, 141, 211n21; Yoruba people and, 175–79. *See also under individual authors and works*; *under* metaphor
Smallwood, Stephanie E., 171–72

Soyinka, Wole, 84, 124, 136, 192; *Death and the King's Horseman*, 175–79
Spillers, Hortense, 133, 152, 164
Starbook (Okri), 192
Structural Adjustment Programs, 32
suffering of survival: fate of the missing unknown, 171; lack of closure and, 173; loss and, 174–75; mourning period, 172–73; ritual mourning, 171–72; slavery as a narrative of victory, 174
"Supplication: Equiano's Mother" (Opoku-Agyemang), 182

Tanyi-Tang, Anne, 149
Things Fall Apart (Achebe), 23–24, 84, 149, 183–84
Trans-Atlantic Slave Trade Database, 1
trauma, 5, 179; archiving the past and, 4, 101, 104; Armah and, 131; Caruth on, 131, 170; characteristics of, 179; colonialism and, 40, 43; Freud and, 69–70; incorporation of, 175; the left behind and, 6; memories of, 63; metaphor and, 10, 21, 31, 39; repression of, 34; transgenerational, 22–23, 73. *See also Fragments* (Armah); *My Life in the Bush of Ghosts* (Tutuola)
trope of the body in the bag. *See* body in the bag, trope of
Truth and Reconciliation, 6, 191
Tutuola, Amos, 1, 4–5, 43, 82, 105; anachronism and, 72–73; body in the bag and, 32, 89–90; as British subject, 50; *The Famished Road* (Okri) and, 81, 82, 89–90, 92–94, 105; on forgetting the past, 74; *My Life in the Bush of Ghosts* (see *My Life in the Bush of Ghosts* [Tutuola]); mythic time in, 49; on novels as allegories, 72; *Simbi and the Satyr of the Dark Jungle*, 63; and Yoruba folk tradition, 51, 54–56
Two Thousand Seasons (Armah), 23, 25–29; call to remembrance in, 28; "the way" in, 27–29; white destroyers in, 27, 28–29
Walcott, Derek, 40
wealth-in-people in West Africa, 108

Wenzel, Jennifer, 30
Wheatley, Phyllis: "On Being Brought from Africa to America," 169
White, Hayden, 39
White, Luise, 3, 10
Whittaker, David, 49, 50
Williams, Sherley Anne, 40
Wilson-Tagoe, Nana, 165
Wood, Marcus, 30–31
Woods, Tim, 43, 125–26
Wright, Derek, 127

Xhosa cattle killing incident, 30

Yan, Haiping, 144
Yoruba, people and culture: British colonialism and, 176–77; drama and, 44; endurance of, 175–76; folklore and, 55, 56; oral tradition and, 54–55; Oshunmare and, 91; Osogun and, 135–36; Sango and, 93; slave trade and, 2; specter of enslavement and, 53, 72–73; Yoruba Wars and, 51–52, 58, 135. See also *My Life in the Bush of Ghosts* (Tutuola)

Zeleza, Paul, 41

www.ingramcontent.com/pod-product-compliance
Lightning Source LLC
Chambersburg PA
CBHW031240290426
44109CB00012B/375